THE OPENNESS OF GOD

CLARK PINNOCK
RICHARD RICE
JOHN SANDERS
WILLIAM HASKER
DAVID BASINGER

A Biblical Challenge to the
Traditional Understanding of God

INTERVARSITY PRESS
DOWNERS GROVE, ILLINOIS, USA

THE PATERNOSTER PRESS
CARLISLE, UK

InterVarsity Press
P.O. Box 1400, Downers Grove, IL 60515, USA
The Paternoster Press
P.O. Box 300, Carlisle, Cumbria CA3 0QS, UK

InterVarsity Press® is the book-publishing division of InterVarsity Christian Fellowship®, a student movement active on campus at hundreds of universities, colleges and schools of nursing in the United States of America, and a member movement of the International Fellowship of Evangelical Students. For information about local and regional activities, write Public Relations Dept., InterVarsity Christian Fellowship, 6400 Schroeder Rd., P.O. Box 7895, Madison, WI 53707-7895.

USA ISBN 0-8308-1852-9
UK ISBN 0-85364-635-X

Printed in the United States of America ∞

Library of Congress Cataloging-in-Publication Data

The openness of God: a biblical challenge to the traditional
    understanding of God/Clark H. Pinnock . . . [et al.].
        p.   cm.
    Includes bibliographical references.
    ISBN 0-8308-1852-9 (alk. paper)
    1. God.   2. God—Biblical teaching.   3. God—Attributes.   4 God—
Attributes—Biblical teaching.   5. God—History of doctrines.
6. God—Attributes—History of doctrines.   I. Pinnock, Clark H.,
1937-
BT102.064   1994
231—dc20   94-3575
                                                                            CIP

British Library Cataloguing in Publication Data

Pinnock, Clark H.
    Openness of God: Biblical Challenge to
    the Traditional Understanding of God
    I. Title
    231
ISBN 0-85364-635-X

---

17   16   15   14
08   07   06

Preface 7

1 Biblical Support for a New Perspective 11
Richard Rice

2 Historical Considerations 59
John Sanders

3 Systematic Theology 101
Clark H. Pinnock

4 A Philosophical Perspective 126
William Hasker

5 Practical Implications 155
David Basinger

Notes 177

Preface

This book presents an understanding of God's nature and relationship with his creatures, which we call the openness of God. In broad strokes, it takes the following form. God, in grace, grants humans significant freedom to cooperate with or work against God's will for their lives, and he enters into dynamic, give-and-take relationships with us. The Christian life involves a genuine interaction between God and human beings. We respond to God's gracious initiatives and God responds to our responses . . . and on it goes. God takes risks in this give-and-take relationship, yet he is endlessly resourceful and competent in working toward his ultimate goals. Sometimes God alone decides how to accomplish these goals. On other occasions, God works with human decisions, adapting his own plans to fit the changing situation. God does not control everything that happens. Rather, he is open to receiving input from his creatures. In loving dialogue, God invites us to participate with him to bring the future into being.

This view resonates deeply with the traditional Christian devotional life. Biblical personalism is widespread among believers, for it allows for a real relationship with God. When we address God in prayer we commonly believe that we are entering into a genuine dialogue and that the future is not settled. Yet traditional theology has had a difficult time allowing for such dialogue. We need a theology that is biblically faithful and intellectually consistent, and that reinforces, rather than makes problematic, our relational experience with God. The view of God presented in this book may seem new to those outside scholarly circles, where it is well known. But if we remember that it presents in a systematic way what most Christians already practice in their devotional lives, then it will not seem strange at all.

The authors came to the view of God reflected in this book from various directions. Some were challenged by certain texts of Scripture that did not fit with the accepted understanding of the divine nature. Others sought to make sense of petitioning a God who was said to know already what we were going to ask, what he was going to do about it and how we would respond. Still others were forced to reconsider classical theism in the light of recent philosophical criticisms. Despite these diverse paths, we have all arrived at the perspective we call the open view of God.

We decided to present this model in book form for several reasons. First, no doctrine is more central than the nature of God. It deeply affects our understanding of the incarnation, grace, creation, election, sovereignty and salvation. Moreover, the doctrine of God is full of implications for daily living. One's view of God has direct impact on practices such as prayer, evangelism, seeking divine guidance and responding to suffering.

Second, many Christians experience an inconsistency between their beliefs about the nature of God and their religious practice. For example, people who believe that God cannot change his mind sometimes pray in ways that would require God to do exactly that. And Christians who make use of the free will defense for the problem of evil sometimes ask God to get them a job or a spouse, or keep them from being harmed, implying that God should override the free will of others in order to achieve these ends. We hope to present an understanding of God that alleviates many of these tensions.

These inharmonious elements are the result of the coupling of biblical ideas about God with notions of the divine nature drawn from Greek thought. The inevitable encounter between biblical and classical thought in the early church generated many significant insights and helped Christianity evangelize pagan thought and culture. Along with the good, however, came a certain theological virus that infected the Christian doctrine of God, making it ill and creating the sorts of problems mentioned above The virus so permeates Christian theology that some have come to take the illness for granted, attributing it to divine mystery, while others remain unaware of the infection altogether. This book, we hope, will be a needed antibiotic to aid the healing process, bringing about a healthier doctrine of God.

Third, we believe that the open view of God needs to be appraised by a broader public, one beyond the confines of professional theologians and philosophers. Contemporary Christian thought is witnessing something of a renaissance on the doctrine of God. A fair number of today's most prominent theologians and philosophers are affirming the openness of God. A new wave of critical reappraisal and competent reconstruction of the doctrine of God is sweeping over the intellectual landscape. Unfortunately, these reflections are generally tucked away in technical journals and books and so remain out of the reach of many who are interested. It is our conviction that a book-length treatment of the model is needed to provide a clear presentation of and call attention to this exciting understanding of God.

Last of all, proponents of two other views of God, classical theists and process theologians, both sometimes speak as though they have the only two models of God. This book presents an understanding of God that is distinctively different from each of them. Many people are looking for an alternative vision but have difficulty formulating one. We hope this work will benefit such seekers.

Though the model proposed has affinities to the classical view of God, we see sufficient problems in the traditional understanding to warrant a different paradigm. We do not claim that the open view is the only model with biblical or philosophical support. The Bible is not unambiguous on the subject and the various conceptions of God have each received thorough philosophical defenses. We do claim, however, that the open view is a superior paradigm in light of the relevant biblical, theological, philosophical and practical material. At the same time, we do not believe that this view is capable of "proof" in any hard sense. We know that our arguments are open to question, and we welcome the discussion we hope they will generate. We also recognize that this articulation of the openness of God is not the final word on the topic. Much more needs to be said in explaining and defending this particular view of God. This book raises numerous issues for future research projects, and we invite others to join us in exploring the paradigm.

Finally, a word about the composition of the book. Though there are five authors, the book is designed to read like a monograph. Like a five-course dinner prepared by five chefs, each author was asked to write a specific section. Each prepared a particular chapter while keeping in mind how it contributed to the whole. After an author completed a draft of his chapter, he sent it to the other four for comments and suggestions. The spirited and enjoyable interchange that ensued greatly improved each chapter and resulted in views on which we all generally agree. The issues on which we are not of one mind are duly noted.

Richard Rice begins by exploring the biblical materials that support the openness of God. John Sanders then asks why traditional theology does not interpret this biblical material in the same way as the open view. Next, Clark Pinnock presents a theological perspective on the open view of God, followed by William Hasker's philosophical defense of the model. David Basinger concludes by spelling out some of the practical implications of the open view and comparing them with the implications of other models.

We pray that this book will foster a passion for God, enable us to understand better how God relates to us, and lead God's people to glorify God.

1 Biblical Support for a New Perspective

Richard Rice

W hat kind of God created the world? What kind of world did God create? Over the centuries no questions have attracted more philosophical and theological attention, stirred up more controversy or generated more vigorous differences of opinion. The reason, of course, is that no questions are more fundamental to our understanding of who we are and what purpose our existence serves. As Christians, the answers we give to these questions influence everything we believe and, perhaps more important, have a profound impact on the way we live.

The Traditional View of God

For most of Christian history, one idea of God and his relation to the world has dominated the church's perspective, among thinkers and general believers alike, and it prevails in the attitudes of most Christians today. This traditional, or conventional, view emphasizes God's sovereignty, majesty and glory. God's will is the final explanation for all that happens; God's glory is the ultimate purpose that all creation serves. In his infinite power, God brought the world into existence in order to fulfill his purposes and display his glory. Since his sovereign will is irresistible, whatever he dictates comes to pass and every event plays its role in his grand design. Nothing can thwart or hinder the accomplishment of his purposes. God's relation to the world is thus one of mastery and control.

In this perspective God is supreme in goodness as well as in power; he is caring and benevolent toward his creatures. Yet God is equally glorified and his purposes are equally well served by the obedience of the righteous, the rebellion of sinners, the redemption of the saints and the destruction of the wicked.

According to this influential view, God dwells in perfect bliss outside the sphere of time and space. From his lofty vantage point, he apprehends the whole of created reality in one timeless perception: past, present and future alike appear before him. But though he fully knows and cares for the created world, he remains essentially unaffected by creaturely events and experiences. He is untouched by the disappointment, sorrow or suffering of his creatures. Just as his sovereign will brooks no opposition, his serene tranquillity knows no interruption.

Millard J. Erickson's *Christian Theology* clearly reflects this perspective, especially when it discusses "the divine plan." According to Erickson, God's plan is "from all eternity," so "there is no temporal sequence to God's willing. It is one coherent simultaneous willing." Moreover, God is not affected by any outside influence when he decides something, particularly not by human input. His sovereign will is the only consideration. The purpose of God's plan is God's glory, "the highest of all values, and the one great motivating factor in all that God has chosen and done." True, God provides for salvation in order to fulfill his love for human beings and his concern for their welfare. But these are strictly "secondary motivations." The "greater end" is God's own glory.

God's plan is also all-inclusive. "There are no areas that fall outside the purview of his concern and decision." This includes human actions and decisions too—evil ones as well as good. Nothing happens that God's will has not ordained. Finally, God's plan is efficacious; it cannot fail to reach fulfillment. "What he has purposed from eternity will surely come to pass." "He will not change his mind, nor will he discover hitherto unknown considerations which will cause him to alter his intentions."[1]

Proponents of this traditional perspective find support in a number of biblical statements. The most important of them emphasize the radical difference between God and everything else. Many texts, of course, affirm the majesty and glory of God: "Who is he, this King of glory? The LORD Almighty—he is the King of glory" (Ps 24:10); "I saw the Lord seated on a throne, high and exalted, and the train of his robe filled the temple" (Is 6:1); "God, the blessed and only Ruler, the King of kings and Lord of lords, who alone is immortal and who lives in unapproachable light, whom no one has seen or can see" (1 Tim 6:15-16). God transcends all creaturely reality. He is unique and utterly incomparable: "Who among the gods is like you, O LORD? Who is like you—majestic in holiness, awesome in glory, working wonders?" (Ex 15:11); "You shall have no other gods before me" (Ex 20:3); "Who is God besides the LORD?" (Ps 18:31); "You alone are God over all the kingdoms of the earth" (Is 37:16); "I am God, and there is no other; I am God, and there is none like me" (Is 46:9). He cannot be equated with anything finite. In contrast to all finite things, the traditional view maintains, God is utterly changeless: "I the LORD do not change" (Mal 3:6); "Every good and perfect gift is from above, coming down from the Father of the heavenly lights, who does not change like shifting shadows" (Jas 1:17).

According to Stephen Charnock's classic work on the divine attributes, immutability is one of God's central characteristics.[2] It applies most obviously to God's existence. In the creaturely sphere, things come and go, begin and end, live and die. Unlike them, God has the attribute of eternity. He has always existed and will never cease to exist. "Before the mountains were born or you brought forth the earth and the world, from everlasting to everlasting you are God" (Ps 90:2). His life alone is independent and underived: "who alone is immortal" (1 Tim 6:16).

Divine transcendence also applies to God's power. In fact, the possession of supreme power is one of the most obvious things that distinguishes God from everything else. Certain texts seem to indicate that God's power is limitless. Unlike mortals, God does whatever he chooses and nothing can resist his might. "Is anything too hard for the LORD?" (Gen 18:14); "Power and might are in your hand, and no one can withstand you" (2 Chron 20:6); "With God all things are possible" (Mt 19:26); his power is "incomparably great" Eph 1:19), and he "is able to do immeasurably more than all we ask or imagine" (Eph 3:20). Biblical writers use the expression "almighty" of God numerous times, occasionally as a proper name: "I am God Almighty," he announced to Abraham (Gen 17:1); "The Almighty is beyond our reach and exalted in power," Elihu told Job (Job 37:23); "Holy, holy, holy, is the Lord God Almighty" is the constant refrain of the four creatures in the book of Revelation (Rev 4:8).

In light of certain biblical statements, God's plans or intentions also appear changeless. Unlike human beings, God does not change his mind. "God is not a man, that he should lie, nor a son of man, that he should change his mind," Balaam exclaimed. "Does he speak and then not act? Does he promise and not fulfill?" (Num 23:19). When Samuel told Saul that the Lord had torn the kingdom of Israel from him and given it to another, he added, "He who is the Glory of Israel does not lie or change his mind; for he is not a man, that he should change his mind" (1 Sam 15:29).

Like many other theologians, Charnock applies changelessness to God's knowledge. Since God's being is timeless, his knowledge is timeless too. "His knowledge being eternal, includes all times; there is nothing past or future with him."[3] Consequently, nothing ever enters God's knowledge; it is already there. "God hath known from all eternity all that which he can know. . . . He knows not at present any more than he hath known from eternity: and that which he knows now he always knows: 'All things are open and naked before him' (Heb 4:13)."[4] God's infinite knowledge also includes an exhaustive understanding of the future. "God knows all things before they exist," Charnock asserts.[5] "Before a word is on my tongue you know it completely, O LORD"; "All the days ordained for me were written in your book before one of them came to be" (Ps 139:4, 16).

Charnock sees a close relation between God's plans and his knowledge. God knows the future completely because he has planned it completely: "his declaration of things to come, is founded upon his appointment of things to come." "God's knowledge doth not arise from things because they are, but because he wills them to be; and therefore he knows everything that shall be."[6] "I make known the end from the beginning, from ancient times, what is still to come. I say: My purpose will stand, and I will do all that I please" (Is 46:10).

It is not difficult to see why this elevated view of God has attracted widespread support over the centuries and even why many people find it religiously helpful. It preserves God's radical transcendence and affirms God's sovereignty by giving him complete control over the universe. It conveys the assurance that everything in our lives happens in precise accordance with God's will. And it enjoys the apparent support of many biblical passages.

The Scriptures contain such vast and varied material that it is not difficult to surround an idea with biblical quotations. The crucial question is whether the idea is faithful to the overall biblical portrait of God—the picture that emerges from the full range of biblical evidence. My contention is that this familiar concept does not reflect faithfully the spirit of the biblical message, in spite of the fact that it appeals to various biblical statements. The broad sweep of biblical testimony points to a quite different understanding of the divine reality. In what follows I shall not attempt a point-by-point refutation of the conventional view of God. Instead, I shall identify some central elements in the biblical portrait of God and show that this portrait is compatible with some of the passages that seem to raise questions about it.

The Open View of God

The view of God and his relation to the world presented in this book provides a striking alternative to the concept just described. It expresses two basic convictions: love is the most important quality we attribute to God, and love is more than care and commitment; it involves being sensitive and responsive as well. These convictions lead the contributors to this book to think of God's relation to the world in dynamic rather than static terms. This conclusion has important consequences. For one thing, it means that God interacts with his creatures. Not only does he influence them, but they also exert an influence on him. As a result, the course of history is not the product of divine action alone. God's will is not the ultimate explanation for everything that happens; human decisions and actions make an important contribution too. Thus history is the combined result of what God and his creatures decide to do.

Another consequence of this conviction concerns God's knowledge. As an aspect of his experience, God's knowledge of the world is also dynamic rather than static. Instead of perceiving the entire course of human existence in one timeless moment, God comes to know events as they take place. He learns something from what transpires. We call this position the "open view of God" because it regards God as receptive to new experiences and as flexible in the way he works toward his objectives in the world. Since it sees God as dependent on the world in certain respects, the open view of God differs from much conventional theology. Yet we believe that this dependence does not detract from God's greatness, it only enhances it.

Later chapters in this book will explore the theological and practical implications of this view of God and address some of the philosophical questions it raises. My task here is to examine the biblical evidence that supports it. Every Christian account of God claims to have the support of the Bible, including, as we have just seen, the conventional view of God's relation to the world. There is good reason for this: agreement with Scripture is the most important test for any theological proposal. By definition, the task of Christian theology is to interpret the contents of the Bible. So, unless the perspective on God presented in this book can claim biblical support, it has little to recommend it to believing Christians.

What, then, is the biblical view of God? It is a challenge to ascertain the biblical view of almost anything, let alone the most important idea of all. The Bible contains an enormous range of material, and on almost any significant topic we can find diverse statements if not diverse perspectives as well.[7] This is certainly true of the idea of God. Thousands of texts refer to God, and they are immensely varied. Sometimes the language employed seems clearly figurative or symbolic: God is often compared to things in the natural world like wind, rocks, plants and animals. The Bible also applies many human qualities to God—physical, mental and emotional. God performs various human roles, including those of a king, a shepherd, a warrior, a potter and a mother. Other biblical language sounds more literal than symbolic or figurative. Occasionally we find lists of divine characteristics or qualities, and a couple of passages read like straightforward definitions of God.

Nearly all of the Bible's descriptions of God fall within the broad designation of "metaphor," a topic that has received massive scholarly attention in recent years. Put very simply, a metaphor is a comparison; it describes one thing as if it were another, or attributes to one thing the qualities of something else. If we insist that every description of God be labeled either "literal" or "symbolic," as some theologians seem to do,[8] then biblical metaphors obviously belong to the latter category. But most scholars would reject a sharp division between literal and figurative theistic language in the Bible. This implies that all metaphors are alike, and such a view obscures the rich variations within the biblical descriptions of God.[9]

While no metaphor provides us with a literal account of the divine reality—a one-to-one correspondence to its object—this does not mean that all metaphors are equally distant from the object represented. For example, the Bible variously refers to God as a rock (Ps 31:2-3), a shepherd (Ps 23:1) and a human parent (Hos 11:1). But most Christians would agree that God is more like a shepherd than a rock, and more like a parent than a shepherd. So within the broad spectrum of biblical metaphors, some are more important than others. These metaphors bear a stronger resemblance to the divine reality—they are closer, so to speak, to the intended object—and they play a more prominent role within the overall biblical account of God. To use Terence Fretheim's expression, these are "controlling metaphors": "they are able to bring coherence to a range of biblical thinking about God; they provide a hermeneutical key for interpreting the whole."[10]

The purpose of this chapter is to restore some important biblical metaphors to the prominence they deserve in our thinking about God, in particular metaphors such as divine suffering and divine repentance. Giving such metaphors more weight will enable us to achieve an understanding of God that is much more faithful to the Bible than is the familiar alternative.

Due to the immense scope and variety of the biblical material that deals with God, this study will attempt neither a comprehensive survey nor a historical reconstruction of biblical thought. At the same time, we must avoid being narrowly selective. Accordingly, I will review some representative passages of Scripture that support the open view of God, and then look at some of the passages that raise questions about it. Let us begin with the most important description of God in the Bible, explore its meaning for human existence, and then examine several Old and New Testament passages that extend and illuminate this conception of the divine reality.

Two streams of biblical evidence support an interactive view of God's relation to the world. One consists of statements that affirm in one way or another that God is responsive to what happens in the creaturely world, that what happens there affects God somehow—by evoking a certain emotion, a change in attitude, a change in plans. The other consists of statements that indicate creaturely freedom in one way or another. These include various divine warnings and promises and calls to repentance, as well as fairly straightforward assertions that presuppose creaturely alternatives.

Divine Love and the Openness of God

From a Christian perspective, *love* is the first and last word in the biblical portrait of God. According to 1 John 4:8: "Whoever does not love does not know God, because God is love." The statement *God is love* is as close as the Bible comes to giving us a definition of the divine reality.[11] And, as Eberhard Jüngel observes, Christian theology has always given this expression pride of place among the many descriptions of God.[12]

The immediate context of these familiar words is instructive. "This is how God showed his love among us: He sent his one and only Son into the world that we might live through him. This is love: not that we loved God, but that he loved us and sent his Son as an atoning sacrifice for our sins. . . . If anyone acknowledges that Jesus is the Son of God, God lives in him and he in God. And so we know and rely on the love God has for us" (1 Jn 4:9-10, 15-16). As these verses show, God's love was completed in sending his Son.

Although it appears only in 1 John, the assertion *God is love* succinctly summarizes a pervasive biblical theme. The psalmist describes God as "abounding in steadfast love" (Ps 103:8 NRSV; cf. v. 13). He has everlasting love for his people (Is 54:8). According to many passages, his love or kindness goes on forever.[13] God's love is the rationale for Israel's beginning as a nation: "It was because the LORD loved you and kept the oath he swore to your forefathers that he brought you out with a mighty hand and redeemed you from the land of slavery, from the power of Pharaoh king of Egypt" (Deut 7:8). It explains God's steadfast commitment to his people in spite of their infidelities: "I have loved you with an everlasting love; I have drawn you with loving-kindness" (Jer 31:3); "in his love and mercy he redeemed them; he lifted them up and carried them all the days of old" (Is 63:9).

God's love comes to its fullest expression in the life and death of Jesus. According to numerous New Testament passages, the giving of his Son is the greatest manifestation of God's love: "He who did not spare his own Son, but gave him up for us all—how will he not also, along with him, graciously give us all things?" (Rom 8:32); "God demonstrates his own love for us in this: While we were still sinners, Christ died for us" (Rom 5:8); "For God so loved the world that he gave his one and only Son, that whoever believes in him shall not perish but have eternal life" (Jn 3:16).

So the statement *God is love* embodies an essential biblical truth. It indicates that love is central, not incidental, to the nature of God. Love is not something God happens to do, it is the one divine activity that most fully and vividly discloses God's inner reality. Love, therefore, is the very essence of the divine nature. Love is what it means to be God.

There is widespread theological support for the idea that love is central to both the revelation and the reality of God. Abraham Joshua Heschel, a Jewish theologian, notes the striking contrast between God's anger and love as the two are described in the Hebrew Scriptures.[14] He points out a profound difference in their duration. God's anger is temporary, his love is permanent: "His anger is but for a moment; his favor is for a lifetime" (Ps 30:5 NRSV); "In overflowing wrath for a moment I hid my face from you, but with everlasting love I will have compassion on you" (Is 54:8 NRSV).

God is also reluctant to get angry, but eager to show mercy (Ex 34:6; Ps 103:8). Heschel concludes that in the prophetic view of God love is essential, while anger is only incidental. God's "normal or original pathos," he observes, "is love or mercy." "The pathos of anger is . . . a transient state," "by no means regarded as an attribute, as a basic disposition, as a quality inherent in the nature of God."[15] It is always described "as a moment, something that happens rather than something that abides." "The prophets never speak of an angry God as if anger were His disposition."[16] In contrast to the numerous applications to God of such words as *good, righteous, merciful* and *gracious,* the expression *angry God* appears in the Old Testament only once (Nahum 1:2).[17]

A similar emphasis on God's love appears in "The Being of God as the One Who Loves," a section of Karl Barth's great *Church Dogmatics.* For Barth, divine revelation does not add to our understanding of God's essence, it defines that essence. Accordingly, God's revelation is nothing less than his "self-revelation": we see who and what God is only where he reveals himself. And what does revelation tell us? That God is "He who, without having to do so, seeks and creates fellowship between Himself and us."[18] God is therefore "the One who loves." Indeed, "that He is God—the Godhead of God—consists in the fact that He loves."[19] "God loves because . . . this act is His being, His essence and His nature."[20]

Numerous theologians echo Barth's emphases. According to Emil Brunner, the assertion *God is love*—the "most daring statement that has ever been made in human language"—means that love is not a mere quality or attribute that God happens to have in common with other beings; it is the very nature of God himself. Moreover, we understand God's love only in the event of divine revelation.[21] We come to see that God is love only through his self-giving in Christ. Similarly, Walter Kasper concludes that God "must in himself be freedom in love and love in freedom" because God shows himself, especially through the cross of Christ, to be "the one who loves in freedom and is free in loving." "From eternity, therefore, God must be self-communicating love."[22] And Wolfhart Pannenberg states, "Only in the love of God does the concrete form of his essence come to expression."[23]

The crucial importance of love requires us to revise a great deal of conventional thought about God. According to standard definitions, "gods" are beings who surpass humans in power and intelligence, and the Christian concept of God is one that includes love in its list of divine attributes. Such an account is misleading, however. According to the Bible, God is not a center of infinite power who happens to be loving, he is loving above all else. Consequently, when we enumerate God's qualities, we must not only include love; to be faithful to the Bible we must put love at the head of the list.

In the thinking of many Christians, however, even this fails to capture the biblical emphasis. As they interpret the Bible, love is not only more important than all of God's other attributes, it is more fundamental as well. Love is the essence of the divine reality, the basic source from which *all* of God's attributes arise. This means that the assertion *God is love* incorporates all there is to say about God. In Barth's words, "All our further insights about who and what God is must revolve round this mystery—the mystery of His love. In a certain sense they can only be repetitions and amplifications of the one statement that 'God loves.' "[24] For Pannenberg as well, the attributes of God's essence that appear in various Old Testament passages like Exodus 34:6[25] and throughout the New Testament "may be understood through and through as the attributes of his love." So, "the goodness, grace, righteousness, faithfulness, wisdom and patience of God do not take us beyond the thought of divine love but describe different aspects of its reality."[26] Love is the concrete reality that unifies all of the attributes of God.[27] A doctrine of God that is faithful to the Bible must show that all of God's characteristics derive from love.[28]

It is not surprising that the topic of divine love has received so much theological attention. A well-known feature of the New Testament writings is the use of *agapē* to express God's love. Unlike other Greek words whose meanings are broadly covered by the English word *love, agapē* has an unconditional element. It refers to affection motivated by the subject, not the object of love. God loves us, not because we are lovable but because he is loving. Spontaneous and unconditional though it is, God's love is not a mechanical outpouring, an inexorable natural process. God's love can never be taken for granted. The Bible indicates that God is deeply sensitive to the ones he loves.

With this initial summary in mind, let us look more closely at some of the important biblical evidence that emphasizes God's love and thus supports the open view of God.

■ Old Testament Evidence for the Openness of God

In recent years a number of biblical scholars have explored some neglected themes in the Hebrew Scriptures that support the open view of God. Their work indicates that God interacts with the world in a give-and-take fashion and that God's inner experience of the world is rich with emotion. As they interpret the Old Testament perspective, God's life exhibits two important qualities: it is social, and it is dynamic. God enters into relationships and genuinely interacts with human beings. He affects them, and they, in turn, have an effect on him. As a result, God's life exhibits transition, development and variation. God experiences the temporal world in a temporal way.

Following one scholar's review of the Old Testament material,[29] I will explore three specific elements in the divine life that point to its social and dynamic character: God's emotions, intentions and actions.

God's Feelings

The Old Testament attributes to God a wide range of feelings, including joy, grief, anger and regret. Many references involve divine pleasure. The repeated exclamation of Genesis 1, "and God saw that it was good," seems to express warm personal satisfaction. A number of passages speak of God as taking delight in various things. "For the LORD takes delight in his people; he crowns the humble with salvation" (Ps 149:4). "The LORD will again delight in you and make you prosperous, just as he delighted in your fathers" (Deut 30:9). " 'I am the LORD, who exercises kindness, justice and righteousness on earth, for in these I delight,' declares the Lord" (Jer 9:24). " 'Is not Ephraim my dear son, the child in whom I delight? Though I often speak against him, I still remember him. Therefore my heart yearns for him; I have great compassion for him,' declares the LORD" (Jer 31:20).[30] According to one memorable description, God takes such great delight in his people that he rejoices over them with singing (Zeph 3:17).

The most touching descriptions of God's inner life involve his reaction to the unfaithfulness of his chosen people. The Hebrew prophets speak of God and Israel in familial terms, drawing on the relations of parent and child, husband and wife. The most dramatic of these is Hosea's description of Israel as the wanton wife of God.[31] Acting on God's instructions, Hosea married a promiscuous woman. She deserted him, and though deeply wounded, he won her back and their marriage began again. According to the prophet, the experience perfectly illustrates God's relationship with Israel. Like Hosea's faithless wife, Israel abandoned the Lord to pursue other lovers, thinking they were the source of her security.

God responded by rejecting her ("she is not my wife, and I am not her husband," 2:2), resolving to disown her children ("the children of adultery," 2:4), destroy her false sense of security ("Therefore I will take away my grain when it ripens, and my new wine when it is ready. I will take back my wool and my linen, intended to cover her nakedness," 2:9) and subject her to public disgrace ("I will expose her lewdness before the eyes of her lovers," 2:10). His thoughts of revenge give way, however, to the promise of reconciliation: "Therefore I am now going to allure her; I will lead her into the desert and speak tenderly to her. . . . I will betroth you to me forever; I will betroth you in righteousness and justice, in love and compassion. I will betroth you in faithfulness, and you will acknowledge the LORD" (2:14, 19-20).

This powerful poem tracks a succession of intense feelings, from jealousy and anger to hope and joy. God's response to Israel runs the same gamut of emotion a betrayed husband would feel, with the significant exception that God longs for reconciliation beyond rejection. In this respect God's behavior transcends the norms that governed husband-wife relations in Israel. Once a divorced woman had remarried, her former husband was forbidden to marry her again. But God promises to marry Israel in spite of her infidelities.[32]

In a similar way two centuries later the prophet Jeremiah used sexually explicit language (some even think pornographic) to describe Judah and Israel's unfaithfulness to God:

> You have lived as a prostitute with many lovers. . . . Look up to the barren heights and see. Is there any place where you have not been ravished? By the roadside you sat waiting for lovers, sat like a nomad in the desert. You have defiled the land with your prostitution and wickedness. . . . You have the brazen look of a prostitute; you refuse to blush with shame. (Jer 3:1-3; cf. 2:20; 13:26-27)

In Ezekiel, too, we find the idolatrous behavior of Israel and Judah compared to the antics of two promiscuous sisters (Ezek 23). And the thrust of this extended metaphor in all three prophets is the pain that this outrageous behavior inflicts on God. " 'Like a woman unfaithful to her husband, so you have been unfaithful to me, O house of Israel,' declares the LORD" (Jer 3:20). "Since you have forgotten me and thrust me behind your back, you must bear the consequences of your lewdness and prostitution" (Exek 23:35). Still, as in Hosea, beyond the cries of divine anguish we hear a promise of reconciliation and restoration: "Return, faithless people; I will cure you of backsliding" (Jer 3:22).

In this dramatic prophetic poetry, the most acute human feelings provide a window on the inner life of God. The Bible contains many symbols for God's relation to his people, but none exudes the emotional poignancy of this one. "When God is portrayed as betrayed husband," one scholar observes, "then God's own frustrated desires and suffering are brought into focus." "Through this imagery, the people of Israel are enabled to *feel* God's agony."[33]

The prophets use other human relationships to describe divine emotion as well. Hosea compares God's feelings for Israel with a parent's tender longing for a wayward child:

> When Israel was a child, I loved him. . . . It was I who taught Ephraim to walk, I took them up in my arms. . . . I led them with cords of human kindness, with bands of love. I was to them like those who lift infants to their cheeks. I bent down to them and fed them. . . . How can I give

you up, Ephraim? How can I hand you over, O Israel? . . . My heart recoils within me; my compassion grows warm and tender. (Hos 11:1, 3, 4, 8 NRSV)

The husband-wife and parent-child metaphors illuminate the experience of God in a unique and indispensable way. Whereas the metaphors of king and subject, judge and criminal emphasize power and punishment in God's relation to his people, these family metaphors emphasize love and commitment.[34]

It is not uncommon for people to dismiss these emotional descriptions of God, numerous though they are, as poetic flights essentially unrelated to the central qualities that the Old Testament attributes to God. As they see it, the real God of the Bible is made of sterner stuff. He is powerful, authoritarian and inflexible, so the tender feelings we read of in the prophets are merely examples of poetic license. As I understand it, however, the evidence supports a strikingly different conclusion. One scholar links these emotion-filled accounts of God's love for Israel directly to the concept of divine oneness, which lies at the heart of biblical religion.[35]

As generally understood, monotheism concentrates in one divine personage all of the powers that ancient religions typically distributed among various divine beings. God does not share his power or glory with any other being. He describes himself as a "jealous God" (Ex 20:5). He alone sustains the natural order, and his will alone is sovereign. Some people believe that monotheism makes God directly responsible for everything that happens in the world, but Tikva Frymer-Kensky draws a completely different conclusion. She asserts that "the reactivity of God" that we see in his powerful emotions for Israel is essential to monotheism, and shows that the one God grants human beings a central role in determining the course of history. God is the ultimate power in reality, but God's activity consists in large measure in responding to human decisions and actions. What he actually decides to do depends directly on the actions of human beings. Far from detracting from the significance of human initiative, then, monotheism heightens and enhances it.

Abraham Joshua Heschel expresses similar convictions in terms of God's "pathos," a category, he maintains, that is central to the prophets' under-standing of God and basic to God's relation to human beings.[36] The basic idea is that human emotions reflect the inner experience of God. Hosea, for example, came to see that the anguish his troubled marriage brought him was "a mirror of the divine pathos, that his sorrow echoed the sorrow of God."[37] Heschel distinguishes pathos from passion, an emotional con-vulsion that takes possession and drives someone blindly. In contrast to unreasoned emotion, pathos involves free will; it is the "result of decision and determination." The divine pathos points to the fact that "God is con-cerned about the world, and shares in its fate." He is willing to be "involved in history, intimately affected by events in history." "He not only rules the world in the majesty of His might and wisdom, but reacts intimately to the events of history." "God does not stand outside the range of human suf-fering and sorrow. He is personally involved in, even stirred by, the conduct and fate of man."[38] Because human beings are so important to God, their existence acquires a new dimension. "Never in history," writes Heschel, "has man been taken as seriously as in prophetic thinking. . . . Whatever man does affects not only his own life, but also the life of God. . . . He is a consort, a partner, a factor in the life of God."[39]

God's Intentions

The Old Testament description of divine intentions also contributes to a social and dynamic portrait of God. Scripture tells us that God formulates plans and purposes and that he occasionally changes his mind. To use a biblical expression, God repents. A later chapter in this book will deal with the philosophical issues that such an idea raises. But the biblical descrip-tions of divine repentance indicate that God's plans are exactly that—plans or possibilities that he intends to realize. They are not ironclad decrees that fix the course of events and preclude all possible variation. For God to will something, therefore, does not make its occurrence inevitable. Factors can arise that hinder or prevent its realization. Consequently, God may refor-mulate his plans, or alter his intentions, in response to developments.

The notion of divine repentance plays a much larger role in the biblical writings than many people realize. The numerous references to it cannot be dismissed as poetic inventions. It emerges as a prevalent theme in the Old Testament, and it applies to a wide range of divine action. God repents in a variety of circumstances. Sometimes God rejects something that he has already done. "The LORD was sorry that he had made humankind on the earth, and it grieved him to his heart" (Gen 6:6 NRSV). "The LORD was sorry that he had made Saul king over Israel" (1 Sam 15:35 NRSV).

At other times God repents of something that he said he would do or started to do. The best-known example is Jonah's mission to Nineveh. When the prophet finally reached the great city after his famous detour at sea, he delivered the message that God had given to him. "Forty more days," he proclaimed, "and Nineveh will be overturned" (Jon 3:4). In response to his dire warning, the entire city fasted and prayed. "When God saw what they did and how they turned from their evil ways, he had compassion and did not bring upon them the destruction he had threatened" (3:10). This, of course, was just what Jonah had feared. "I knew that you are a gracious and compassionate God," he complained, "slow to anger and abounding in love, a God who relents from sending calamity" (4:2).

In another well-known instance, God repented in response to human intercession. Not long after their dramatic escape from Egypt, the Israelites worshiped a golden calf as the god who had delivered them from bondage. Outraged at this apostasy, God told Moses that he would destroy the Israelites and make of Moses a great nation. Instead of welcoming the offer, however, Moses pleaded for his people. He feared that such an action would damage God's reputation among the Egyptians; he reminded God of his promises to Abraham, Isaac and Israel that he would make a great nation of their descendants. "Turn from your fierce anger," Moses implored; "relent and do not bring disaster on your people" (Ex 32:12). In response to his entreaties, Exodus records, "the LORD relented and did not bring on his people the disaster he had threatened" (Ex 32:14).[40]

In spite of the straightforward assertion that God changed his mind ("repented" or "relented"), biblical commentators often go to great lengths to explain that this is *not* what occurred. The gist of their remarks is that

God did not change, but circumstances did. According to R. Alan Cole, for example, this statement is clearly an "anthropomorphism" (or, more accurately, an "anthropopathism"), a description of God's action "in strictly human terms." It does not mean "that God changed His mind; still less that He regretted something that He had intended to do. It means . . . that He now embarked on a different course of action from that already suggested as a possibility, owing to some new factor." "We are not to think of Moses as altering God's purpose towards Israel by this prayer, but as carrying it out."[41]

Stephen Charnock takes a similar tack. "God is not changed," he writes, "when of loving to any creatures he becomes angry with them, or of angry he becomes appeased. The change in these cases is in the creature; according to the alteration in the creature, it stands in a various relation to God."[42] So when the Bible says that God "turns" from love to wrath, or from wrath to love, this describes a change in the way people relate to God, not in the way he relates to them.

But a significant feature of this passage does not permit this construction. The fact is that God relents in direct response to Moses' plea, not as a consequence of the people's repentance of their apostasy. The repentance mentioned in this case clearly applies to a change that took place in God, not in his people. Of course, God's essential nature and his ultimate purpose did not change—Moses' appeal presupposes this. But this hardly means that nothing in God really changed. To the contrary, his ultimate objectives required him to change his immediate intentions.

A number of Bible scholars do see this dramatic passage as a clear indication that God underwent a real and important change. In his commentary on Exodus, George A. F. Knight maintains that while God's ultimate purpose remained the same, his specific intention regarding Israel *did* change in response to Moses' inquiry. Moses begs God to repent, using the very same word *(shubh)* that the prophets employed in their appeals to backsliding Israel, to change his plan to destroy Israel and so to remain loyal to the great revelation of himself in which he promised to be with them.[43]

In his comments on this passage, Terence Fretheim carefully charts the steps in God's interaction with Moses. He shows that Israel's fate was determined only gradually, and that Moses genuinely influenced God's final decision. At the outset, the future of the Israelites is really up in the air. God's initial outburst shows that he is deeply hurt by the people's behavior and inclined to reject them, but his decision is not final and, in effect, he invites Moses to "contribute something to the divine deliberation."[44] Moses' vigorous entrance into the discussion shows that "God is not the only one who has something important to say."[45] He appeals to God's reasonableness and reputation, and reminds God of his own promise. In response, God immediately changes his mind: he "repented of the evil" he planned to do.[46] Fretheim concludes that this passage reveals God as "one who is open to change. God will move from decisions made, from courses charted, in view of the ongoing interaction with those affected. God treats the relationship with the people with an integrity that is responsive to what they do and say." "This means that there is genuine openness to the future on God's part."[47]

This incident is reminiscent of Abraham's conversation with his heavenly visitor concerning the fate of Sodom. When God announced that he planned to destroy Sodom and Gomorrah, Abraham asked him to spare Sodom in order to avoid killing righteous people along with the wicked. "Far be it from you to do such a thing," he exclaimed, "to kill the righteous with the wicked. . . . Will not the Judge of all the earth do right?" (Gen 18:25). Carefully negotiating in time-honored Middle Eastern fashion, Abraham persuaded God to spare the city if it had as few as ten righteous inhabitants (Gen 18:23-32). Sodom was still destroyed—it must have contained hardly any worthy people—but the story reveals that God sometimes reconsidered his plans in response to human requests.

These incidents indicate that human intercession can influence God's actions. They show that God's intentions are not absolute and invariant; he does not unilaterally and irrevocably decide what to do. When God deliberates, he evidently takes a variety of things into account, including human attitudes and responses. Once he formulates his plans, they are still open to revision. This appears to be true of even the most emphatic assurances on God's part.

God's covenant with David included this promise regarding David's offspring: "My love will never be taken away from him, as I took it away from Saul, whom I removed from before you. Your house and your kingdom will endure forever before me; your throne will be established forever" (2 Sam 7:15-16). In spite of this firm promise, other passages attach an important condition to the fulfillment of this pledge. As his death approached, David advised Solomon to observe all of God's laws, so "that the LORD may keep his promise to me: 'If your descendants watch how they live, and if they walk faithfully before me with all their heart and soul, you will never fail to have a man on the throne of Israel' " (1 Kings 2:1-4). Solomon himself repeated this promise and its condition in his prayer at the dedication of the temple: "Now LORD, God of Israel, keep for your servant David my father the promises you made to him when you said, 'You shall never fail to have a man to sit before me on the throne of Israel, if only your sons are careful in all they do to walk before me as you have done' " (1 Kings 8:25).

The original promise seems to draw a sharp distinction between the way God treated Saul and the way he plans to treat David. Saul's disobedience led to divine rejection, but it will be different for David: God will not reject him. Both David and Solomon, however, understood this promise to depend on the continued obedience of their descendants. Evidently God attached conditions to his promise, even though they were not spelled out at first. What appears to have been an unconditional commitment on God's part turns out to be conditional after all.

We see the importance of divine repentance not only in the number of times it appears but also in the distinctive way in which biblical writers refer to it. Several noteworthy passages present a list of God's essential qualities or characteristics. They catalog the attributes that establish God's identity and that distinguish him from all potential rivals. One such passage describes God's appearance to Moses on Mount Sinai during the giving of the law. "And he passed in front of Moses, proclaiming, 'The LORD, the LORD, the compassionate and gracious God, slow to anger, abounding in love and faithfulness, maintaining love to thousands, and forgiving wickedness, rebellion and sin' " (Ex 34:6-7). The attributes mentioned in such a dramatic moment of revelation have great importance. As we noticed earlier in connection with divine love, these are the qualities that make God what he is, that define the essence of the divine reality.

It is highly significant that several passages of this "defining" sort list divine repentance (or "relenting," as some translations read) among God's essential characteristics. As we have seen, Jonah addressed God as "gracious . . . and merciful, slow to anger, and abounding in steadfast love, and ready to relent from punishing" (Jon 4:2 NRSV). Similarly, Joel said that God is "gracious and merciful, slow to anger, and abounding in steadfast love, and relents from punishing" (Joel 2:13 NRSV). Formulations like these demonstrate that repentance is not an exceptional action on God's part, let alone something that is out of character for him. To the contrary, it is typical of God to relent from punishment (which is why Jonah was so irritated when Nineveh was spared). In fact, it is his very nature to do so. Accordingly, God does not repent in spite of the fact that he is God; he repents precisely *because* he is God.

The Bible's most extensive account of divine repentance deserves careful attention. As recorded in Jeremiah 18, the Lord sends the prophet to the potter's house, where he observes the man at his wheel, throwing pots and reworking spoiled vessels into other designs. The Lord declares that Israel to him is like clay in the potter's hands. Depending on the circumstances, his plans for Israel can change. He will rework his design in response to the actions of his people. Then follows a statement of the general principle that explains God's actions:

> If at any time I announce that a nation or kingdom is to be uprooted, torn down and destroyed, and if that nation I warned repents of its evil, then I will relent and not inflict on it the disaster I had planned. And if at another time I announce that a nation or kingdom is to be built up and planted, and if it does evil in my sight and does not obey me, then I will reconsider the good I had intended to do for it. (Jer 18:7-10)

The passage concludes with an application of this principle to Israel's situation: "Now therefore say to the people of Judah and those living in Jerusalem, 'This is what the LORD says: Look! I am preparing a disaster for you and devising a plan against you. So turn from your evil ways, each one of you, and reform your ways and your actions' " (Jer 18:11).

There are different ways to read these verses. Some interpreters view them as an affirmation of God's absolute control over creation: God exercises the same mastery over human affairs that a potter has over his clay. But a more natural reading of the passage, we believe, suggests something quite different. What happens to nations is not something that God alone decides and then imposes on them. Instead, what God decides to do depends on what people decide to do. His decisions hinge on the way human beings respond to his threats and warnings. If this is so, a description of intended divine judgment is not an announcement of ineluctable fate, it is a call to repentance. Indeed, the very prediction of impending disaster implies the possibility that it may yet be avoided. If the purpose of such prophecies is to awaken repentance, we must conclude that God sends predictions of judgment precisely in hopes that they will not be fulfilled.[48]

Subsequent verses in Jeremiah 18 confirm this reading. They further emphasize that God is not responsible for what happens to Israel. As the nations will testify, the tragedy befalling Israel resulted from her own perversity, not from the inflexible application of divine power.[49]

This important passage indicates that God is not unilaterally directive in his dealings with human beings. Instead, his relation to us is one of dynamic interaction. God expresses certain intentions and waits to see how people will react. What he finally decides to do depends on their response. As a result, the general course of events is not something for which God is exclusively responsible. To a significant extent it depends on the actions and decisions of human beings.

Although two passages assert that God does *not* repent (in comparison to forty or so indicating that he does so), close inspection reveals that they are exceptions that prove the rule that he can repent when he chooses. Balaam's second oracle includes this statement: "God is not a human being, that he should lie, or a mortal, that he should change his mind. Has he promised, and will he not do it? Has he spoken, and will he not fulfill it?" (Num 23:19 NRSV). When Samuel told Saul that the Lord had torn the kingdom of Israel from him and given it to another, he added, "He who is the Glory of Israel does not lie or change his mind; for he is not a man, that he should change his mind" (1 Sam 15:29). If God's rejection of Saul was irreversible, so was his acceptance of David.

Some construe these denials that God will change his mind as general assertions of divine immutability, but this is not the case. For one thing, the word *repent* in both instances is used synonymously with the word *lie*. The point is not that God never changes, but that God never says one thing while fully intending to do something else. Only in this limited sense of the word does God not "repent." Unlike human beings, God will not say one thing and then arbitrarily do another.[50] Second, these statements pertain to specific promises that God declares he will stand by forever; they do not posit a general principle. Third, the assurance that God will *not* repent presupposes the general possibility that God *can* repent when he chooses. God does not repent in certain cases, not because it is impossible or inconceivable for him to do so, nor because he never does so; he does not repent simply because he chooses not to do so.[51] Fourth, it is noteworthy—"striking," one scholar exclaims—that one of the very chapters that asserts that God does *not* repent (1 Sam 15) contains two statements that he *does* repent (vv. 11, 35). So the scope of this denial obviously is very limited. It is not a statement of general principle.

In addition to the assertions that God does *not* repent because he is not human (Num 23:19; 1 Sam 15:29) are the biblical assertions that God *does* repent because he is not human. According to Hosea 11:8-9, God exclaims, "How can I give you up, Ephraim? How can I hand you over, O Israel? . . . My heart recoils within me; my compassion grows warm and tender. I will not execute my fierce anger; I will not again destroy Ephraim; for I am God and no mortal, the Holy One in your midst" (NRSV). In general, then, God's repentance is a genuine possibility, but one that is foreclosed when God pledges himself unconditionally to a particular course of action.

The biblical descriptions of divine repentance combine elements of emotion and decision to provide a striking picture of the divine reality. They indicate that God is intimately involved in human affairs and that the course of creaturely events has profound effects on him. It stirs his feelings and influences his decisions. He is variously happy and sad, joyful and disappointed, disposed to bring blessing or judgment, depending on the behavior of human beings. God works toward his objectives in history in dynamic interaction with human beings. Their experiences and decisions affect his experience and decisions. So important is the notion of divine repentance in biblical thought that it deserves to be regarded as one of the central themes of Scripture. It represents "an important interpretive vehicle for understanding the divine activity throughout the canon."[52]

Such an interpretation conflicts, of course, with the popular and theologically entrenched idea that God lies utterly beyond the reach of creaturely experience, serenely untouched by our joys and sorrows, overseeing the inevitable fulfillment of his will irrespective of human actions and decisions. To those who hold this perspective, the biblical accounts of divine repentance are so many figures of speech. If references to God's physical appearance are anthropomorphic, descriptions of God's feelings are anthropopathic. They attribute human qualities to the divine being. They embellish the biblical account, but they are not to be taken literally.

This is an influential argument. There is no question that the Bible contains a good many anthropomorphisms and employs numerous figures of speech when it talks about God. The book of Genesis describes God as walking in the Garden of Eden and coming down to inspect the tower of Babel. Several passages attribute to God various features of the human body—eyes, ears, hands, an arm, a mouth, a face and even a backside. In other instances God is said to have appeared to men and women in the form of a human being.[53]

Most Christians rightly construe such descriptions as symbolic and deny that physical form and features characterize the divine being itself. The question is whether we should do the same with references to God's thoughts and feelings. If physical descriptions of the divine reality are not to be taken literally, is the same true of descriptions of God as deliberating, deciding, acting and feeling? To avoid turning God into an enlarged human being, must we deny not only that God shares our physical properties but our intellectual, volitional and emotional properties too?

This question actually belongs more to the philosophical than the biblical portion of this volume. But it is difficult to see what, if anything, would remain of the idea of God in the wake of such sweeping denials. They would deprive it of any meaningful content. If human beings and God have nothing whatever in common, if we have utterly no mutual experience, then we have no way of talking and thinking about God and there is no possibility of a personal relationship with him.

More to the point here, the Bible itself provides important reasons for taking many of its descriptions of God's thoughts and feelings at face value. One is the frequency with which they appear in Scripture; another is the strategic significance of the passages where we find them. As we have seen, certain passages have a defining function. They specifically indicate what it is that makes God God. Other passages deliberately distinguish God from other things, such as false gods and human beings. Such evidence indicates that the biblical writers were not employing figures of speech or deliberately contriving analogies when they spoke of such things as divine love and divine repentance. Their expressions faithfully portray the inner life of God.

God's Actions

Besides God's feelings and decisions, a third element in the Old Testament indicates that God's life is social and dynamic. This is divine activity. God does things. In fact, the Bible identifies God primarily by describing his actions. To quote a title that was popular years ago, the Bible is "The Book of the Acts of God."[54] The biblical narrative opens with an account of creation (Gen 1—2). And an important confession of faith recounts the central event in Old Testament history, God's deliverance of the Hebrew people from bondage:

My father was a wandering Aramean, and he went down into Egypt with a few people and lived there and became a great nation, powerful and numerous. But the Egyptians mistreated us and made us suffer, putting us to hard labor. Then we cried out to the LORD, the God of our fathers, and the LORD heard our voice and saw our misery, toil and oppression. So the LORD brought us out of Egypt with a mighty hand and an outstretched arm, with great terror and with miraculous signs and wonders. He brought us to this place and gave us this land, a land flowing with milk and honey; and now I bring the firstfruits of the soil that you, O LORD, have given me. (Deut 26:5-10)

Worshipers were to recite these words as they offered the firstfruits of their harvest to God. The setting underscores the importance of the words. It shows that the Hebrew people identified God by his actions. They understood who he was in light of what he had done.

The Bible attributes to God both general activities and specific actions. Some of what God does is ongoing, or continuous. For example, God acts to uphold the created order and sustain human life (Neh 9:6; Acts 17:28). But some of God's actions are discrete. He causes certain things to happen, and brings about specific states of affairs.

This is not the place to develop a philosophy of action, but we should note that the very concept of an act involves change. An action makes a difference. It brings about something that would not otherwise exist. In the case of specific acts, it brings about something that did not previously exist. To say that God acts, therefore, means that it makes sense to use the words *before* and *after* when we talk about him. God makes decisions and then he acts. He decides before he acts, he acts after he decides. This is so simple that it sounds trivial, but it points to a fundamental truth about God. Not only does he bring about change, but in a significant sense God himself experiences change. After God acts, the universe is different and God's experience of the universe is different. The concept of divine action thus involves divine temporality. Time is real for God.

We also see divine temporality in the relationship the Bible describes between the purposes and the actions of God. God does things to accomplish his purposes. The fact that God acts to achieve his purposes suggests a distinction between the *formulation* of God's plans and the *fulfillment* of those plans.[55] A passage like Isaiah 46:9-11 is instructive in this regard. "I am God, and there is no other; I am God, and there is no one like me, declaring the end from the beginning and from ancient times things not yet done, saying, 'My purpose shall stand, and I will fulfill my intention.' . . . I have spoken, and I will bring it to pass; I have planned, and I will do it" (NRSV). These verses seem to indicate that divine purpose and divine enactment are not one indistinguishable event, but distinct moments in God's experience. God announces his plans; then he acts to implement his plans. Moreover, God acts from time to time throughout the course of human history, not just at the beginning. So the drama of history is not an inexorable outworking of a process instituted at the beginning of time, but a series of events.

This passage fits with some of the others we have seen to demonstrate that the realm of creaturely existence is not a complete and perfect replica of God's design. God has plans, and he acts to bring his plans to fruition. While God contributes to the ongoing course of events, other agents make their contributions, too, and God takes them into account.

When we think of the will of God and the decrees of God, therefore, we must also think of the concrete, dynamic manner in which they are implemented. God's plans are not cast-iron molds to which the course of history passively and perfectly conforms. They are goals that God pursues over time and in different ways. At times, God acts to bring things about unilaterally, as it were. Some things God wants done, so he does them. "In the beginning God created the heavens and the earth" (Gen 1:1). "God said, 'Let there be light,' and there was light" (Gen 1:3). At other times, however, God interacts with creaturely agents in pursuing his goals. He works in and through situations where people are variously receptive and resistant to his influence. God used the hatred of Joseph's brothers to save the Israelites from famine (Gen 45:4-7). God used the hardness of Pharaoh's heart to heighten the drama of Israel's deliverance (Ex 7:3-5). God hoped that Saul would be a good king. When Saul disappointed him, God turned elsewhere (1 Sam 15:35; 16:1). God hoped that his chosen people would remain faithful to him and fulfill their mission. When they proved uncooperative, God revised his plans for them (Mt 21:33-45). God used the treachery of religious and political leaders in offering Jesus as a sacrifice for sin (Acts 2:32). God used the dedication of the apostles to spread the gospel throughout the Mediterranean world (Mt 28:19-20). God will overcome the forces of darkness in their final challenge to his authority (Rev 20:7-10).

To summarize, at times God simply does things, acting on his own initiative and relying solely on his own power. Sometimes he accomplishes things through the cooperation of human agents, sometimes he overcomes creaturely opposition to accomplish things, sometimes he providentially uses opposition to accomplish something, and sometimes his intentions to do something are thwarted by human opposition.

The will of God, therefore, is not an irresistible, all-determining force. God is not the only actor on the stage of history. Other agents, too, play a role. Creatures who bear the image of God are capable of deciding and acting, and God takes their decisions and actions into account as he determines what course to follow. To a significant extent, then, God's actions are reactions—different ways he responds to what others do as he pursues his ultimate purposes. For the most part, the fulfillment of God's will represents a genuine achievement rather than a foregone conclusion.

■ New Testament Evidence for the Openness of God

Many people see a stark contrast between the New and Old Testament views of God. For most of them, probably, the Old Testament God is stern, harsh and unforgiving, while the New Testament God is loving, forbearing and pliable. To them the New Testament is a helpful corrective, if not an outright reversal, of what the Old Testament says about God. Paradoxically, other people find almost the opposite sort of change from Old to New Testament perspectives. As they see it, the Old Testament God is responsive to human behavior and relatively open in his plans and decisions, whereas the New Testament God is much more rigid. He mapped out the entire course of history in advance, and everything that happens fits into his scheme.

In contrast to both versions of the notion that there is a major shift from Old to New Testament views of God, I believe the New Testament extends and intensifies the dynamic portrait of God we found in the Old. It, too, supports the open view of God.

Jesus' Life and Ministry

Various elements in the New Testament support the idea that God interacts with the creaturely world in a dynamic way. They show that God is aware of, involved in and profoundly affected by human events. This perspective on God is vivid in the accounts of Jesus' life and work, especially in these four elements: the basic concept of the incarnation, the identification of Jesus with God; the general portrayal of God in Jesus' life and ministry; Jesus' specific teachings about God; and finally, the nature of Jesus' death.

The familiar word *incarnation* expresses the idea that Jesus is the definitive revelation of God. According to the central claim of Christian faith— "the Word became flesh" (Jn 1:14)[56]—this particular human life was the most important means God has ever used to reveal himself. The fundamental claim here is not simply that God revealed himself in Jesus, but that God revealed himself in Jesus *as nowhere else.* In this specific human life, as never before or since, nor anywhere else in the sphere of creaturely existence, God expresses his innermost reality. Accordingly, from a Christian standpoint it is appropriate to say not only that *Jesus is God,* but that *God is Jesus.* For Christians, Jesus defines the reality of God.

The incarnation reveals many things about the character of God. The fact that God chose to express himself through the medium of a human life suggests that God's experience has something in common with certain aspects of human experience. If human life in its fullness and complexity, with social, emotional and volitional dimensions, represents the supreme expression of God's own nature among the creatures (Gen 1:26-27), it is reasonable to infer that the distinctive features of human experience are most reminiscent of the divine reality. It would therefore seem that God, like us, is personal existence. If so, then God enjoys relationships, has feelings, makes decisions, formulates plans and acts to fulfill them. Naturally, we may not use the "humanity" of God as a pretext for unbridled speculation, but it clearly points to important similarities between our experience and his.

We learn about God not only from the fact that he assumed human nature but also from the distinctive qualities we see in Jesus. As the Word made flesh, Jesus' life and work represent and correspond to the most important qualities of God himself.

While any attempt to summarize the ministry of Jesus would be presumptuous, an obvious feature is the fact that his life was characterized by *service to* and *suffering with* rather than *power over* human beings. Jesus was acutely sensitive to people's needs and feelings, and he devoted himself to uplifting the poor and the sick. "The Son of Man," as the pivotal text in Mark puts it, "came not to be served but to serve" (Mk 10:45 NRSV). In fact, he explicitly rejected the quest for power over others as inappropriate for his followers (Lk 22:25-26). One of the New Testament letters identifies Jesus with the suffering servant of Isaiah 53:

> Christ suffered for you, leaving you an example, that you should follow in his steps. "He committed no sin, and no deceit was found in his mouth." When they hurled insults at him, he did not retaliate; when he suffered, he made no threats. Instead, he entrusted himself to him who judges justly. He himself bore our sins in his body on the tree, so that we might die to sins and live for righteousness; by his wounds you have been healed. (1 Pet 2:21-24)

Through this remarkable portrayal we see the sovereign of the universe as one who reaches to the depths of human need with tenderness and compassion, one who appreciates human sorrows to the fullest.

The Gospels' clearest insights into the nature of God appear in the teachings of Jesus about his heavenly Father, and the most striking element in these teachings is what Jesus says about God's attitude toward sinners. According to the opening verses of Luke 15, the great parables of recovery—the lost sheep, the lost coin, the prodigal son—were intended to illuminate God's attitude toward those the world designates as "sinners." Their message is that God rejoices with the recovery of his lost sons and daughters. But these parables illuminate this point in a most instructive way.

In each parable, something of great value is lost, and its recovery is the occasion of great excitement. As we all know from personal experience, the thrill of recovery is quite different from the satisfaction of predictable achievement. It is gratifying to achieve a goal you have worked toward; it brings a deep sense of accomplishment. Loss and recovery involve a much wider range of emotions. Losing something of value can inflict enormous pain. We feel the threat of permanent deprivation. The uncertainty as we search or wait to get it back can be agonizing. And then, if we're fortunate, the moment of recovery brings a rush of surprise, relief and joy.

Now the purpose of these parables is to illustrate God's reaction to repentant sinners, and the climax of each parable is the exhilaration of recovery. Jesus says in effect, "Do you know how it feels to lose something you love and then get it back again? That's just how God feels when sinners return to him." These parables thus portray God as one who has a capacity for deep and diverse feelings, who is intimately aware of and keenly sensitive to men and women, and who reacts differently to different situations. In the words of Jesus, "There will be more rejoicing in heaven over one sinner who repents than over ninety-nine righteous persons who do not need to repent" (Lk 15:7).

It is worth noting how the poignancy of emotion increases in the last of these three parables. The joy of recovery on the part of the shepherd and the woman is entirely understandable. We can easily imagine ourselves in their position. The joy of the waiting father is different. In contrast to the lost items in the first two parables, the lost son is responsible for his predicament. His headstrong determination to leave home and family, his disdain for his family's values and disregard for his parents' feelings, his outrageous demand for a share of the family estate while his father was living (in effect, wishing his father were dead), his reckless, self-destructive behavior in the far country, even his pathetic, inadequate apology—all these things make it highly unlikely that an ancient Middle Eastern father would receive him, let alone welcome him with open arms.

If the first two parables show us how much like our feelings God's feelings are, the last one discloses a vast difference between them. The wayward son deserves to be rejected. At the least he merits a public rebuke. But instead of humiliating his son, the father humiliates himself by unceremoniously running to him—in full view of curious villagers, no doubt—embracing him, restoring him instantly to his honored position in the family and then even throwing a party to celebrate his return.[57] There is not a trace of recrimination or a hint of resentment in his actions. To rejoice with the return of an irresponsible, insensitive son, rather than turn him away or shower him with reproach, contradicts normal behavior. It reveals a depth of feeling that transcends our natural human emotions. It is actually the vindictive older son, not the father in this story, who displays the natural human response to this situation. He deeply resents what his brother has done and refuses to celebrate his return—just what most of us would do in the same situation. His reaction to his brother's homecoming is entirely understandable. But the joy of the father mystifies us. It is as unexpected as it is profound.[58]

These parables suggest that God's feelings involve a broad spectrum of emotion, and they relate God's experience to ours in a very interesting way. They show us, first, how like and then how unlike ours is God's experience. God's love is like ours in its openness to pain and joy, but his capacity for these experiences is greater than anything of which we are capable.

It is significant that Jesus not only taught what God felt with the sinner's return but in his own actions demonstrated it. In receiving and eating with sinners and social outcasts, he behaved in a manner that conflicted with conventional humanity. And yet precisely here, in his departure from conventional behavior, he most vividly portrayed what God is like. In the words of Adrio König, "Jesus Christ is both the consummation and the explicative history of 'God is love.' "[59]

So the open view of God draws some important parallels between divine and human experience, but it does not by any means equate the two. God is like us in being sensitive to the experiences of others, but radically different from us in the profound depth of his feelings. Like traditional theism, the open view of God affirms divine transcendence, the radical difference between God and all things human. But whereas traditional theism seeks to safeguard God's transcendence by denying divine sensitivity, the open view of God does so by maintaining that his sensitivity and love are infinitely greater than our own.

This is the sort of difference that lies behind the familiar prophetic exclamation, "My thoughts are not your thoughts, neither are your ways my ways. . . . As the heavens are higher than the earth, so are my ways higher than your ways and my thoughts than your thoughts" (Is 55:8-9). This is no general affirmation of divine inscrutability, in spite of the use theologians often make of it.[60] It refers specifically to God's willingness to forgive, in contrast to our typical reluctance to do so. "Let the wicked forsake his way and the evil man his thoughts," states the preceding verse. "Let him turn to the LORD, and he will have mercy on him, and to our God, for he will freely pardon" (Is 55:7).

The fact that Jesus' life most clearly revealed the nature and character of God has important implications for the Bible's use of anthropological language. When the Scriptures compare God with humanity, the clearest parallels are not between God and fallen human beings, but between God and our essential humanity, specifically Jesus Christ. To draw from König's work again, when the biblical writers deny that God is like human beings, sinful humanity is typically the point of comparison. But when the same writers continue to speak of God in anthropomorphic terms, "it is obvious that it is in another sense that they refer to God as being like man. Here it is intended that the comparison is between God and man as the image of God, and not between God and man as sinner." In particular, "the anthropomorphisms in the Bible represent the proclamation about God in terms of the person and work of Christ."[61] Not only what Jesus taught about God, then, but the way he manifested God in his treatment of people, in particular the undeserving and the unwanted, provides powerful indications that God is deeply sensitive and responsive to human experience.

Jesus' Death
Descriptions of Christ's passion also suggest that God dynamically interacts

with the creaturely world. According to well-known biblical testimony, Jesus' death was the fulfillment of a plan established far in advance. Christ was "chosen before the creation of the world" (1 Pet 1:20) and handed over to his executioners "by God's set purpose and foreknowledge" (Acts 2:23). The Bible also indicates that Jesus came to a full acceptance of his Father's will through a process of intense spiritual struggle.

The New Testament describes Jesus as engaged in fierce battles with temptation. The letter to the Hebrews asserts that Jesus, our high priest, "has been tempted in every way, just as we are—yet was without sin" (Heb 4:15). Matthew and Luke vividly recount his temptations in the wilderness following his baptism (Mt 4:1-11; Lk 4:1-13). And, perhaps most important, the Synoptic passion narratives record Jesus' heart-rending pleas on the eve of his crucifixion that he be spared the suffering that lay ahead. "My Father, if it is possible, let this cup pass from me; yet not what I want but what you want" (Mt 26:39 NRSV). According to the Gospels, Jesus reached the point of complete commitment—"Your will be done"—after a period of deep anguish.

The biblical references to Jesus' temptations thus indicate that his moral victory was a genuine achievement, not just a foregone conclusion. He ultimately submitted to God's will while facing tremendous pressure to avoid it. So while God formulated specific plans for Jesus' life, the fulfillment of these plans required Jesus to accept the suffering that God assigned to him. This supports the conclusion that the fulfillment of God's plans for humanity generally requires the cooperation of human agents. It is not something that God's will unilaterally brings about.

The New Testament presents the cross, of course, as the central act in the drama of human salvation. Christ's death is the major concern of all four Gospels, with the passion narratives occupying fully one-third of Mark. As the Gospel of John emphasizes, the cross is the high point in divine revelation as well. For if God was personally present in Jesus, and if the cross was the climactic moment in Jesus' life, it follows that the cross is the supreme moment in the history of God's self-disclosure. According to John, the cross is the place where Jesus' identity is fully known (Jn 12:32-33; cf. 3:14) and where God's name is glorified (Jn 12:27-28). What the cross reveals is therefore central to the nature of God. Through Calvary we peer, as it were, into the very heart of the divine reality.

What does it reveal about God? We can view the cross both as something God does and as something God experiences. In each case, we find God deeply involved in human life. First of all, it demonstrates that God takes an active role in salvation. The cross is a prominent theme in the writings of Paul, who connects a number of sacrificial terms with Christ's death, including "atonement" (Rom 3:25), "blood" (1 Cor 11:25) and "Passover lamb" (1 Cor 5:7). Using such expressions Paul interprets the cross as an act of reconciliation on God's part. One passage in particular describes it as something that God himself provides:

> God . . . reconciled us to himself through Christ and gave us the ministry of reconciliation: that God was reconciling the world to himself in Christ, not counting men's sins against them. And he has committed to us the message of reconciliation. . . . We implore you on Christ's behalf: Be reconciled to God. (2 Cor 5:18-20)

This text underscores the central New Testament truth that God is always the subject, and never the object, of reconciliation. He is the agent, not the recipient, of reconciliation. The apostle's call, therefore, is not for sinful human beings to reconcile God, but to be reconciled *to* God, to accept the reconciliation that God freely offers. Clearly, then, the cross was God's action. He was working in Christ to accomplish our reconciliation. Appreciating this fact, many Christian scholars now perceive the suffering of Calvary not as something Jesus offers to God on human behalf, still less as something God inflicts on Jesus (instead of on other human beings), but as the activity of God himself.

Pursuing God's role in reconciliation a step further, we see that the cross is a divine experience as well as a divine action. Humanity and divinity were united in the suffering of Calvary. God was in Christ, himself enduring the agony that Christ underwent. As Kenneth Leech puts it, "It is necessary to see God in the pain and the dying. There must have been a Calvary in the heart of God before it could have been planted on that hill outside . . . Jerusalem."[62]

The idea of a suffering God is the antithesis of traditional divine attributes such as immutability and impassibility. It contradicts the notion that God is immune to transition, to anything resembling the vicissitudes of human experience. To quote Leech again, "The cross is a rejection of the apathetic God, the God who is incapable of suffering, and an assertion of the passionate God, the God in whose heart there is pain, the crucified God."[63] Strange as it seems to some, this idea faithfully reflects the central affirmations of the New Testament concerning God's relation to Jesus. Identifying God with Jesus leads ultimately to the conclusion that what Jesus experienced in the depths of his anguish was experienced by God himself. If the Word truly became flesh, if God was indeed in Christ, then the most significant experience Jesus endured was something God endured as well. The cross is nothing less than the suffering of God himself.

A careful look at the center of Christian faith, the life and death of Jesus, thus supports the idea that God is intimately involved in the creaturely world and experiences it in a dynamic way. He is aware of, involved in and deeply sensitive to human events. His inner life is not static or impassive at all. It surges with powerful emotions.

■ Problem Passages

While impressive biblical evidence supports the openness of God, a number of passages seem to call it into question. Since we are striving for a perspective on God that reflects the broad sweep of biblical testimony, we need to take these into account as well. Can we reconcile the open view of God with the sort of statements we noted earlier to the effect that God never changes, that God can do anything and that God knows everything? And what about the biblical concepts of prophecy, providence and predestination? Can the open view of God accommodate these ideas? As we shall see, the answer is yes. In fact, not only is the open view of God compatible with these important biblical ideas, but they actually support it.[64]

Divine Changelessness

As we saw earlier, the idea of changelessness, or immutability, is central to the traditional view of God. A number of biblical statements seem to support it (see Mal 3:6; Jas 1:17; Num 23:19; 1 Sam 15:29), and they speak of several ways in which God does not change. One is the fact that, unlike his creatures, the Creator cannot fail to exist. Several texts associated with divine changelessness indicate that God has always existed and will never cease to exist. "Before the mountains were brought forth, or ever you had formed the earth and the world, from everlasting to everlasting you are God" (Ps 90:2 NRSV; cf. Ps 9:7). He enjoys unending life, or immortality. He is "the King eternal, immortal, invisible, the only God" (1 Tim 1:17; cf. 6:16).

Most of the biblical references to divine changelessness pertain to God's character rather than his existence. They assure us that God is completely reliable. He will not be kind and caring one day, spiteful and vengeful the next. He does not promise something only to retract it a moment later. The familiar statement in Malachi, for example, relates God's changelessness to his mercy: "For I the LORD do not change; therefore you, O children of Jacob, have not perished" (Mal 3:6 NRSV). Although God's people have been wayward, the prophet proclaims, God's changelessness—his abiding mercy—provides a basis for calling them to return. As one scholar observes, the concern of such statements is really divine faithfulness rather than immutability.[65] The God who "changes not" is not fickle and capricious. His love and care are steadfast. In fact, the most important Hebrew words for God's love carry the meaning of "steadfastness," "loyalty" and "faithfulness."[66]

This is the thrust of two texts that deny that God repents, or changes his mind, Numbers 23:19 and 1 Samuel 15:29.[67] The issue in these verses is the constancy of God's character, not the content of his experience. In both cases, the author's point is that God does not lie, but tells the truth. He does not say one thing while planning to do something else, or make promises with no intention of keeping them. God is changeless in the sense that he is faithful to his word.

As these texts indicate, the Bible clearly supports a concept of divine changelessness. In certain respects God never varies, he is always the same.

The notion that God is changeless is perfectly compatible with the open view of God. In fact, it is just as important to this position as to the conventional alternative. The difference between them is not that one views God as changeless while the other doesn't. The difference is that everything about God must be changeless for the traditional view, whereas the open view sees God as both changeless and changeable.

We can attribute both change and changelessness to God if we apply them to different aspects of his being. God's existence, God's nature and God's character are just as changeless as he could possibly be. These aspects of divinity are completely unaffected by anything else. God would be God no matter what happened in the world. Indeed, God would be God whether the creaturely world existed or not.[68]

When it comes to God's concrete relation to the world, however, the situation is different. God is dynamic in respect to his experience of the creaturely world, his response to what happens in the world, his decisions about what to do in the world and his actions within the world. He is deeply affected by what happens to his creatures.

For the open view, then, God is both changeless and changeable, in distinctly different ways. So while proponents of divine openness emphasize the biblical evidence that God is affected by what happens in the world (suffers) and that he changes his mind (repents), they fully accept the biblical affirmations of divine changelessness. They apply the "changeless" statements to God's existence and character, to his love and reliability. They apply the "changing" statements to God's actions and experience.

Far from creating a conflict in God, these different aspects of divinity are closely related. The reason that God is open to change in some respects is the fact that in other respects he never changes. It is God's nature to love, to love without measure and without interruption. And precisely because this is God's essential nature, he must be sensitive and responsive to the creaturely world. Everything that happens in it has an effect on him. Because God's love *never* changes, God's experience *must* change. In other words, it is part of God's unchanging nature to change.[69]

When we distinguish between God's unchanging nature and his dynamic experience, we can make sense of a wide range of biblical evidence. We can accept at face value the biblical statements that attribute powerful emotions to God. We do not have to dismiss them as "anthropomorphisms" or "anthropopathisms," which have no application to his real life. The open view of God does justice to a broad spectrum of biblical evidence and allows for a natural reading of the Bible.

In contrast, proponents of the traditional view of God have great difficulty with the many texts that attribute change to God, and they often resort to elaborate measures to avoid their plain import. In the words of one scholar, the response of several influential theologians to biblical assertions of divine repentance is simply "a laboured effort to avoid the obvious meaning of passages."[70] So those who deny that God ever changes have a real problem with texts that indicate that he does, while those who accept the notion that God changes do not face a comparable problem with passages that say that God does not change. By attributing change and changelessness to different aspects of God, proponents of the open view of God achieve a perspective that is both logically consistent and faithful to the full dimensions of the biblical portrait.

An expression often construed as pointing to divine immutability is the name by which God identified himself to Moses in the wilderness, "I AM WHO I AM" (Ex 3:14). In a move widely deplored by biblical and systematic theologians today, Scholastic thinkers interpreted this as a metaphysical statement and applied it to God's being or existence. God thus says to Moses, "I am the self-existent one."[71] It is more in harmony with the biblical view to see this as expressing God's freedom to act and as relating God's identity to his action, since it occurs at an important moment in salvation history—just prior to God's dramatic deliverance of his people from Egypt. Thus, according to Wolfhart Pannenberg, it asserts that God "will show himself in his historical acts."[72] In effect, God says, "I will be there for you."[73] Or, to risk putting it too colloquially, "I am the one you can always count on." At any rate, the text points to the dynamic quality of God's activity rather than to the static quality of the divine nature.

While the biblical writers do affirm respects in which God is changeless, their primary emphases—in fact, their consistent preoccupation—concern the ways in which God is active within and affected by human history. Accordingly, writes König, "anyone who describes God's being in terms of disengagement, remoteness and self-sufficiency, the ground or origin of all that is, has listened wrongly to the biblical message in general and the preaching of Jesus in particular." To be sure, these aspects do enter the picture. "But they are peripheral concepts, subsidiary matters which do not belong to the discussion of the being of God."[74]

Prophecy

There is no question that prophecy plays a prominent role in the biblical description of God. As the work of the biblical prophets indicates, prophecy involves much more than predicting the future, but this is certainly a part of it, and it is what most of us think of when we hear the word. Many people regard the ability to foretell future events as one of God's distinguishing characteristics.[75] A well-known text seems to indicate this: "I am God, and there is no other; I am God, and there is none like me. I make known the end from the beginning, from ancient times, what it still to come" (Is 46:9-10).

According to traditional theism, God predicts the future on the basis of absolute foreknowledge. He can tell us what lies ahead, because he already sees everything that is going to happen. Familiar examples of prophecy include God's announcement to Moses that he would harden Pharaoh's heart so that he would refuse to let the Israelites leave Egypt (Ex 4:21), and the prediction that Cyrus would help the Jews rebuild Jerusalem (Is 44:28). The Bible contains divine predictions that did not come to pass, of course, but these represent "conditional prophecies," that is, prophecies whose fulfillment depended on certain human responses (which God knew would not occur). The best-known description of conditional prophecy is Jeremiah 18:7-10 (discussed above), and the best-known example of conditional prophecy is Jonah's prediction of Nineveh's downfall (Jon 3:4). According to the traditional view of God, conditional prophecies do not conflict with the notion of absolute foreknowledge, because they were not genuine predictions. Rather, they were the means by which God achieved his purposes. In Jonah's case, for example, getting the Ninevites to repent. God knew that these predictions would not be fulfilled and never intended them to be.[76]

Both Calvinist and Arminian supporters of traditional theism appeal to prophecy to refute the notion that the future is open for God. For Calvinists like Jonathan Edwards, God's knowledge of future human actions and decisions demonstrates that there is no such thing as libertarian freedom.[77] For Arminians, who affirm creaturely freedom, it shows that all free decisions and actions are somehow foreknown by God.[78] For those who espouse the open view of God, predictive prophecy is compatible with genuine creaturely freedom, provided we recognize that there is no simple model that fits all prophecies. Instead, prophecy is a subtle and varied phenomenon, and a divine prediction may represent one of several things.

A prophecy may express God's intention to do something in the future irrespective of creaturely decision. If God's will is the only condition required for something to happen, if human cooperation is not involved, then God can unilaterally guarantee its fulfillment, and he can announce it ahead of time. This seems to be the case with a number of prophecies, including the famous passage in Isaiah. After announcing that he makes known the end from the beginning, God states, "I will do all that I please. . . . What I have said, that will I bring about; what I have planned, that will I do" (Is 46:10-11). Of course, God can predict his own actions.

A prophecy may also express God's knowledge that something will happen because the necessary conditions for it have been fulfilled and nothing could conceivably prevent it. By the time God foretold Pharaoh's behavior to Moses, the ruler's character may have been so rigid that it was entirely predictable. God understood him well enough to know exactly what his reaction to certain situations would be.

A prophecy may also express what God intends to do *if* certain conditions obtain. This is what a conditional prophecy represents—a prediction as to what will happen if human beings behave in one way rather than another. According to Jeremiah 18, prophecies of destruction will not come to pass if people turn from their evil ways, nor will prophecies of blessing be fulfilled if people disobey. As we have seen, conditional prophecies are better interpreted in the open view of God than in the traditional view. They indicate that God's relation to the creaturely world is one of dynamic interaction. Conditional prophecies express a genuine divine intention. When God had Saul anointed king of Israel, he really intended it to be permanent.

The problem with the traditional view on this point is that there is no *if* from God's perspective. If God knows the future exhaustively, then conditional prophecies lose their integrity. They do not express a genuine divine intention. They are nothing more than hypothetical assertions that God fully knows will never be realized. In the traditional view, Jonah's announcement that Nineveh would be destroyed did not represent something that God really intended to do, since he knew exactly how the Ninevites would respond. It was simply a ploy that produced the desired result.

Most people apply the category of conditional prophecy only to unfulfilled predictions (and regard all fulfilled predictions as indications of absolute foreknowledge). But there is good reason to believe that a number of fulfilled prophecies, like the one concerning Cyrus's aid to the Jews, were conditional too. For example, Jeremiah predicted that the Babylonians would destroy Jerusalem, as in time they did (Jer 32:4; 52:12-14), so the prophecy was fulfilled. Jeremiah also predicted that the city would be spared if Zedekiah would surrender instead of holding out (Jer 38:17-18). If the latter was a conditional prophecy, which seems obvious, then so was the former. It, too, depended on certain conditions that might or might not have obtained.

Instead of posing a problem to the open view of God, therefore, the phenomenon of prophecy actually supports it. In light of the full range of biblical predictions, we see God sometimes acting on his own within the world, but more often interacting with creatures whose behavior is not entirely predictable—not even by him. God told Jeremiah, "I thought that after [Israel] had done all this she would return to me but she did not" (Jer 3:7). " 'I thought you would call me "Father" and not turn away from following me. But like a woman unfaithful to her husband, so you have been unfaithful to me, O house of Israel,' declares the LORD" (Jer 3:19-20). So the typical prophecy expresses God's intentions to act a certain way, depending on what his creatures decide to do.

Foreknowledge and Predestination

For many who see prophecy as evidence that the future is entirely foreseeable to God, biblical expressions such as "foreknowledge" and "predestination" indicate that God determines the entire course of history, or at least substantial portions of it. A number of biblical words convey the idea that God chooses, wills or ordains certain things to occur, sometimes as long ago as the origin of the world. Although God occasionally planned seemingly mundane things in advance, such as the building of a reservoir in Jerusalem (Is 22:11), most of what he planned relates to the history of salvation. Christ, for example, was "chosen before the creation of the world" (1 Pet 1:20) and handed over to his executioners "by God's set purpose and foreknowledge" (Acts 2:23; cf. 4:27-28).

Similarly, God's people are the object of divine calling, foreknowledge and predestination. God's elect "have been chosen according to the foreknowledge of God the Father" (1 Pet 1:2). God chose us in Christ "before the creation of the world to be holy and blameless in his sight. In love he predestined us to be adopted as his sons through Jesus Christ, in accordance with his pleasure and will" (Eph 1:4-5). In a famous passage Paul speaks of those who "have been called according to his purpose": "For those God foreknew he also predestined to be conformed to the likeness of his Son. . . . And those he predestined, he also called; those he called, he also justified; those he justified, he also glorified" (Rom 8:28-30).

From time to time the Bible also indicates that certain individuals had very specific roles to play in fulfilling God's plan. God called Abraham to leave his country, promising to make of him a great nation through whom all peoples on earth would be blessed (Gen 12:1-2). His covenant included giving Abraham's descendants the land of Canaan (Gen 15:18-19). God preferred Jacob to Esau (Gen 25:23; Rom 9:10-13). He told Jeremiah that he had been appointed to be a prophet "before I formed you in the womb

. . . before you were born" (Jer 1:5).

On the negative side, those who oppose God also serve his purposes. God used Pharaoh to magnify his power: "I have raised you up for this very purpose, that I might show you my power and that my name might be proclaimed in all the earth" (Ex 9:16). The writer of Exodus attributed the hardness of Pharaoh's heart both to God ("I will harden his heart so that he will not let the people go" [Ex 4:21]) and to the monarch himself ("Pharaoh hardened his heart" [Ex 8:32]). He also stated that Pharaoh sinned in hardening his heart (Ex 9:34). Similarly, the New Testament speaks of Judas' betrayal of Jesus as a fulfillment of prophecy. Quoting Psalm 41:9, Jesus said, "This is to fulfill the scripture: 'He who shares my bread has lifted up his heel against me' " (Jn 13:18). He also said, "None has been lost except the one doomed to destruction so that Scripture would be fulfilled" (Jn 17:12). Following Jesus' ascension Peter told the believers, "the Scripture had to be fulfilled which the Holy Spirit spoke long ago through the mouth of David concerning Judas, who served as guide for those who arrested Jesus" (Acts 1:16).

Are these accounts of foreknowledge and predestination compatible with the open view of God? Or do they require us to conclude that the future is entirely foreseen by him and to a significant extent, if not entirely, determined by him? The first thing to bear in mind is the wide range of biblical testimony. In addition to the sort of passages just noticed, which speak of God's plans being fulfilled, numerous passages (including a number already examined) indicate that this is not always the case. To cite a general example, the Bible asserts that God does not want "anyone to perish, but everyone to come to repentance" (2 Pet 3:9); he "wants all men to be saved and to come to a knowledge of the truth" (1 Tim 2:4; cf. Tit 2:11). Yet it appears that not all will be saved. According to Jesus' statement, all of the dead will come back to life—"those who have done good, to the resurrection of life, and those who have done evil, to the resurrection of condemnation" (Jn 5:29 NRSV). Other passages indicate that some human beings set themselves against God for eternity (Mt 21:41-46; Rev 20:14-15; cf. Mt 7:13-14). In this important respect, then, God's will does not guarantee the outcome that he desires.

The same seems to be true in more specific cases as well. According to Isaiah's beautiful song of the vineyard, the Lord did everything he could to ensure the prosperity of his chosen people, only to be bitterly disappointed: "he looked for justice, but saw bloodshed; for righteousness, but heard cries of distress" (Is 5:7). On the individual level, too, God's plans are often thwarted. King Saul's behavior is a clear example.

Even when God's plans are fulfilled, there are often indications that things might have turned out otherwise. Some of the greatest prophets were reluctant to accept God's call. Moses offered up a long series of excuses before finally agreeing to return to Egypt as God's representative (Ex 3—4). Jeremiah felt too young for the responsibility (Jer 1:6). Could Moses or Jeremiah have rejected God's call? Nothing in the biblical accounts rules out that possibility.

But what about the specific predictions concerning individual behavior? What about the hardness of Pharaoh's heart, Judas' betrayal of Jesus and Peter's denial, for that matter? All of them fulfilled predictions and the first two, at least, seemed to be part of a prior plan. Was their occurrence therefore inevitable? Not necessarily. It is logically possible that they represent conditional prophecies. In the case of Peter's denial this seems especially likely, since Jesus had prayed that his faith would not fail (Lk 22:32). We have already remarked on Pharaoh's behavior. By the time the prediction was made, his character may have been so fixed that his response to Moses' request was a foregone conclusion. It may also be that he actually could have responded positively when he first received the request, even though he denied it, but then became increasingly resistant as time went by until his refusal was adamant.[79] While Judas's behavior fulfilled prophecy (Ps 41:9), it is possible the prophecy in question could have found fulfillment in some other way. After all, the Gospels tell us that "all the disciples deserted him and fled" (Mt 26:56; cf. Mk 14:50).

The traditional view of foreknowledge and predestination draws broader conclusions than the evidence warrants in three important ways. The fact that God foreknows or predestines something does not guarantee that it will happen, the fact that God determines part of history does not mean that he determines all of history, and the fact that God extends a specific call to certain people does not mean that he similarly calls all people.

First, although certain things did (and do) happen in harmony with divine predestination, this does not mean that these events could not possibly have failed to occur. As we have seen, the Bible clearly indicates that God has often experienced disappointment and frustration.

Second, it may be true that God occasionally acts by fiat and directly causes something to happen. Yet even if he determines one event, it does not necessarily follow that he determines all events. If God wants something specific to happen—say, the parting of the Red Sea—and his power alone is a sufficient condition of its occurring, then he can bring it about entirely on his own initiative. Where human decision is presupposed, however, God cannot achieve his objectives unilaterally. He requires our cooperation. Endowing creatures with significant freedom means that God gave them the ability to decide a good deal of what occurs. Consequently, the actual course of history is not something God alone decides all by himself. God and the creatures both contribute.[80] So even though some things happen as a direct result of divine action, this is not true of everything that happens.

Third, the concept of calling does not imply that God directly decides the eternal destiny of each human being. In fact, we misunderstand the biblical notion of calling, or election, if we think it applies either primarily to individuals or primarily to ultimate human destiny. Throughout the Bible divine election typically represents a corporate call to service.[81] It applies to groups rather than to individuals, and it involves a role in God's saving work in the present world rather than in the future life (although this may be an extension of the former). There were specific calls to individuals, of course. It was characteristic of prophets and apostles to be directly called to their work (see Gal 1:1). But in certain cases calls to individuals were really calls to the groups they represented. This was true of Abraham and Jacob, for example. In calling them, God was in effect calling their descendants, the "children of Israel."

An extensive survey of biblical references to election and foreknowledge leads William W. Klein to similar conclusions.[82] He finds that biblical election is fundamentally a corporate category. It pertains primarily to groups, not to the individuals who make up the group. "Plural language dominates [New Testament] election texts," he writes, creating "the overwhelming impression—in keeping with the Old Testament pattern of a chosen people—that God has chosen the church as a body rather than the specific individuals who populate that body."[83] Similarly, the central point of predestination is the goals God sets for his people as a whole, "not the selection of who will become his people."[84] And when God's call does focus on specific individuals, it represents a summons to service, not a guarantee of personal salvation. He appoints them to "perform tasks, functions, or ministries in his service."[85]

Conclusion

What kind of God created the world? What kind of world did God create? As with any important inquiry, the portrait of God's relation to the world that emerges from the Bible depends heavily on the angle of vision from which we approach it. Assuming that the supreme Monarch exercises complete control over the reality he created, and that its entire past and future lie perpetually before him, proponents of the traditional view of God find support in the biblical affirmations of divine changelessness and in biblical notions like prophecy and election. They emphasize biblical statements to the effect that God never changes, that he does whatever he chooses, and that he knows the future in detail. And they typically construe accounts of divine suffering and divine repentance as literary inventions, figures of speech that are not to be taken literally.

Our objective in this discussion has been to explore the scriptural evidence for the open view of God. If we shift our angle of vision in light of some powerful biblical themes, a quite different portrait of God emerges. A number of important ideas converge in the view that God's experience is open and that his relation to the creaturely world is one of dynamic interaction. The most fundamental of them is divine love, God's unswerving commitment to the welfare of his creatures and his profound sensitivity to their experiences. We find the clearest manifestation of this love in the life and ministry of Jesus, the Word become flesh who shares our human lot with us. We also see it throughout the history of creation and salvation that preoccupies the writers of the Bible. We see it in the biblical accounts of God's inner life—in his actions, decisions and, perhaps most vividly, in his feelings.

Various passages reveal a God who is deeply involved in human experience. The failings of his human children disappoint him and their sufferings bring him grief, but he seeks their companionship and rejoices when they return his love. These passages also reveal a God who is active within human history, patiently pursuing his objectives for his creatures, while taking into account their decisions and actions. They show that God adjusts and alters his plans to accommodate changes in human behavior.

The view of God proposed in this book thus rests on a broad spectrum of biblical evidence. A host of biblical themes support the openness of God.

2 Historical Considerations

John Sanders

W hy do we not usually read the Bible in the way suggested in the previous chapter? After all, many of us do read the Bible initially as saying that God responds to us and may change his mind, but once we become more "theologically informed" we tend to reinterpret those texts in a way that does not allow for such theologically "incorrect" views. Where does this "theologically correct" view of God come from? The answer, in part, is found in the way Christian thinkers have used certain Greek philosophical ideas. Greek thought has played an extensive role in the development of the traditional doctrine of God. But the classical view of God worked out in the Western tradition is at odds at several key points with a reading of the biblical text as given in chapter one. In the classical tradition the prima facie meaning of the texts cited in favor of the openness of God is commonly overturned in favor of another interpretation. The task of this chapter is to explain how this turn of events came about.

The answer, as I see it, lies in an understanding of the cultural framework within which the early church developed its view of God. The early church fathers lived in the intellectual atmosphere where Greek philosophy (especially middle Platonism) dominated. Scholars customarily describe the Christian use of Greek philosophy as the "Hellenization" of Christian theology. Yet we must acknowledge that what transpired was just as much the Christianization of Hellenism as Christian writers, brought up in the

Hellenic tradition, worked out how to be a Christian in that context. Moreover, they saw a need to proclaim that the Father of Jesus was the universal God and not merely the ethnic God of the Jews. Hence, they sought to demonstrate that the Christian God was the author of all creation according to the idea of the universal God articulated by the philosophers.

In seeking to accomplish these objectives the early fathers did not sell out to Hellenism, but they did, on certain key points, use it both to defend and to explain the Christian concept of God to their contemporaries. The view of God worked out in the early church, the "biblical-classical synthesis," has become so commonplace that even today most conservative theologians simply assume that it is *the* correct scriptural concept of God and thus that any other alleged biblical understanding of God (such as the one we are proposing) must be rejected. The classical view is so taken for granted that it functions as a preunderstanding that rules out certain interpretations of Scripture that do not "fit" with the conception of what is "appropriate" for God to be like, as derived from Greek metaphysics.

In what follows I will document the manner in which I believe the Greek metaphysical system "boxed up" the God described in the Bible and the tremendous impact this has had in shaping the Christian understandings of the nature of God, the Trinity, election, sin, grace, the covenant, the sovereignty of God, prayer, salvation and the incarnation. Most of this chapter is given over to demonstrating older expressions of the synthesis rather than the contemporary conversation. The reason for this is that the tradition sets the stage in a particular way that both contemporary conservative and progressive theologians generally accept, with some modifications.

Greek Philosophical Conceptions of God

The roots of Greek philosophy lie in Greek religion, which contained both an affirmative, positive stance toward life and a pessimistic, fear-laden side. Greek philosophy, in general, seized upon the positive while writers of tragedy focused on the negative. Philosophy could take the more affirmative route because it, in part, saw the human mind as in some sense one with divinity, sharing the immutable realm of being. Both philosophy and religion were interested in the ultimate source and explanation of why things happen. But whereas religion spoke in terms of fate or destiny, philosophy preferred the notion of necessity. The major distinction here, as Gilson explains, is that "behind necessity, there is a law; behind the gods, there is a will."[1] Whereas religion had tended to think of ultimate reality as personal in nature (even if somewhat fickle), philosophy posited a belief in something impersonal above (and hence more real than) the personal gods. Greek philosophy did not reject religion, but it did seek to purify it by submitting it to the constraints of an abstract and impersonal notion of ultimate reality. Utilizing the methods of natural theology, philosophers deduced their understanding of deity from the concept of "perfection" since nothing less than perfection would be appropriate for God *(theoprepēs)*. In this way they critiqued the older mythology and sought to rid the conception of deity of anthropomorphism.

Several of the philosophers before Socrates produced ideas that were discussed by Plato and eventually, though him, influenced Jewish, Christian and Islamic thinking about God. Though there were a great many thinkers, only a few may be mentioned here. The first is Thales, who claimed that all reality was water. This is not a ridiculous remark, for what he was actually trying to discover was the one ultimate metaphysical principle, that which is most real and to which even the gods are subject. Thales did not deny the existence of the gods but subordinated them to the ultimate principle.

Anaximander thought Thales to be on the right track but said that the ultimate reality behind all appearances (elements) should not be called water, which is one of the appearances. Rather, the ultimate metaphysical principle should be called "the unlimited." The unlimited is indescribable in human language (ineffable) since it is beyond all reality that humans can know. It can have no description or definition because it has no predicates.

Anaximenes took exception to this, saying that if ultimate reality is unlimited, then it is beyond all human thought and we cannot know anything of it (agnosticism). If the unlimited has being, he said, then it must have characteristics and so be capable of some definition. An indefinite something that is nothing in particular is nothing at all.[2]

Heraclitus used the term *logos* to denote the one thing that remains constant when everything else is changing. The logos is the principle of change, which does not itself change, but gives order and understanding to the changing world. Xenophanes ridiculed the anthropomorphic deities of the Olympian religion and claimed that the One or God was "motionless."

Finally, Parmenides held that "being," the One, is eternally full and complete and so is unchangeable. He also introduced the definition of eternity as timelessness. The One is "uncreated and imperishable, for it is entire, immovable and without end. It was not in the past, nor shall it be, since it is now, all at once."[3]

Plato

Many of these ideas made their way into Plato's thinking. Regarding the nature of God, most scholars agree that it is impossible to derive a single consistent view in Plato. Plato can speak like a monotheist, polytheist or even pantheist. Some scholars discount the religious and mystical elements in his thought, claiming that this is not the real Plato. It seems best, however, to say that Plato combined the logic of Parmenides with the otherworldliness of Pythagoras and the Orphics and so included both rational and mystical strains. Even if Plato did not end up with a wholly consistent view of God, his ideas became the spawning ground from which came many influential schools of thought regarding divine reality.

Scholars disagree concerning what Plato considered God.[4] Some believe that he refers to the "Good" as the highest of the forms (eternal truths that are the patterns of all reality) as deity. Others believe that his God is what he called the "Demiurge," who fashioned the preexisting matter into the present universe. Some believe that he equates the Demiurge with the Good. I believe that Plato (following those before him) distinguished between a personal God (the Demiurge) and an impersonal principle (the Good) and then elevated the principle above the personal in the order of being. For Plato the Good is not a mind (let alone a soul) but the cause of mind; it is an Idea or Form, not a God. The Demiurge or Maker, on the other hand, possesses intelligence, which can exist only in a soul, and is a God. But what the Demiurge possesses, whether wisdom or goodness, he has because, like everything else, he appropriates it from the Good. Consequently, the Demiurge or Maker is Plato's God, but this God is dependent on the Good, which is Plato's ultimate metaphysical principle. The Good is completely self-sufficient whereas everything else depends on it.

Nevertheless, even though God is in some sense dependent on the Good, God is "in every way perfect."[5] By "perfect" he means without lack or in need of anything or dependent on other persons (self-sufficient). Because he is perfect, change is impossible since "if he change at all he can only change for the worse." God must be immutable, for if he changed he would no longer be perfect. Plato's natural theology posits the idea that God is "the fairest and best that is conceivable" and then deduces implications from it, concluding that God measures up to the ideal conception of what is rational, good and beautiful. These are the best ideas and values his culture has to offer—which happen to be those of immutability, timelessness and impassibility.

This notion of perfection carries with it several related ideas. First, Plato says that incarnations of the gods are impossible, as that would imply change. Hence, we must reject the writings of the poets about visitations of the gods. Second, God is a most blessed and happy being experiencing no "joy or sorrow or pleasure."[6] God is beyond such emotions, as they would disturb the perfection of his soul. Moreover, God does not love (eros), for one loves only what one lacks, and God lacks nothing.[7] A self-sufficient being has no need of love.

Does this mean that God has no concern with the affairs of men?[8] Plato does not appear to give a consistent answer here. On the one hand he wants to say that because of God's perfection he "mingles not with man."[9] In this passage he says that love serves as an intermediary between God and humanity. Elsewhere, however, he rejects the claim that God has no concern for human affairs.[10] Yet even here the care God has for us consists primarily in his establishing the best possible world, not in his being active in human history.[11] In this regard Plato intellectualizes the religious conception of the gods of the poets (the Olympians). He rejects the anthropomorphic expressions of the gods since they fail to measure up to what a perfect being would be like.

Continuing this line of thought, since God is the best being we can imagine, we must think of God as perfectly good and never the author of evil or of lies.[12] God would never change in any way regarding virtue, beauty or truth. Plato also says that God is all-knowing and all-powerful in the sense that he knows everything that is a matter of sense and knowledge and has all the power that mortals and immortals can have.[13] Furthermore, God has these qualities "timelessly."[14] It is not proper to speak of God in the past or the future, that he "was" or "will be." Rather, "the truth is that 'is' alone is properly attributed to him." Though Plato himself does not develop it, the idea will emerge that God's knowledge and will could never change, as this would reflect badly on God's timelessly perfect goodness and omniscience.

Though the Demiurge is all-powerful, Plato does qualify his understanding of omnipotence by saying that the Demiurge is not a "creator" in the biblical sense. God did not create the realm of the Forms (the Good). Rather, the Good and the Demiurge are coeternal. Furthermore, the Demiurge did not "create" matter but rather "gave it form" or shaped it, much as a potter molds clay. Greek philosophy considered matter to be coeternal with God and not created ex nihilo (out of nothing). A couple of points are worth noting about Plato's understanding of "creation." First, the world did not arise as the product of blind chance, but rather through the will of an agent.[15] Second, the Demiurge is limited in two senses: by necessity—for "not even God himself can fight against necessity"; and by matter—"for God desired that all things should be good and nothing bad, so far as this was attainable."[16] God had to work with the laws of necessity and the matter at his disposal and so fashioned the best world that he could.

The fecundity of Plato's mind is extraordinary, and, as we will see, in the centuries following him one thinker after another accentuated one or more aspects of his musings on God.

Aristotle

Aristotle's writings on God are relatively few and are scattered throughout his works.[17] In fact, he is not that interested in the "problem of God." Rather, his interest lies in the "problem of change"—explaining how and why there is change or motion in the universe. In searching for an explanation for change he arrives at a God that is essentially a metaphysical principle needed only to explain motion. Though Aristotle has a supreme God he does not deny the existence of lesser gods. Some lesser deities move the planets by efficient causation (pushing them) and others exercise concern for humanity (the Olympian gods). He does not seem to take these latter gods seriously, however. His main objective is to discover the highest form of being in the universe that causes all else to move.

Viewing Plato's Forms as inadequate for the task of explaining motion, Aristotle argued that there must be an "unmoved mover" as the first cause of all motion.[18] He rejects the possibility of an infinite series.[19] There must be a first cause on which all other motion depends. Though the universe is eternal, it must be eternally dependent on something. But the unmoved mover must move the universe without itself moving or changing in any way.[20] For if it itself moved then it would no longer be perfect, for any "change would be change for the worse." The unmoved mover moves the universe by "final causation," not "efficient causation." If God actually pushed or fashioned the world (as did Plato's Demiurge) in any way, then that would mean a change in God. Instead, God is the final cause or goal (telos) of the universe. God starts motion not because he acts as an agent but rather by simply being so beautiful and perfect that the universe desires (eros) to be like him. And so it moves toward God—but God does not move toward the world. If God entered into any sort of relation to the world then God would in some sense be dependent on the world, just as a master is dependent on the slave in order to be master.

This unmoved mover is an immaterial substance whose being is pure actuality and possesses no potentiality. Since matter is corruptible and changeable God is immaterial, and since to have potential is to be susceptible to change God must have only actuality. This God is absolutely immutable. It also follows that this God cannot be affected by any other being (impassible) since he has no room for change.

What does this completely actual substance do? It thinks! For thinking is that which is most divine. Here Aristotle again diverges from Plato by believing that the ultimate metaphysical principle (the unmoved mover) has consciousness and is divine. Aristotle's ultimate God is a mind (not a soul) that thinks about what is perfect and unchangeable—itself. "It must be of itself that the divine thought thinks (since it is the most excellent of things), and its thinking is a thinking on thinking." This sounds rather narcissistic to us but it makes sense in Aristotle's system. What he means is that for God there is no subject-object distinction. Because God (the subject) thinks about himself as perfect thought (the object), the subject and the object of thought are one and the same.

Several conclusions follow from this. First, this self-thinking thought is so radically independent (aseity) and is such pure actuality that it cannot *receive* the knowledge of other beings. To receive anything would imply dependency and deficiency. Second, because God cannot receive anything (including knowledge) from any other being, God is unaware of the existence of anything but himself. Aristotle's supreme God is unaware of the existence of the world and certainly has no need of entering into relations with others.[21] "Since he is in need of nothing God cannot have need of friends, nor will he have any."[22] God is literally apathetic toward the world as he has no concern or feelings toward it. God does not interact with the world nor enter into covenantal relations with humans—God only "contemplates."[23] God is neither providential nor righteous in regard to the world: "God is not an imperative ruler."[24]

In sum, Aristotle says that this supreme God "is a substance which is eternal and unmovable . . . without parts and indivisible . . . impassive and unalterable."[25] This God, he says, "compels our wonder," but Aristotle does not worship it.[26] The unmoved mover is, for him, a metaphysical necessity that he needs to explain motion in his philosophical system. Though this God may not be religiously satisfying, several aspects of Aristotle's unmoved mover have found their way into the Christian tradition.

The Stoics

Though Stoic philosophers span several centuries there is general agreement among them regarding the nature of divinity. They espoused a monistic materialism whereby God was in the world (pantheism). They believed that the universe must be self-sufficient and so must be composed of only one essence (no dualism). Ultimately, only one principle exists, but that principle manifests itself in various ways—including gods and humans. The universe is a "great chain of being." God is the eternal and uncreated One who begets out of himself the whole of being by distributing the rational sperms *(logoi spermaktikoi)* and then resumes them all back into himself in never-ending cycles. The idea of procession and return to God, anticipated by Plato, is articulated by the Stoics and neo-Platonists and utilized by many Christians.

Though God is identified with the world *(kosmos)* he can be logically distinguished from the world. The Stoics use a variety of names for God: Zeus, nature, providence, logos, fate, fire and world soul. They tend to speak of God in personal rather than impersonal terms. Rejecting the Aristotelian and Epicurian denial of providence the Stoics affirmed that the logos so orders the world that nothing occurs that was not providentially ordained by God.[27] All events in world history are placed into a single causal system amounting to absolute predestination. But they qualified this cosmological determinism by admitting that humans have control of their "inner responses."

Yet the belief that God causes everything exterior to us raises the problem of evil: How can God be said to be wholly good if such evil things happen to us? The Stoic solution is that there really is no evil in the world if one would only look at things from God's point of view.[28] From God's perspective there is no gratuitous or pointless evil; each individual "evil"—say, liver cancer or the death of your child—is actually for a good purpose when it is considered as part of God's overall plan. If a tragic event happens to you, you should not necessarily consider it a "good" for you individually, but it is certainly good for the universe as a whole.

Thus, God is the "playwright" who assigns us our parts in the play. Pious humans will acknowledge this and "resign" themselves to their destiny and use whatever happens to them as opportunities for building character. It is useless to pray for God to change your situation since your circumstances are exactly what he has providentially arranged for the benefit of the whole.

A significant dissenter from this determinism was Cicero. Though sympathetic to Stoicism he made some notable qualifications.[29] For him the future is open depending on what God and humans decide to do. Human desires and wills are not the result of natural and antecedent causes or there would be no freedom of the will at all. Instead of viewing all tragic events as being specific parts of the divine plan, he counsels: "the gods attend to great matters; they neglect small ones." In line with his rejection of determinism, he denies that God has foreknowledge of future events. If God knows everything that is to happen, then everything will happen in accordance with divine foreknowledge—which would remove human freedom. Thus if humans have free will, says Cicero, then God does not foreknow what they will choose.[30] Yet, as we will see, Cicero's views would not become widely influential.

From this very limited survey of Hellenistic rational theology four tendencies emerge that had a profound impact on Jewish and Christian thinking about the divine nature. (1) The Greek philosophers were looking for that which was stable and reliable in contrast to the earthly world of change. Something of this attitude had perhaps been anticipated in the myths where Chronos (time) devoured his children: time destroys what it creates. It seems an almost cultural value they shared that change and time denoted weakness and corruption while immutability and timelessness represented strength, immortality and perfection. (2) This leads to the distinction between being and becoming or reality and appearances. Appearance involves time and change while reality is timeless and immutable. (3) The "world" was understood as a "natural order," a system of universal relations that implies an eternal, immutable order. (4) Above the personal gods exists the impersonal principle of sufficient reason, which is the ultimate explanation for why the world is the way it is. Deity, in this sense, is the universal principle of order presupposed to explain the natural order. God, then, is characterized by rationality, timelessness and immutability.

Philo: The Bridge from the Greeks to the Christians

Philo of Alexandria (c. 25 B.C.-A.D. 45) was a Jewish thinker who sought to reconcile biblical teaching with Greek philosophy. To him goes the distinction of being the leading figure in forging the biblical-classical synthesis. Both the method and the content of this synthesis were closely followed by later Jewish, Christian and Muslim thinkers. Philo's was a creative synthesis that did not wholly forfeit the God of the Bible to Greek thinking. Indeed, as we will see, on several key issues Philo rejects or significantly modifies Hellenistic formulations in defense of the biblical revelation. Nevertheless, in the end philosophical presuppositions are placed over the God described in the Bible and so serve as the preunderstanding that guided his reading of Scripture.

For Philo, God's essence is unknowable since it is beyond both human reason and sensation. All that we can know of God is that he exists, and certain of his activities (creation and providence). His favorite term for God is "that which is" (Greek, *to on*).[31] God is the being whose nature it is to be. Philo understood Exodus 3:14 ("He who is," *ho on* in the Septuagint) to mean "My nature is to be, not to be described by name."[32] God is anonymous or nameless, for to name is to define and to define is to limit.[33] We know that to ascribe limitation to God would be inappropriate (the method of *theoprepēs*), and so God must remain anonymous.

Philo's God is absolutely transcendent and so is ineffable. Human language may say that God is the prime Good, but in reality God is "beyond Good." God is so transcendent that he has no contact with human reason, let alone with matter. God does not leave us in a hopeless situation, however, for he creates a host of intermediary beings that help us to know God's existence and activities.

Philo, following the Hellenistic pattern, adopts a three-leveled cosmology.[34] At the top is the true God *(to on)*, the unknowable super-essence.[35] Between this utterly transcendent being and the world lies a knowable realm full of intermediary beings. This is the realm of the logos, the world of the forms, which exemplifies God's justice *(theos)* and providential love *(kyrios)*. "Justice" and "love" are not names for God and do not refer to God's essence but only to his activities of creating and ruling the world. At the bottom of the scale of being is matter, the knowable, sensible realm. The true God is anonymous while the biblical God is named, and so the biblical God must refer only to God's activities and not to the essence of God.[36] Hence, the God revealed in the Bible is subordinated to the "true" God of Greek thought.

God, or "that which is," has the typical list of properties developed in Greek philosophy, though Philo does make some modifications. God is timeless, for his "life is not a time, but eternity, which is the archetype and pattern of time; and in eternity there is no past nor future, but only present existence."[37] God is perfect, omnipotent, omniscient (including foreknowledge), omnipresent, simple, incorporeal, alone, self-sufficient, immutable and impassible. Concerning the last three of these properties, Philo made some qualifications in light of his biblicism. Regarding God's self-sufficiency, Philo disagreed with Aristotle that God had no relations with humanity.[38] Aristotle had maintained that anything that enters into relation with another being enters a reciprocal relationship and becomes dependent on that being. But Philo claims that though God's self-sufficiency cannot allow reciprocal relations, God's activities produce effects on the world that are not true relations but "quasi relations."

Philo wrote an entire treatise on the subject of God's immutability and impassibility. He believes that it is God's nature to act, not to be acted upon, and that "God is not susceptible to any passion at all." He does not, however, wish to end up with a static conception of deity. His desire is to protect God from fickleness and capriciousness and to affirm God's faithfulness in love and trustworthiness. In this regard, his biblical understanding would seem to have subdued his philosophical preunderstanding. That this is not the case, however, is made clear in his handling of the biblical texts where God is said to repent. Philo is well aware of the many texts that say that God repents (changes his mind) or feels anger. In Philo's mind such texts are not to be taken literally; rather, they are anthropomorphisms for the benefit of the "duller folk" who cannot understand the true nature of God. "For what greater impiety could there be than to suppose that the Unchanging changes?" Philo leans on Numbers 23:19, which in the Septuagint reads: "God is not as man."[39] Because God is not like us, he cannot change his mind. Moreover, since God foreknows all that will happen, divine repentance is impossible. Consequently, though Philo struggled against a static conception of immutability, in the end, the Greek metaphysical understanding of divinity ruled his interpretation of the biblical texts that describe God as genuinely responsive.

Philo breaks with the Greek tradition not so much in the nature of God but in the activities of God. He does not allow for an eternal world. Instead he opts for the biblical doctrine of creation, appropriately baptized, of course, with Platonic overtones. According to Philo, God first created the ideal Forms (patterns), then created matter, then fashioned matter in accordance with the Forms. Moreover, he says that God was not under necessity to create at all nor to create this particular world. When asked to explain why God created the world, he says that it is because God looked "to his eternal goodness, and thinking that to be beneficent was incumbent on His blessed and happy nature," he created. But this seems to suggest that God had to create because that is the sort of thing perfect goodness does. If so, then God's will would be subordinate to his nature. At the very least there is a tension in Philo's thinking concerning the freedom of God.

Another area where Philo takes issue with the Hellenistic perspective is the doctrine of providence. Philo rejects the determinism of the Stoics and affirms that humans have "libertarian" freedom (the ability to do otherwise). God providentially cares for us but does not determine all that happens. Humans have the freedom to produce events that God did not determine. Moreover, earthquakes, diseases and the like are not visitations from God but are merely events generated by changes in the elements. God can and does intervene miraculously in human history (through the intermediary beings). When he does, such providential activity is dependent on his foreknowledge of our future. That is, God can plan to provide for a certain situation based on what he foreknows will occur.

These ideas and many more Philo passed on in the development of classical theism.[40] Merging the two streams of Greek philosophy and the Bible, he established the method and content for arriving at the biblical-classical synthesis regarding the nature of God that would become so prevalent in Jewish, Christian and Islamic thought.

The Church Fathers' Appropriation of the Philosophical God

According to H. P. Owen, "so far as the Western world is concerned theism has a double origin: the Bible and Greek philosophy."[41] Despite different attitudes taken by the fathers toward philosophy, the influence of Greek philosophical notions of God is universal, even among those who "repudiate" philosophy.[42] The fathers had several noble reasons for making use of Greek thought. In seeking to overthrow the gods of paganism they found in philosophy some helpful critiques of the polytheistic gods. Moreover, they desired to show that the God of the Bible was the universal God, that this God was compatible with the best thinking of their day, and that the Christian God was the fulfillment of the God sought by the philosophers. Furthermore, like Philo, the fathers did critique certain aspects of the Hellenic worldview. They did not believe that it had the total truth about God— otherwise there would have been no need for Jesus. On the other hand, though the fathers do retain many important features of the biblical God, they seldom allow these features to call into question the philosophical understanding of the divine nature. Instead, a tensive relationship developed between the two conceptions: the idea of God as a world principle and God as the free Lord of history. In so doing, the fathers exhibit a subtle shift of emphasis from the God of revelation history to the God beyond history.

It is somewhat astonishing how quickly Christian thinkers adopted the philosophical vocabulary in discussing the nature of God and the nature of the incarnation. Though the early fathers do not always carefully define their terms and certainly did not develop their theologies as fully as later writers, they nevertheless pave the way as early as A.D. 100 for the synthesis of the biblical and philosophical God concepts. What follows is not an exhaustive coverage; rather, I will provide selections from a wide variety of writers to show the impact of Greek philosophical reflection on the nature of God in the Christian tradition.

Ignatius (d. 107), for instance, describes God as timeless, invisible and impassible.[43] Though he does allow for suffering in Jesus, he does not seem to allow that God, as God, can suffer.[44]

According to Justin Martyr the Christian God is not a completely new revelation but is a fuller one compared to Hellenic thought.[45] Consequently, he is comfortable in saying that God is unchangeable, eternal, incomprehensible, impassible, noncorporeal and anonymous. The ineffable God is nameless: not even terms such as God, Father, Creator or Lord actually apply to God due to his immutability.[46] But Justin is careful not to allow these ideas to overthrow totally the biblical portrait of God as patient, compassionate and loving. He rejects the Epicurean notion that the gods do not concern themselves with human affairs when he declares that though there are no passions in God, he does care for us: God, after all, is "not a stone."[47]

Justin also addresses the issue of divine foreknowledge and human freedom. He argues for a libertarian definition of freedom as the mark God bestowed on humanity to distinguish them from the rest of creation and by which God can hold humans morally accountable for their choices.[48] Yet he also believes that God foreknows all the decisions humans will make, which explains the prophecies in Scripture. This does not, he believes, lead to determinism, because God only foresees the free choices of individuals and bases his election on their choices.[49] In this respect God's decisions are in some sense dependent on human choices. Consequently, God is "responsive" for Justin.

In his polemics against the religions, Athenagoras says that God is "uncreated, eternal, invisible, impassible, incomprehensible, illimitable, [and] is apprehended by the understanding only."[50] He also foreshadowed the doctrine of divine simplicity when he said that God was indivisible, having "no parts."[51] The picture is the same in the writings of Irenaeus.[52] He furthers the discussion by affirming the biblical doctrine of divine wrath on evildoers but explaining it as being indirect in the sense that the evil deed is its own punishment.[53] In this way Irenaeus sought to remove any hint of change in the divine blessedness. Significantly, he rejected the Platonic need for intermediaries between God and creatures: God can deal directly with his creation.[54] Finally, like Justin Martyr, Irenaeus affirms libertarian human freedom and rejects any predetermination on God's part concerning human decisions.[55]

Tertullian sought to do away with all attempts at combining Christianity with various philosophies. To his credit he affirmed that God can change his mind, clearly seen in God's repentance of his intention to destroy Nineveh.[56] He sought to break free of the limitations of the doctrines of immutability and impassibility and allow for a reading of the biblical text that affirmed divine responsiveness to changes in the world.[57] God's will can change in response to human decisions. For Tertullian, God has many of the same feelings that we do but in a way that is "fitting" for God so that the divine nature remains unaffected by them.[58] Moreover, he is willing to speak of the "crucified God" who suffered on our behalf.[59] God, he says, is not in control of everything that happens, because he has chosen to grant humans free will by which they may participate with or fight against God's purposes. God foresaw the evil that would happen in the world but would not recind the liberty he had granted. Instead, he has chosen to respond with blessings and punishments depending upon human actions.[60]

All this makes it sound as though Tertullian was unaffected by the classical God concept, but such is not the case. Elsewhere he writes that God the Father, God the Son and God the Holy Spirit are incapable of suffering—only the humanity of Jesus suffered.[61] God, being eternal, must be incapable of change since a change would imply loss.[62] "Eternity has no time. It is itself all time. It acts; it cannot then suffer."[63] Tertullian, more than those before him, emphasized the personhood of God in dynamic, responsive relationship with humans. Yet tensions remained in his understanding of God.[64]

In Origen the tension between the biblical language of God and the Greek philosophical notions of God is much more pronounced. Origen follows Clement of Alexandria's lead on this subject but with more sophistication. Like Clement he believes that God is impassible, immutable, uncreated, simple, all-powerful and all-knowing.[65] He believes that because God has foreknowledge of the free choices humans will make, God has providentially arranged his responses. He steadfastly maintains that God's foreknowledge of human decisions is not their cause and does not necessitate what will happen. Interestingly, some friends asked Origen why they should pray if God foreknows everything or if he has predestined all things. In response he rejects predestination, upholds human freedom and insists that prayer is still valuable even though God foreknows our prayers.[66]

In a couple of famous homilies Origen seems to break free from the bonds of classical theism when he affirms that God rejoices at human conversion and experiences sorrow for human sin. Moreover, the Son of God felt compassion for us in our sin and so condescended to take on human flesh and suffer the cross for us. He even goes so far as to claim that God the Father experiences the human emotions of suffering, pity and love. It seems that Origen desired to defend a genuine relationship between God and humanity, but he found it difficult given the constraints of Hellenic thought. For he goes on to say that God is truly impassible, immutable and has no passions, but experiences uninterrupted happiness. All of the scriptural references to the passions of God (such as anger and joy) are anthropomorphisms used because of human weakness and cannot be taken literally.[67]

In a similar manner he explains away the biblical references to the repentance of God. They must be figures of speech, he says, because God is immutable and knows the future. It is thus impossible for God to make a poor decision and need to change his mind later. God only appears to be joyful or angry and only seems to repent, but in actuality God never does such things. What then of the incarnation? If Jesus is truly God, then did he not suffer and experience change and emotions? Origen struggles with this issue and ends up repeating those before him, saying that only the human side of Jesus suffered while his divinity remained untouched by the incarnation.[68] Though Origen sensed the tension in his thought here, he was unable to resolve it.

One third-century writer made a more successful attempt at breaking with the philosophical understanding of divine immutability and impassibility. Supposedly written by Gregory, one of Origen's students, the text claims that though God cannot be forced to suffer, he can voluntarily choose to suffer for the sake of human salvation.[69] But even this is not genuine suffering, since God is not subject to suffering but only wills to share in suffering. Since God chose to suffer of his own free will and was successful in obtaining redemption, it can be said that his nature remained impassible. The key point in Gregory's argument is that God's free will is not subject to the necessity imposed by the divine nature. If God does only what his nature dictates, then God, being impassible, could never suffer even if he wanted to. But if God cannot even will to suffer, then he is subject to great suffering, since his will is confined. Instead, Gregory says that we should understand that God is free to do as he wills and his will is not determined by his nature. Gregory forged an important path that, had it been followed, might have allowed Christian thinkers to be more open to divine responsiveness.

Lactantius, a Latin writer, also criticized the supposed impassibility of God, producing a treatise on God's anger in which he defended the reality of divine emotions.[70] Arnobius, Lactantius's contemporary, held to the completely transcendent, impassible God to whom our prayers make no difference, as they are merely for our benefit.[71] In his rejoinder, Lactantius says that God's blessedness does not prohibit the experience of joy, benevolence, anger or pity. If you remove these from God, he says, you remove any genuine religion and relationship with God. Against those who claimed that God is perfectly impassible and at rest, Lactantius replied that to be perfectly at rest is to be dead. Lactantius seemed to grasp that the Christian understanding of God's personhood and his relationship with humanity clashes with the Hellenic conception of God's transcendent immutability and impassibility. However, like those before him, he did not hold this insight consistently.

The Arian Controversy

The Arians denied that the Son of God was fully divine because the incarnation involved change and suffering.[72] The true God is immutable, impassible, simple and self-sufficient and cannot enter into time and human history except through an intermediary. The divine Son did enter history as an intermediary and so could not be completely God. The Arians saw that the incarnation calls for the reality of divine suffering and change and so rejected the full divinity of the Son. While they spoke of a "crucified God," Jesus—as savior, due to his connection with suffering and time— could not be fully divine.

In response Athanasius desired to begin, not with a discussion of the being of God, but with the historical salvation accomplished in the incarnation of the Son of God.[73] Though agreeing with the Arians that God is by nature impassible, immutable and ungraspable, he, in contrast, affirmed the full divinity of the Son. For Athanasius, since the Son is fully God he could not have changed or suffered. Then what of the sufferings of Christ? Athanasius insists that these must be ascribed only to the body of Jesus and not to the divine Son. Nevertheless, he defended the relationality of the Godhead by affirming that God truly is Father and Son: to be Father is to be in relation.

This idea was established as orthodoxy at the councils of Nicea and Constantinople, where it was affirmed that the divine Son shares the same being as the Father: the two having an internal relation in the Godhead. Robert Jenson points out two important modifications of the classical God concept implied in these declarations. First, "to be God is to be related. With that the fathers contradicted the main principle of Hellenic theology." Second, if the Son is "begotten," then "to be God is not only to give being, it is also to receive being. And there went the rest of Plato."[74] The church, however, continued to wrestle with the biblical-classical synthesis.

In the East the Cappadocian fathers (Basil, Gregory of Nyssa, Gregory of Nazianzus) helped to shape orthodox belief on the incarnation. They agreed with the Arians that the divine nature was impassible, immutable, illimitable and transcended all characteristics. However, using the newly developed doctrine of the two natures of Christ (human and divine), they were able to rebut the charge that the suffering of Christ implied that the

Son was not of the same substance as the Father. The Son, sharing the divine substance, was incapable of change. Since Jesus is both the Son of God and human, and since only the human nature of Christ underwent change, it could be argued that the Son was fully God. This became the orthodox answer to the Arian challenge.

Another problem raised in the debate pushed the Cappadocians toward a new understanding of the Trinity. The neo-Arian Eunomius claimed that God was a simple essence (not composed of any parts) and so the Son and Spirit could not be fully God. He believed that God could not communicate (share) nor beget anything from the divine essence since God is a unitary being devoid of internal relations.

In response the Cappadocians claimed that the term *Father* did not refer to the divine essence *(ousia)* but to the *relation* between the Father and the Son. In so doing they held that person not substance was the ultimate metaphysical category, and so, in opposition to Eunomius, they could claim that God was supremely relational.[75] The Father can beget the Son because the Father, as personal, has self-emptying love for another. God is then not alone, in isolation from relationships, but eternally related within the God-head as Trinity. God is then not an "in-itself," apart from others, but the epitome of community and love for others.

Moreover, the Cappadocians had a different understanding of God's external relation to history and the created order.[76] For them the Creator is absolutely different from the creature, but this does not mean that God is distant, since to be Creator is to be actively related to the creature. This is especially seen in salvation history, where the *activity* of the Father, Son and Holy Spirit is the essence of God! Regarding God's relationship to time, Gregory of Nyssa chastises the Arians for defining God's being as having no beginning (ungenerate) rather than as having no end. He suggests they reverse this since the unending God is Lord over history, which provides genuine hope.[77] In fact, Gregory claims that the Arian's timeless God is inactive, whereas his God keeps things moving. This understanding of God as involved with time and as a relational being (both internally and exter-nally) was a tremendous break with Hellenic thought.[78]

Some summary comments about the early fathers are in order here. Overall, whether Eastern or Western, their understanding of God is a mix of Greek metaphysics and biblical faith. They wrestled with how to explain the Christian God as the universal God of philosophical reflection. In faithfulness to the Bible they upheld God's love for and grace upon us, and they sought to affirm God's faithfulness and moral constancy and to safeguard God from compulsion or force. They also wished to maintain that God entered freely into relationship with humanity and in grace saves us. The doctrines of immutability and impassibility were intended to safeguard divine freedom and prevent anyone from confusing the Christian God with the fickle gods of the pagan religions. In addition they understood the incarnation to be a decisive action of God in human history that dramatically altered the course of world history. Finally, for the most part, they held that God freely created ex nihilo, denying the eternality of the world.[79]

On the other hand, many of these same desires are in conflict with other guiding beliefs drawn from Greek metaphysics. If God is utterly transcendent and immutable, then every change in the relationship between God and humanity must be explained as a human change. God does not have the sort of relationship with his creation by which he can be affected by what he loves. This begins to undermine God's freedom and the reality of his action in history.[80] The doctrine of simplicity exacerbates this tension, forming a gap between the God of biblical history and the God of theological reflection, between the God for us and God in himself.

Early prayers, liturgies and creeds followed the language of the Bible emphasizing who God is in relation to us in the economy of salvation. But after Nicea such language was replaced with abstract terminology about God in himself.[81] The focus on the eternal (timeless) relationship between the Father and the Son meant that the Father's relationship to the historical Jesus faded in importance. The "self-relatedness" of God takes precedence over God's relationship to us in incarnation and salvation history. Jesus of Nazareth fades in importance and is replaced by the eternal divine Son. Arguing from what is "fitting" for God to be *(theoprepēs),* significant aspects of the biblical revelation (such as suffering and temporality) were revised to fit this understanding. Though they had good intentions in applying the ideas of immutability and impassibility, they used them in an absolute sense and so distorted the faithfulness and love of the biblical God. In the end the true understanding of the divine nature was derived from metaphysics and the biblical revelation was made to conform to it.

Augustine

The last of the church fathers to be surveyed is also the most important for Western theology, as his thinking profoundly affected the understanding of God for both Catholics and Protestants. For the history of the biblical-classical synthesis there is no more significant Western theologian than Augustine. He was deeply influenced by the neo-Platonism he learned from Plotinus, which, even in his mature years, he used to interpret the Bible.[82] The neo-Platonic notions of God as creative force rather than one who fashions the world, the immutability of ultimate reality, seeking the truth by turning inward into our souls, and evil understood as a lack of goodness (connected to mutability and finitude) all vied with Augustine's biblical sensibilities for preeminence in his thinking.

Augustine maintains the traditional list of divine attributes describing God as self-sufficient, impassible, immutable, omniscient, omnipotent, timeless, ineffable and simple.[83] It could be argued that, for Augustine, immutability, simplicity and spirituality are the three most important divine attributes, because they cannot be revised without placing his entire conception of God in jeopardy. He writes: "Whatever is changeable is not the most high God," and "that is truly real which remains immutable."[84] God's immutability implies that neither his knowledge nor his will ever changes. Augustine made God's immunity to time, change and responsiveness to his creatures axiomatic for Western theology.

Yet does not the act of creation itself imply a change in God? What seems to have been a popular question in the early church was, What was God doing before he created the world? In one place Augustine facetiously replies, "Making hell for those who pry too deep"[85]—but he also gives a theologically developed response. He declares that God did nothing before he created the world, because time was not created until the world came into being.[86] Hence, the word *before* has no meaning until the creation of time. Augustine connects divine timelessness to the immutability of God's knowledge and will. God does not will one thing now and another later, because he wills once and for all everything that he wills.[87] If it were not so, then God would be mutable and hence would not be the eternal and simple. Furthermore, God cannot be said to know one thing now and another thing later, since he knows everything, including all future events, in one eternal moment of "spiritual vision."[88]

Augustine believes that divine foreknowledge and human freedom are compatible.[89] If God does not know the future then he is not God. God knows what is going to happen, but his knowledge is not the cause of those future events. God simply sees what is going to happen.[90] This would make God in some sense dependent on the world.

Elsewhere, however, when Augustine discusses the nature of election he takes back this concession.[91] The fathers had taught that God uses his foreknowledge to see who will have faith and then elects those who will. In this respect they thought we had the freedom to become Christians. Augustine, however, rejects this belief for two reasons: his anthropology and his doctrine of God. The sort of freedom necessary to respond positively to God was lost, he says, in the fall of Adam, so God must choose who will become believers. Second, if God's predestination for salvation depended on his foreknowledge of who would come to Christ, then God's will would be dependent on humanity and would be a violation of divine immutability and impassibility. God is not dependent on anything or anyone, so the gift of salvation must be totally independent of human agents.[92] Human wills cannot interfere with God's decisions, for "the will of the omnipotent is always undefeated."[93]

In light of his conception of divine power Augustine interprets the texts about God desiring all people to be saved (such as 1 Tim 2:4) as meaning either that no person is saved unless God wills her salvation or that the "all people" refers not to every individual, but some individuals from all classes and ranks of people (such as kings and slaves).[94]

Augustine saw other implications for this conception of divine sovereignty. For instance, what about those people who for a time profess faith in Christ but do not hold it to the end of their lives? According to Augustine, some people, though professing Christians, are not genuine Christians since God has not granted them persevering faith. Unless God willed from eternity that a believer in Christ (even a pastor) persevere to the end, then that person was never truly predestined for salvation.[95] Regarding infants who suffer or die, he says that God has good reasons for such events: "perhaps God is doing some good in correcting parents when their beloved children suffer pain and even death."[96] Though God's will is immutable, he always acts justly in the circumstances of life, so we should never question God's judgment.

When Augustine applies the doctrines of divine immutability and impassibility to the incarnation he arrives at the same conclusions as did those before him. He holds that the self-abasement of the Son is in no way a change in the divine nature since the incarnation is the assumption of an inferior human nature, not a transformation in the superior divine nature.[97] Consequently, only the human nature of Jesus experienced emotions.[98]

Regarding divine repentance, Augustine is well aware of the numerous biblical texts that speak of God "changing his mind." Such texts, however, are written for "babes" and do not properly refer to God.[99] There are, he says, a few texts in Scripture that truly describe God's nature—namely, those which say that he does not change. Augustine knows what is fitting for God to be *(dignum Deo)* and uses this understanding to filter the biblical message. He maintains that divine repentance is literally impossible, since God has complete foreknowledge of all that will happen and all that he has willed to do from eternity.[100] When God "changed his mind" by removing the kingship from Saul and giving it to David, God did not change his will but only his "work."[101] In other words, the effects of what God has eternally willed change, but the will of God remains immutable. An immutable God may act upon but not *interact* with others.

Augustine treats the divine "passions" similarly. When God shows pity his heart is not changed, and when God displays anger his will remains the same. God experiences no emotion of pity or anger despite the fact that his work effects salvation and punishment.[102] The Bible, when speaking of divine wrath, anger, love and mercy, must not be taken literally. After all, God has known from all eternity who would be punished and who would be saved, so it would make no sense to ascribe temporal upset to God.[103] All change is to be explained as a change in us and not in God. People who develop eye problems may no longer be able to tolerate the light of the sun—but the change is in them, not in the sun. Likewise, when people sin and experience the effects of God's judgment, it is they who have changed, not God.[104]

The same line of thought can be applied to God's love and mercy. Though God begins to be our Father when we are regenerated by his grace, God himself does not change. God's love is the activity by which he causes us to exist and (for some) to be regenerated.[105] God's mercy is his eternally foreknown and predestined grace to the elect. The biblical references to divine love, mercy and wrath refer only to God's works and not to any emotions or any change in God's relationship to us and certainly not to any change in God's substance. How then can God be said to be Lord over creation when there was no creation? Must not God in some sense become Lord when he creates? Augustine's reply is that being Lord does not belong to the nature of God, otherwise the creation would have to be eternal. God may be said to "become" Lord, but that is only an "accidental" relation and does not affect the being of God.[106] God's relationship to us in the economy of salvation is not constitutive of what God is. God remains unaffected by every "relation" between God and the creature.[107]

According to Augustine, God has internal and external relations. The internal relations between the Father, Son and Spirit are eternal and immutable but do not convey the being (or substance) of God. The being of God is one, a simple substance. The Father is God in respect to substance, but we may not say that God is *Father* in respect to substance because that would make relations an aspect of the being of God—which would conflict with divine simplicity.[108] Augustine says that God's external relations with the temporal creation are accidental and so do not affect the being of God.

Since neither internal nor external relations involve the essence of God, God has no "real relationship" with any other, including creation.

This idea did not appear to bother Augustine, for three reasons. First, it agreed with his notions of absolute immutability and simplicity in the Godhead. Second, it conformed to his understanding of the nature of personhood.[109] Augustine has been called the theologian of individual inwardness, and his ideas have been formative in the development of Western individualism. For him, the true self (image of God) is to be found in the individual's inherent faculties (memory, understanding and will), not in our relations with others.[110] The true nature of God and the image of God in humans is that which constitutes a nature (having a substance), not relationality. The essence of God is to be alone. The nature of the Trinity is known by turning within ourselves and examining our faculties. The soul images God, so by knowing itself, the soul comes to a true knowledge of God. Though God affects human history, the best analogies for God exist in the higher intellect, away from the transitoriness of history and human relations. Due to his intense sensitivity to the suffering involved in friendships and love, Augustine developed a permanent dislike for interpersonal models of the Godhead. Consequently, he relocated the search for God within the unchanging human soul instead of in relationships with others and the history of salvation.

Third, Augustine makes divine substance rather than the tripersonal God the highest ontological principle. The substance of God is what is ultimately real, not the relationships between the Father, Son and Spirit—let alone the relationships between the triune God and creatures. The divine essence, for Augustine, is defined as Pelikan notes: "in relation to absoluteness and impassibility rather than on the basis of the active involvement of God in creation and redemption."[111] Though it is not his intention, he makes God a remote deity, perilously close to being impersonal.[112]

Augustine's ideas have had a profound effect on Western thought. His understandings of creation, psychology, anthropology, soteriology, politics and history have influenced Christian and non-Christian thinkers alike. On some issues Augustine traces out more fully the views of the fathers, and on other issues he brings about innovations. His understandings of grace, faith and God's "relationship" to creation are seen in mechanistic terms rather than in personalistic and covenantal categories. His emphasis on divine immutability and simplicity takes precedence over God's suffering love and faithfulness. Augustine always believed in the biblical God, but in my opinion he allowed neo-Platonic metaphysics to constrain that God. He quotes the Bible extensively but interprets it within the neo-Platonic framework.[113] His consistent rejection of any sort of changeability or passibility in God leads to problems in understanding the nature of God's love for his creatures and how God can have any sort of covenant relationship with them. "The immunity of God to all 'real relationship' with creation will become axiomatic in scholastic theology."[114]

The Middle Ages

Enough has been said to establish the contours of the biblical-classical synthesis and the tensions in the doctrine of God this produced. It remains only to sketch out how this synthesis has generally been taken for granted in Western theology. Though some thinkers have modified certain points of the synthesis, it remained largely intact through the Reformation and continues to dominate conservative theology today.

A fellow claiming to be Dionysius the Areopagite, a convert of Paul (Acts 17:34), but actually a neo-Platonic theologian of the late fifth century, produced some writings that carried immense authority throughout the Middle Ages and were widely quoted by theologians such as Erigena and Aquinas.[115] Pseudo-Dionysius, as he is now called, pushed the notion of divine simplicity to its limits by claiming that we cannot know what God is. We may say that God is wise, loving or existing, but we may also say that God is not wise, loving or existing because he actually is more than these. God is superessential, that is, "nonbeing," due to his surplus of being. God is super-vital or lifeless through a surplus of life. He even describes God as the darkness beyond the light. God is such an absolute unity of being as to be beyond our thoughts and language. Thus it is best to say that God is ineffable, anonymous and incomprehensible. The biblical language about God only occasionally hits the truth about God.

John Scotus Erigena (born c. 810), whose main authority was Pseudo-Dionysius, said that the biblical descriptions of God are for the simple-minded.[116] In truth the infinite God is unknowable, for to know is to define and to define is to limit. In fact, God does not even know himself. God is absolutely immutable and impassible, so "God neither acts nor is acted upon, neither moves nor is moved, neither loves nor is loved."[117] Although the Bible "shouts on all sides" that this view is false, he argues that we must take the Bible metaphorically, whereas the method of what is fitting for God to be *(dignum Deo)* gives us the literal truth. Hence, God is said to love because he is the cause of all love and is said to be loved because all things long for him. God is completely removed from all relationships with humanity. Finally, God's absolute immutability implies that the creation is eternal. Otherwise, there would be a change in God once the creation existed.

Anselm of Canterbury developed the famed ontological argument for the existence of God based on the conception of the most perfect being that we can conceive. Anselm's perfect-being theology leads him to define God as timeless, immutable, impassible, ineffable and so forth. In a well-known passage he explains how God can be simultaneously compassionate and impassible: in actuality God is not compassionate; rather, it is *we* who experience compassion as the result of God's works.[118]

Thomas Aquinas, the apex of medieval theology, sought to harmonize the biblical-classical synthesis he inherited from the Christian tradition with the newly discovered works of Aristotle.[119] Hence, he blends Aristotelian ingredients into the neo-Platonic/Christian recipe. He believes that God is pure actuality, containing no potentiality. That is, there can be no "becoming" for God since he is eternally actualized. The best name for God, then, is "He who is"—for God is the only being whose essence it is to exist.

Aquinas uses the traditional list of divine attributes but adds a few touches of his own. For instance, he defines omnipotence as the ability to do anything that is not logically contradictory for God to do. God cannot, he says, make square circles, as that is a logical contradiction. Regarding predestination he took up Augustine's view that divine election of individuals to salvation does not depend on his foreknowledge, as that would make God dependent on the creature.[120] Instead, God simply chooses those he will save without regard to his foreknowledge of their lives. God is, in fact, so radically independent that his knowledge of the world is not caused by the world.[121] God knows the world by knowing himself. This knowledge is direct, involving no deliberation or reasoning from premises to conclusion, as either of these options entails transition from ignorance to knowledge. Moreover, if God's knowledge of what would happen in history depended on the creature, then God would be dependent and passive. But God is completely independent, immutable and impassible. This, of course, makes God's "relationship" with the world suspect. For Aquinas, the creatures' relationship with God is "real" while God's relationship to the creation is only "logical." God is like a stone column, he says, to which we stand in relation. The column may be on our right or our left, but the relation to the column is always in us and not in the column. As the zenith of medieval thought, Aquinas epitomizes the tensions of the biblical-classical synthesis in attempting to reconcile the God of historical action depicted in the Bible with the understanding of God as metaphysical principle, which was needed to explain the cosmos.

The Reformation Era

In many respects the Reformers were able to reorient theology toward the experience of salvation through the cross of Christ. Nevertheless, the Reformers achieved much greater success in revising ecclesiology and soteriology than in the doctrine of God proper. Moreover, they did not turn their backs on the entire Christian tradition to go directly to the Bible for their theologies; rather, they were deeply influenced both by Augustine's thought and by Scotist and Ockhamist tendencies that affirmed an absolute divine sovereignty.

Martin Luther instigated a tremendous revolution in theological method when he began with the "God for us" of redemptive history instead of the God known purely by rational thought *(dignum Deo)*. For him there is no

God beyond the God revealed in Jesus. He boldly asserts that in Jesus of Nazareth, God suffered and was crucified. He is well aware that this is an affront to both philosophical thought and human political experience, as kings do not voluntarily suffer for their subjects.[122] Luther's theology of the cross allows him to return to the "fatherhood" of God by which he contrasts the God of the Bible and the God of Greek metaphysics. On the one hand is God in himself, the absolute God apart from the world. On the other hand is the God of Israel who reveals himself to us, binds himself to his word, manifests himself in Jesus and limits himself to our understanding. All of this is done *for us,* thus emphasizing God's loving relationship with his creatures. Regarding the two natures of Christ, Luther used the "communication of attributes" in order to say that in Jesus, the divine nature of Christ suffered and even died. That the early Luther did not break completely free from the tradition is clear in his discussion of predestination.

In *The Bondage of the Will* Luther follows Augustine in arguing that God's will is the sole reason for individual salvation, for two reasons. First, human wills are so depraved that they cannot choose the good and God must choose for them. Luther thought that humans are still responsible for their actions, however, because he held to a compatibilist or soft-determinist definition of freedom. Accordingly, freedom means the ability to do what you want to do. Since we all want to sin, we are free to sin, and since none of us desire God we are not free to seek him. We cannot change our desires—only God can do that. We are like donkeys who go where the rider bids but cannot choose the rider.

Second "God foreknows nothing contingently, but that He foresees, purposes, and does all things according to His own immutable, eternal and infallible will."[123] God gets whatever he desires, including every human circumstance and eternal destiny. God's will is the ultimate cause for everything. Even God's foreknowledge is a function of the divine will; thus God cannot be said to "respond" to human sin.[124] God wills what is to happen, and that is the cause of his foreknowledge. Consequently, individual salvation and damnation is solely up to God and not humanity. In his later years Luther retreated from this position as he came more and more to understand the being of God as love for others that desired a mutual relationship. He warns against searching for a hidden divine decree for individual salvation and instead locates predestination in the election of Jesus Christ. The early Luther, however, "did not yet see clearly that the inmost Being of God, that which He is in himself, must be identical with that which He is for us."[125]

In a similar way, John Calvin sought a return to biblical theology, away from speculation. Calvin uses the Bible extensively in his writings, seeking to develop an edifying and practical theology. He often speaks of God's great compassion and love for the saints. In speaking of the attributes of God, Calvin prefers to use biblical terms. He describes God as eternal, wise, kind, merciful, good, just, powerful and truthful.[126] Though he explicitly repudiates Scholastic theology, he shows that he has not escaped neo-Platonic influence when he defines God as self-existent, simple, impassible and immutable.[127] Moreover, like Luther, he used Augustine as a theological mentor and was influenced by Ockhamist thinking in that he understood God to have an absolutely free and sovereign will. This is a crucial break with much speculative theology, since it frees the will of God from willing only what the divine nature determines. It had been commonplace to assert that God could will only what his nature necessitated, thus placing the divine will under the divine nature. This is an attempt to establish greater freedom for God by allowing for volitional decisions that we cannot fully explain by logical deduction from the goodness of the divine nature. God does not will something because it is good; rather, it is good because God wills it.[128]

Nonetheless, Calvin came to some of the same conclusions as had Aquinas and the Scholastics before him. He understood God's knowledge and will to be absolutely independent of the creation. God does not look ahead and see what is going to happen, for that would make God dependent on the creatures' decisions. God does not decide what he will do in response to anything that the creatures do. All that God knows and wills is not in relation to the creation but simply in relation to his own will. This effectively denies any sort of mutual relationship between God and his creatures. It is all a one-way street or, better, a novel in which the characters do exactly what the novelist decides. Calvin followed his feudal culture in interpreting divine kingship as domination and control so that "nothing happens except what is knowingly and willingly decreed by him."[129]

On the subject of predestination, Calvin asserts that God's election of individuals to salvation is based solely on his will. He repudiates the notion that God foresees faith in humans and then elects them. On the contrary, God "foresees future events only by reason of the fact that he decreed that they take place."[130] In fact, God decreed even the fall into sin. Yet Calvin seeks to deflect the charge that God is then responsible for sin by defining human freedom in compatibilistic terms and by making use of the Scholastic notion that God works through secondary causes. As long as God does not directly determine events but only establishes the causes by which they come about, God is thought to be absolved of blame.[131] Furthermore, whatever God wills is right, because his will is the criterion of justice. Lastly, Calvin says that we are not to question God's will in such matters (Rom 9:20-21). In whatever happens to us in this life, even should a mother lack breast milk for her child, God has good reasons for bringing it about.[132] In predestination God is the solely active and never receptive agent, while humans are solely receptive and never active agents in the process of regeneration. Once one is regenerated, the human response of repentance follows. Nevertheless, "the personal relation between God and Man became a causal relation: God the cause, faith the effect."[133]

It will come as little surprise that Calvin believes God incapable of changing his mind. Repentance of any decision would contradict God's immutable and impassible will as well as his foreknowledge. In his commentary on Genesis 6:6, where it says that God repented and was grieved, Calvin writes that the text cannot mean what it says since such activities are impossible for God. "Certainly God is not sorrowful or sad; but remains for ever like himself in his celestial and happy repose." Moreover, Calvin's hermeneutic presupposes that sovereignty means "domination," and so biblical texts that go against this understanding are read differently.[134] Calvin's high view of Scripture did not prevent him from denying the obvious meaning of the text. God uses such anthropomorphisms because "we cannot comprehend him as he is." Calvin says that the texts referring to divine repentance do not reveal the truth of God and must be taken figuratively.[135] Two biblical texts, however, teach in a literal (truthful) way the immutability of God: 1 Samuel 15:29 and Numbers 23:19. An interesting tension in Calvin's thought, of which he was apparently unaware, is that when he discusses the nature and value of prayer he speaks a very different language, as though God does, in fact, respond to our prayers, is receptive and enters into reciprocal relationships with his creatures.[136]

The Reformers evince aspects of the biblical-classical synthesis. They utilized the doctrine of God drawn from Hellenism while qualifying it with more dynamic and active analogies from Scripture.[137] They raised a challenge against the biblical-classical synthesis, yet in the end it was not overcome.

Jacob Arminius, like Calvin, displays the tensions of the biblical-classical synthesis. For him, the attributes of God involve love, mercy, wisdom, justice and patience. But he also describes God as immutable, impassible, pure act, simple and eternal.[138] Arminius decisively modified the Reformed thought in which he was educated, however, when it came to the will and knowledge of God. God's foreknowledge of what will happen is caused by what the creatures freely decide to do and is not based on his immutable will.[139] God uses his prevision of who will, through grace, come to Christ as the basis for divine predestination. Consequently, God genuinely *responds* to his creatures. Divine sovereignty grants the creatures genuine freedom. Arminius thus introduces a degree of dependency in God that allows God to enter freely into covenantal, reciprocal relations with creatures. He apparently never saw, however, the conflict between these ideas and those of the classical attributes such as impassibility.

Progressive Views of God

Modern theology has witnessed a remarkable reexamination of the nature and attributes of God. For purposes of discussion I will divide the survey into three sections, examining the views of progressives, moderates and conservatives.

Progressive theology ranges from antirealism, where God is merely *our* religious discourse or lifestyle, to process theology, where God is ontologically dependent on the world. Progressives still wrestle with the biblical-classical synthesis as they seek to explain God in light of modern knowledge. Among them one finds an emphasis on divine immanence and a movement beyond biblical personalism. The theology of Paul Tillich is exemplary in this regard.

Tillich self-consciously drew upon many elements of classical theism, modifying them for the modern age. Utilizing classical theism's emphasis on the ineffable and unnamed God, he calls God "Being-Itself."[140] For Tillich, God is the explanation for the metaphysical question: "What is being itself?" The God that explains all being is not *a* being existing alongside other beings, as that would make God finite. All existing beings are a mix of being and nonbeing, but God is infinite, containing no potentiality or mutability. God, as Being-Itself, does not even exist, since to exist is to experience estrangement and to possess nonbeing, which are obviously inapplicable to God. Interestingly, Tillich's understanding of God as fully immanent in the cosmos arrives at the same conclusion as had many classical theists who emphasized divine transcendence: God can have no external relations with creatures. To think of having personal relations with God or being his partner in action is impossible if God is Being-Itself, since to have such a relationship is to posit two beings existing alongside each other. "It is an insult to the divine holiness to treat God as a partner with whom one collaborates or as a superior power whom one influences by rites and prayers."[141]

Though Tillich often denigrates biblical personalism, he does see the need to speak of God in personal terms, since "man cannot be ultimately concerned about something which is less than he is, something impersonal."[142] Though God as Being-Itself is beyond the categories of personal and living, Tillich repeatedly speaks of the "living" God utilizing personal terms. To understand this we must keep in mind his notion that biblical ideas such as personal, living and acting, when applied to God, are "symbolic." They are not the literal truth about God, but are pragmatic means for making life meaningful. The one nonsymbolic statement about God is that God is Being-Itself. In line with the classical tradition, the true God is the God of abstract reflection, beyond predication, not the biblical (symbolic) God. This is what Tillich meant by the "God above God." But a question arises at this point. It is one thing to claim that "God carried Israel in his arms" is symbolic of the action of a personal God. It is quite another to say that the "action of a personal God" is symbolic. Of what is it symbolic? It would seem that, for Tillich, the living, forgiving, judging God is a description of *our* participation in Being-Itself. God is not a separate being acting in and upon the world, but is immanent within our living and acting. Hence, concerning prayer he says, "we can only pray to the God who prays to himself through us."[143]

Tillich's panentheism led him to revise radically the doctrines of creation and incarnation. For him, creation denotes our dependence on God rather than an event that happened. Aware that classical theism had always had difficulty explaining why the creation was not coeternal with God, Tillich holds that it is. Regarding the incarnation, he does not believe that God actually became flesh, as that would posit God as a being distinct from the cosmos. Instead, Jesus, as the Christ, exemplified to a high degree a new way of life that is not unique but is available to all human beings if we would only participate in it. Similar ideas are found in process theology.

Since process theology is discussed more fully elsewhere in this book, only a few comments here will suffice. In process thought all things are essentially related. God and the world are involved in an ontologically interdependent relationship. Process theology criticizes classical theism for its overemphasis on absolute transcendence, immutability and impassibility. Instead, God is seen as an ever-changing being evolving toward the perfection that is potentially his. God is creative, but only in the sense that God "creates" as *we* act, since this God cannot unilaterally act upon the world. God does not coerce us, but "lures" the world by love (eros) toward his purposes. In general, process thought tends to stray from any biblical moorings and substitutes the metaphysics of change for the metaphysics of static substance, ending up with a God that, if personal at all, cannot act in history.[144] What sort of relationship can we have with a God who cannot act or communicate clearly? Consequently, the doctrines of creation, incarnation and salvation are radically revised.

In progressive theology the biblical-classical synthesis is still evident, but the subjugation of biblical personalism to metaphysics is even more pronounced. The focus is on abstraction instead of on the concrete God who comes to us in the history of Israel and Jesus. Yet where the classical tradition overemphasized divine transcendence and immutability, these views reverse it, radicalizing divine immanence (as did Stoicism). This returns us to Hellenism, where the world is not created but is eternally dependent on God.

Conservative Protestant Views of God

Modern conservative theologians, like the Protestant Scholastics before them, have sought to maintain the God of the biblical-classical synthesis with its emphasis on divine transcendence. Standard theology texts remain filled with references to the classical attributes of immutability, timelessness, omnipotence, simplicity, exhaustive foreknowledge and the like.

Stephen Charnock's classic work *Discourses on the Existence and Attributes of God* has had a tremendous impact on conservative theology in this regard. Though he claims to arrive at all the classical attributes simply by exegesis, it is clear that he is controlled by the presuppositions of the biblical-classical synthesis. All biblical texts that suggest that God changed his mind, was surprised by human action or suffered are explained as anthropomorphisms and do not tell the truth. Since God is perfect, immutable, pure spirit and completely blessed, it is impossible that God repent or have emotions. In Charnock one finds the tension between God as he really is and God as he reveals himself. Of course, some biblical texts do describe the reality of God—those which speak of divine transcendence and immutability. Consequently, the data of the Bible are divided into two levels: the upper level, which defines God as he really is (transcendent, independent, alone and immutable), and the lower level, which describes God as he appears to us (immanent, suffering, changeable).

This two-layered approach to Scripture is evidenced in the writings of William G. T. Shedd, A. H. Strong, Louis Berkhof, Herman Bavinck, Lewis Sperry Chafer, A. W. Tozer, Charles Ryrie and J. I. Packer.[145] It is also found in standard biblical commentaries concerning the texts on divine repentance. These texts cannot mean what they say, since we know *(dignum Deo)* what God is really like. God, it is said, always knew what he would do, so he could not have repented.

When conservatives apply the doctrines of divine immutability and omniscience to the subject of prayer, the typical conclusion is that it is impossible to change God's mind. God could not change his will, for he has always known what he was going to do. "All change," as Tozer says, "must be on our part."[146] In his book on prayer, W. Bingham Hunter claims that texts such as Exodus 32:9-14, which asserts that God changed his mind in response to a human prayer, are simply anthropopathisms.[147] After all, he says, the Bible explicitly says that God does not change his mind (Num 23:19; 1 Sam 15:29). These texts actually claim only that in these specific situations God is not going to reverse his decision. But because such texts more easily fit within the framework of the philosophical conception of God, they are taken literally while the more numerous texts affirming divine changeability are taken anthropomorphically.

Carl Henry, a leading evangelical theologian, concurs with these ideas, arguing that God is timeless, immutable and simple, and that divine omniscience is not dependent on the creation. God foreknows because he foreordains. Consequently, prayer cannot change God's mind and divine repentance is impossible. Scriptures that indicate otherwise are anthropopathisms. Following Plato he says, "God is perfect and, if perfect, can only change for the worse."[148] Even the charismatic theology of J. Rodman Williams evinces this tension, claiming that God is personal and loving and relates to his creatures but also is timeless and immutable, does not repent and wills only what the divine nature necessitates.[149]

These thinkers exhibit the problems inherent in classical theism. Their view of the doctrine of God is the same as that worked out in the long history traced above, whereby the loving, interactive God of the Bible is conjoined with the static, independent God of Greek metaphysics. Sometimes this results in an unusual understanding of God's love. Louis Berkhof, for instance, says that God's love cannot find complete satisfaction in any object less than perfect. Hence, God loves his creatures for his own sake— he loves them in himself.[150]

This is not the whole picture within conservatism, however, for its hymnody and piety often speak of God's genuine relationship and response to us. It is even common to find clergy and laity alike asserting that petitionary prayer can change God's mind (while at the same time affirming all the classical attributes!).

Moreover, there has also been some movement regarding the divine attributes, especially the doctrines of immutability and impassibility. The great Princeton theologian Charles Hodge says that God has feelings because the Bible says so, and that if God has no feelings then he has no love. Hodge rejects the traditional attempts that defined divine love merely as the causation of existence or happiness (such as Augustine). Rather, God as a personal being experiences genuine emotions and so the Bible is correct when it ascribes joy, pity, anger and love to God. "We have to choose," he says, "between a mere philosophical speculation and the clear testimony of the Bible, and of our own moral and religious nature."[151] Millard Erickson, a contemporary Baptist theologian, concurs and modifies certain aspects of the God of classical theism (especially in light of the critique by process theology), arguing that there is no God beyond the God of the Bible and that the traditional understanding of immutability must be reformed.[152]

Moderate Views of God

Moderate theology represents an emerging perspective on the nature of God standing between the classical theism of the conservatives and the radical revisions of the progressives. A new movement is afoot that seeks to modify classical theism in the direction of an open God. Though all of those cited below would not agree with everything we say in this book, there is general agreement that God, though ontologically distinct from creation (contra process theology), enters into genuine give-and-take relations with his creatures and is resourceful, creative and omnicompetent rather than all-determining and immutable. God has made significantly free creatures on whom he conditions some of his actions. God is truly involved in human history, opening up new possibilities in overcoming sin. Moreover, many tend to have a relational understanding of the Trinity where the Father, Son and Holy Spirit relate to one another in self-giving love. God is not the "alone," absolute substance of Greek metaphysics, but the God who is for others.

From the evangelical tradition, James Oliver Buswell Jr. calls for a major shift in our understanding of God when he rejects the ideas of divine timelessness, immutability, impassibility and God as pure act. "We should," he says, "shake off the static ideology which has come into Christian theology from non-Biblical sources."[153] Buswell's plea has not gone unheeded. Nicholas Wolterstorff and Stephen Davis have given serious philosophical attention to divine temporality and passibility.[154]

Evangelicals advocating a more open view of God break decisively with those theologians who "cannot bring themselves to admit that anything God does can be conditioned by man or can be a reaction to something in creation. This sort of thing is regarded as a contradiction of sovereignty. As sovereign, God must always *act* and never *react*."[155] But God does react and enters into genuine responsive relationships with his creatures. In his relationships God is faithful, but God can and does, at times, change his mind. God may genuinely repent as the Bible repeatedly says. Evangelicals especially think of prayer in this regard.

Prayer, according to Richard Foster, is genuine dialogue with God.[156] In a particularly forthright declaration Foster says,

We have been taught that everything in the universe is already set, and so things cannot be changed. And if things cannot be changed, why pray? . . . It is Stoicism that demands a closed universe not the Bible. . . . In fact, the Bible stresses so forcefully the openness of our universe that . . . it speaks of God constantly changing his mind in accord with his unchanging love. . . . We are working with God to change the future![157]

Echoing similar sentiments, Donald Bloesch writes that through prayer "God makes himself dependent on the requests of his children."[158] This dependency and openness of God result from the fact that the divine love does not force its will on the creatures. Instead, according to Gabriel Fackre, God makes himself vulnerable by taking the risk of being rejected.[159] A growing number of evangelicals such as Philip Yancey, Gilbert Bilezikian, Greg Boyd, John Boykin, Harry Boer and others either affirm the full openness of God or at least seek to make room for genuine divine responsiveness.[160]

From the mainline and Roman Catholic traditions several notable theologians also see the need for understanding God in more relational terms. Especially helpful are the works of Terence Fretheim, who demonstrates the openness of God from the biblical texts.[161] Thomas Torrance speaks of the "openness of God" to his creatures.[162] Thomas Oden, drawing heavily on the fathers, says that God has a name, enters into history, has emotions, responds to us and takes new initiatives.[163] Theologians such as Jürgen Moltmann and Wolfhart Pannenberg see God's actions in the incarnation of Jesus as paramount for understanding the essence of God.[164] For them, Jesus reveals that God is involved in history and is willing to become vulnerable and even suffer because of and on behalf of us. God is a subject who acts in history and who involves himself in genuine relations with humans in time. Robert Jenson is highly critical of the biblical-classical synthesis, replacing it with a dynamic trinitarianism.[165] The theologies of Emil Brunner, Hendrikus Berkhof, Thomas Finger, Eberhard Jüngel, Adrio König, Colin Gunton and C. S. Lewis manifest a movement back toward a more biblical understanding of God as personal and essentially relational.[166] Roman Catholic feminist theologians Catherine LaCugna and Elizabeth Johnson marvelously demonstrate sensitivity to the classical tradition while evincing a truly relational and responsive trinitarian God.[167] Finally, contemporary philosophers of religion Richard Swinburne, J. R. Lucas, Peter Geach, Richard Purtill and Keith Ward defend the openness of God.[168]

Concluding Reflections

This has been a lengthy answer to the question of why we do not usually interpret the Bible as was done in chapter one. The inevitable encounter between biblical and classical thought generated many significant insights and helped Christianity to evangelize pagan thought and culture. Along with the good, however, came certain negative elements that gave rise to the biblical-classical synthesis that so permeates Christian theology that it often serves as the preunderstanding for the reading of the Bible. Hence, the biblical texts that speak of God's temporality, repentance and being affected by his creatures are dismissed as anthropomorphisms. If God is immune to time then biblical personalism must be left behind as an initial truth (for the simple-minded) while the correct understanding of the divine nature is pursued according to the canons of what is fitting for God to be *(dignum Deo)*. Biblical statements such as "I AM WHO I AM" (Ex 3:14) are understood to express the true divine nature as atemporal and pure actuality while statements that describe God as the "one who is, was, and will be" (Rev 1:4) are ignored or written off as figures of speech. Whence did Christian theologians get the criterion for making such distinctions?

It came from Hellenic thought with its quest to find that which escapes the ravages of time. Time divides life into parts, so the Greek philosophers sought a God for whom there was only unity and absolute oneness, one who never waits for his desires to be fulfilled. The eternity of God, then, is the abstraction from time, without a past or a future, the persistence of the beginning and by no means forward-looking.[169] Opposed to this is the biblical teaching that Yahweh is eternal in his faithfulness through time. The God of salvation history is the one who leads us into the future with hope, patiently working through time to achieve his ends.

In both Greek and progressive thought God is used as the ultimate principle that explains the natural order. Yahweh, however, is not a principle of explanation, but the name for a specific being who acts in history to fulfill his purposes.

Classical theism's root metaphor of motion with God as the nonrelating pillar around which we move makes it difficult to speak of a God who covenants with humanity and who makes humans significant partners in the building of the kingdom. It also affects the Christian understanding of divine love since it is seen as a one-way, purely active benevolence with no receptivity or passion: a benevolent despot in no way conditioned by or dependent on his creatures.[170] Western thought has tended to define the divine freedom as unaffectedness from time and others instead of openness to the future with others. The openness of God view sees persons in loving relation as the root metaphor from which theology should grow.

Furthermore, when Christian theology applied the classical divine attributes of impassibility, immutability, timelessness and simplicity to the God incarnate in Jesus, a whole host of problems arose for Christology and the Trinity. It became commonplace to deny any real suffering of the Son and it was difficult to speak of relationality within the Godhead. The God of Greek thought is anonymous, self-sufficient, alone (unrelated), invulnerable, self-thinking thought, changeless and egocentric. The triune God of the Bible is "named" (as Yahweh to Israel and then as Father, Son and Spirit through Jesus), is God for others, makes himself vulnerable and is self-giving love. This God, as Nicea established, is essentially related between the Father, Son and Spirit. Moreover, since the creation, the Trinity enjoys genuine external relations with us creatures. This personal God uses the divine freedom to enter into relationships of love involving reciprocity and mutuality. Though the tradition, with good intentions, employed immutability and impassibility in order to protect God's freedom, they were taken too far and left no room for speaking of divine openness where God, in vulnerability, binds himself to others in love. Christian theology, I am arguing, needs to reevaluate classical theism in light of a more relational metaphysic (not all philosophy is bad!) so that the living, personal, responsive and loving God of the Bible may be spoken of more consistently in our theological reflection and not merely in our devotional practice.

3 Systematic Theology

Clark H. Pinnock

Now that we have surveyed how the Bible construes God's identity in personal terms (chapter one) and how that portrait was (mis)handled in the tradition (chapter two), our task is to propose a more biblical and coherent doctrine of God. I want to overcome any distortions caused by excessive Hellenization and allow biblical teaching to operate more normatively. My aim is to do greater justice to mutuality and relationality in both the triune God and the God-human covenant.[1]

The concept of God is the most important topic in theology—and the most mysterious. Dealing with it makes one aware of the limitations of our finite understanding. We are not starting from scratch, though, or operating only from the light of human wisdom, but are reflecting on those perfections that must be ascribed to the divine Being on the basis of God's own self-disclosure in Jesus Christ. On the basis of revelation we strive for a biblically and conceptually sound understanding of God and of the package of divine properties that contribute to a coherent understanding. Each attribute needs to be explained coherently and the attributes together shown to be compatible with one another and with the vision of God as a whole. I believe that unless the portrait of God is compelling, the credibility of belief in God is bound to decline.[2]

In Christian theology we are not dealing with just any old concept of God, but with the surprising God and Father of our Lord Jesus. This is a God who does not remain at a safe distance, worrying about his own honor, but one who bares his holy arm and rescues humankind through sharing their distress and affliction. We are not dealing with an unapproachable deity but with God who has a human face and who is not indifferent to us but is deeply involved with us in our need.

Doctrines are important because they express the truth-claims of religion both for insiders and outsiders. They try faithfully to state what we believe and to describe the realities that underlie these commitments in a timely way. Doctrines explore the cognitive substance of the Christian message. A doctrine of God seeks to distill in conceptual form what we know about God through revelation, truth that bears ultimate significance for humanity.[3]

No doctrine can be more important than the doctrine of God. It is the principal doctrine in any theology, because apart from it the vision of faith cannot be stated. The whole creation is grounded in God, and the flow of history is the sphere of the outworking of his purposes. The doctrine is of more than academic interest; it is also of great missiological and practical importance.[4] How can we commend belief unless we have formed a convincing conception of God for ourselves? Modern atheism has resulted in part from distortions that were allowed to enter the doctrine of God from the direction of philosophy. We cannot believe if we have conceptualized God in existentially repugnant ways. It makes a difference whether God is portrayed as genuinely related to human life or as standing aloof from it and indifferent to human needs. On the other hand, formulating this doctrine in a way that shows the relevence of belief in God has great apologetic value as people learn that God shares in their sorrows and is touched by the feelings of their infirmities.

Humility is essential when thinking about such lofty matters. What the apostle said about our knowing "only in part" is very apt and his exclamation rings true: "O the depth of the riches and wisdom and knowledge of God! How unsearchable are his judgments and how inscrutable his ways!" (Rom 11:33 NRSV). In theology, as in the Christian life generally, we are pilgrims traveling en route to God's kingdom. Some things are too high for us, and we can always learn more in conversation with others. Nevertheless, we hope to get a little closer to the truth by our efforts; if we reach a dead end, we will not be too proud to retrace our steps and try a different path. We insist on distinguishing between the Bible and our attempts to interpret it, and we believe that God always has more light to shed on his Word than we have received.[5]

Basic Models

Interpretation is a human activity in which we distinguish between the primary biblical data and any presuppositions and interests we bring to the task. In theology, as in science, we also make use of models. Models help us to deal with complex subjects like Christology, ecclesiology, salvation and so forth. We face a great variety of data needing interpretation and are compelled to choose an angle of approach to them. In the case of the doctrine of God, we all have a basic portrait of God's identity in our minds when we search the Scriptures, and this model influences our exposition. What a great difference it makes, for example, whether we think of God as a stern judge, a loving parent or an indulgent grandfather. In theology we experiment with plausible angles of vision and try them out.[6]

Two models of God in particular are the most influential that people commonly carry around in their minds. We may think of God primarily as an aloof monarch, removed from the contingencies of the world, unchangeable in every aspect of being, as an all-determining and irresistible power, aware of everything that will ever happen and never taking risks. Or we may understand God as a caring parent with qualities of love and responsiveness, generosity and sensitivity, openness and vulnerability, a person (rather than a metaphysical principle) who experiences the world, responds to what happens, relates to us and interacts dynamically with humans. These correspond to the differences Sanders has noted between the God of Greek philosophy and the God of the Bible. God is sovereign in both models, but the mode of his sovereignty differs.

In this book we are advancing the second, or the open, view of God. Our understanding of the Scriptures leads us to depict God, the sovereign Creator, as voluntarily bringing into existence a world with significantly free personal agents in it, agents who can respond positively to God or reject his plans for them. In line with the decision to make this kind of world, God rules in such a way as to uphold the created structures and, because he gives liberty to his creatures, is happy to accept the future as open, not closed, and a relationship with the world that is dynamic, not static. We believe that the Bible presents an open view of God as living and active, involved in history, relating to us and changing in relation to us. We see the universe as a context in which there are real choices, alternatives and surprises. God's openness means that God is open to the changing realities of history, that God cares about us and lets what we do impact him. Our lives make a difference to God—they are truly significant. God is delighted when we trust him and saddened when we rebel against him. God made us significant creatures and treats us as such. We are significant to God and the apple of his eye (Ps 17:8).[7]

We hope to persuade people both inside and outside the church to regard God in this fashion, because we believe it is more biblical and meaningful to do so. Some critics may speak of "a battle of the gods," as if we were advocating a God other than the God of historic Christianity.[8] What we are really doing is conducting a competition between models of God. We are trying to understand the God of Christian revelation better. I realize that reconsidering one's model of God may be a delicate issue for some readers. It may feel as if, when a familiar way of thinking about God is questioned, God himself is lost or has become distant. But the experience of reconceptualizing can be positive. After the initial anxiety of rethinking, one will find God again in a fresh way around the next bend in the reflective road. Rather than worry about *our* discomfort, perhaps we should be concerned about *God's* reputation. Does it not concern us that God's name is often dishonored because of poor theologies of God? How can we expect Christians to delight in God or outsiders to seek God if we portray God in biblically flawed, rationally suspect and existentially repugnant ways? We cannot expect it.

Systematic Theology
Many contemporary Christians will not be surprised by the model we call

the openness of God or free will theism. They already enjoy a vital personal relationship with God and experience God as dynamically responding to them. Few doubt that what they do in life has an impact on God and calls forth appropriate responses from God. The problem actually lies more in systematic theology than it does in religious experience. For some reason, when we do theology we lose sight of the openness of God that we experience. There is resistance to conceptualizing it, even though it is existentially familiar.

This is because of tradition. The history of doctrine has seen a tilt toward divine transcendence over against God's immanence. Theology emphasized one set of divine properties to the neglect of another and disturbed the delicate balance between them. Though God is both transcendent and immanent, theology has tended to be one-sided. In Isaiah we hear the balance as God says: "I dwell in the high and holy place, *and* also with him who is of a contrite and humble spirit" (Is 57:15 RSV). Though acknowledging the truth of divine immanence, theologians usually place the preponderance of their emphasis on God's transcendence. They prefer to speak more of God's power than of weakness, more of God's eternity than of temporality, and more of God's immutability than of loving changeableness in relation to us. This represents a theological distortion that must be corrected, without being overcorrected.[9] I hope the reader will not see my position as an overreaction; it is not my intention.

It is important to recognize that God (according to the Bible) is both transcendent (that is, self-sufficient, the Creator of the world, ontologically other than creation, sovereign and eternal) and at the same time immanent (that is, present to the world, active within history, involved, relational and temporal). Combining the two, we say that God is so transcendent that he creates room for others to exist and maintains a relationship with them, that God is so powerful as to be able to stoop down and humble himself, that God is so stable and secure as to be able to risk suffering and change. Theology must strive to do greater justice to the two truths and hold them in proper balance. God must not be situated in our thinking so far away that he becomes irrelevant to human life or so near that he becomes dependent on the world, not by volition but necessarily.

Traditional theology has been biased in the direction of transcendence as the result of undue philosophical influences. Greek thinking located the ultimate and the perfect in the realm of the immutable and absolutely transcendent. This led early theologians (given that the biblical God is also transcendent) to experiment with equating the God of revelation with the Greek ideal of deity. However, a price had to be paid in terms of faithfulness to Scripture and relevance to human life. A striking example of this is the way they distorted the divine self-ascription "I AM WHO I AM" (Ex 3:14). This text, which points to the living God of the exodus, was transmuted into a principle of metaphysical immutability, as the dynamic "I AM" of the Hebrew text became the impersonal "being who is" of the Greek Septuagint (LXX), enabling theologians like Philo and Origen to link a changeless Greek deity with the God who acts in history. What God is saying to Moses in this verse is not "I exist" or even "I will be present." God is saying that he will be a faithful God for his people. This is an example of the way in which the image of God as defined on the horizon of Greek thinking threatened to replace the image of the living God of the biblical revelation in theology. The God of promise who acts in history tended to be replaced by a metaphysical statement about abstract being.[10]

No one should criticize the fathers for trying to integrate current philosophical beliefs and biblical insights. If God is the God of the universe and if truth is one, theologians should try to integrate all of the truth that they know from any quarter. But it is essential to integrate the various insights in such a way that the biblical message is not negated or compromised. In the integration the insights of revelation must be normative and not swept aside.[11]

Fortunately the tilt toward transcendence in traditional dogmatics was not always extreme. Christians did not consistently lose sight of the dynamic portrait of God in the Scriptures. It was present in hymns, sermons and liturgies, which tend to be more conservative in relation to biblical language. It was even present in theology, particularly in dealing with a subject like the incarnation. When contemplating this mystery, the same theologians would often admit that in becoming flesh the logos underwent change, because of God's desire to be gracious to humanity. The doctrine of the incarnation requires nuanced thinking about God's immutability, and this was not lost upon the fathers.[12] Nevertheless, the one-sided stress on God's transcendence (on God turned away from us, not toward us) would continue to distort Catholic and Protestant theology to the present time.[13]

My task here is to correct this imbalance in the handling of the transcendence and immanence of God. This requires allowing Scripture to challenge tradition and not permitting theology to be Hellenic where that would be unbiblical. While open to everything that is good in Greek thinking, we must discard what is not good. We cannot allow undue loyalty to traditional paradigms and esteemed theologians to prevent needed revision of the doctrine of God for today.[14]

Modern culture can actually assist us in this task because the contemporary horizon is more congenial to dynamic thinking about God than is the Greek portrait. Today it is easier to invite people to find fulfillment in a dynamic, personal God than it would be to ask them to find it in a deity who is immutable and self-enclosed. Modern thinking has more room for a God who is personal (even tripersonal) than it does for a God as absolute substance. We ought to be grateful for those features of modern culture which make it easier to recover the biblical witness.[15]

Let me attempt now to correct the imbalance in theology's handling of transcendence and immanence by expounding on the relevent divine perfections. In doing so, I will take care not to engage in overcorrection or to reverse the tilt, this time in the direction of immanance, as liberal theology has customarily done. Let us seek a way to revise classical theism in a dynamic direction without falling into process theology.[16]

The Trinity

The doctrine of the Trinity is the centerpiece of Christian theism. The church has always confessed that the God who created all things is one and many (not an undifferentiated simple unity) and embodies a relational fullness and richness of being in himself. Given the fact that Father and Son are persons and that the Spirit is spoken of in personal terms in the Scriptures, it is appropriate to speak of God as a community of persons rather than as modes of being.[17]

This doctrine is relevant to the openness of God because the social trinity is an open and dynamic structure. It does not portray God as a solitary, domineering individual but as the essence of loving community. When presented as a solitary potentate, God appears as the enemy of human freedom and atheism flourishes, but when seen as social trinity, God is the ultimate in community, mutuality and sharing. The doctrine enables us to break with substantialist assumptions about God being a "thing" and puts the idea of three relationally interconnected persons in its place. The Trinity points to a relational ontology in which God is more like a dynamic event than a simple substance and is essentially relational, ecstatic and alive. God exists as diverse persons united in a communion of love and freedom. God is the perfection of love and communion, the very antithesis of self-sufficiency.[18]

The Trinity lets us say simultaneously two very important things about God—that God is (on the one hand) self-sufficient in fullness and (on the other hand) open to the world in overflowing love. It sheds light on God's genuine delight in creatures as social beings themselves and on why he would invite them to share the richness of the divine fellowship as his friends. His love for us is not the benevolence of a distant king but like the tender love of a nursing mother (Is 49:15).[19]

The trinitarian model seems superior to process theism in this matter of the divine openness. It lets us criticize classical theism without moving in that direction. Process thinking does not have a patent on the dynamic, relational and temporal nature of God. The triune God (unlike God in process theism) does not need the world to make up for a love and mutuality lacking in his nature. The Trinity allows the church to confess that God is both self-sufficient and loving at the same time. The problem in process theology seems to be the fact that it requires us to view the world as necessary to God, with the implication that God is not free in creation but necessarily tied to a world. The Trinity, being an event of relationship, can be open to the world by choice and can work toward the mutuality in history already present in God's being.

The Trinity depicts a relational God who is ontologically other and a dynamic world that has real value. As internally social and self-sufficient, God does not need the world but creates it out of the abundance of his rich inner life. This makes God free to create and respond to the world, free to be gracious and take the initiative where necessary. Gregory Boyd writes:

> Only if God is antecedently actual, relational, and self-sufficient in relation to the world can God be free enough to do what scripture proclaims that God did in fact do in Jesus Christ. Only a God who is internally social within Godself can perform the more than necessary feat of opening up this sociality to what is fundamentally other than Godself. Only a God who is socially and self-sufficiently triune as lover, beloved, and loving can take the radical and completely unprovoked initiative to take on within this One's self the full nature of a non-divine self in order to effect wholeness in the whole of the non-divine creation.[20]

The Creation

The triune God is the Creator of the world out of nothing. This means that God does not simply influence preexisting matter but that everything depends on God for its existence. Belief in creation captures an essential dimension of the theistic worldview because it posits the world as the creation of God, as having its origin in God. Each being owes its existence to God, whose own being is independent of any world, making any relationship with the world voluntary, not necessitated. It also implies that God has the power to intervene in the world, interrupting (if need be) the normal causal sequences.

However, contrary to the opinions of some, this act of creation does not entail that God controls and determines everything. God is free to make such creatures as he wills and has chosen to make some with the capacity for choice. God has given them a relative and derived autonomy. As H. P. Owen puts it, "God can create such beings as as he wills; and has chosen to make some creatures with the capacity for free choice."[21]

Being socially triune, God has made a world with freedom, in which loving relationships can flourish. It is an ecosystem capable of echoing back the triune life of God. We may think of humanity as the created image of God's social nature, enacting on the finite level the relational movements that occur eternally in God. This must be why in the beginning God said the creation was "good"—because it brings such pleasure to God in this respect. As triune, God would be self-sufficient without creating any world, but as triune, God delights in a world in which he can interact with creatures for whom his love can overflow. God does not need a world in the sense of having a deficiency in his nature but wants one that delights his heart and pleases him.[22]

This helps to explain why God made human beings—because they are able to respond to God and to hear his Word. Their lives, like God's own life, are dynamic and oriented toward fulfillment in the coming kingdom. God wanted a world where personal relations and loving communion could occur. It would be a world not wholly determined but one peopled with creaturely free agents. Without having to do so metaphysically, God seeks fellowship with us, out of grace and overflowing love. Sovereign and free, God chooses to be involved with us.[23] He does not remain in spendid isolation but enters into relationship with his creatures. In the incarnation God stoops down, shares our lives and involves himself in our joys and sorrows. God chooses to express his deity not in the mode of aloofness, independency and total control but in creating free beings on the finite level and entering lovingly into their lives.[24]

Thus God has created a world that in a creaturely way reflects the goodness that characterizes God's own experience as triune. At great cost, God is leading the world forward to the place where it will reflect more perfectly the goodness that God himself enjoys. God does all this without having to do it, without being compelled by anything outside of himself. God's bliss cannot be increased, but it can express itself in the world. The creation is an occasion for the expression of God's experience outside of God. In the spirit of the ancient image of the ecstatic dance of the triune God, we can say that the purpose of creation is to express this same delightful movement on the level of the creature, ever summoning new partners to the dance. Beyond metaphysical necessity, God creates a nondivine world with real significance and accepts the risks of entering into a relationship with it. The aim was to create an echo in space and time of the communion that God experiences in eternity, a reflection on the creaturely level of the loving movement within God. The decision gave God the possibility of reflecting on himself in the created other and of enjoying the delight of real inter-action. It should be plain why the creation is so dear to God's heart.[25]

Transcendence and Immanence

In relation to the world, God the Creator is both transcendent and imma-nent. There are many polarities in theology: one and many, three persons and one essence, one person and two natures, and so forth. In a dialectical way, God both transcends the world and participates in it, is both high and lifted up and at the same time very close to it. God transcends and surpasses the world as its Maker but also indwells it and is active within it. Though transcendent, God is committed to us and wills to be in relation with us. As Isaiah says, God the Holy One is in our midst (Is 12:6). Though sovereign and free, God decides not to dwell alone but to establish communion with us. He has chosen to be God for us, even God for us in a human form.

A partial analogy is that of the artist, one who transcends her work and shapes it outside of herself and yet also imparts something of herself to it. The analogy cannot capture the intimacy and penetration of God's indwell-ing the world, though, for in a much greater way God, though ontologically distinct from created forms, creates a world external to himself and chooses to be present and immanent within it. On the one hand, God is sovereign and free and does not need the world; on the other hand, God has decided not to be alone but uses his freedom to establish communion with creatures and to exist in openness to the unfolding world.

By divine immanence I mean that God is everywhere present in all that exists. The world and God are not radically separated realities—God is present within every created being. As Paul said, quoting a Greek poet, "In him we live and move and have our being" (Acts 17:28). Today we understand the world as an interconnected ecosystem, a dynamic and developing whole, which has made this idea of God's immanence even more meaningful. It has become easier for us to imagine God the Spirit everywhere working as creativity in the whole cosmic situation. God is not detached from the world. Creation is not an event that happened and is done with. It is an ongoing process in which every particle, every atom, every molecule is held in existence by the Creator. Divine creativity has been taking place from the beginning until now, respecting what has already been made and calling forth new possibilities for the future. The whole world in which we dwell expresses God's continuous activity.

Process theology denies ontological independence, maintaining that God needs the world as much as the world needs God. This drops out the crucial distinction between God and the world so central to the scriptural portrayal. It makes God too passive, able only to experience the world and to organize the elements that present themselves to him. The Bible describes God as more present to the world than that, as a deity working out salvation in history and moving all things forward to a new creation.

The relation of God and creation is asymmetrical. The Creator gives life and freedom to the creature and voluntarily limits the exercise of his power in relation to it. God's openness to the world is freely chosen, not compelled. Process theism deserves commendation for opposing a static concept of God and for seeking a dynamic model, but not just any dynamic model will do. It is important to have a dynamic model that is biblically and theologically sound. Social trinitarian metaphysics (a relational ontology) gives us a God who is ontologically other but at the same time is ceaselessly relating and responsive.

In the second verse of Genesis we read about God's Spirit soaring over the creation. God not only created out of nothing—God also sustains the world, calls forth life and renews the face of the ground. God is on the inside of creation, in the processes not in the gaps. God is immanent throughout the universe in all of its changeableness and contingency and active in the whole long process of its development. The Creator has a mysterious relationship with every bit of matter and with every person. We need to recover the immanence of God, which helps us to relate to the new creation story being supplied by modern science.[26]

The Power of God

As Creator, God is unquestionably the superior power. His is the power to exist and the power to control all things. God depends on nothing else in order to be and is therefore free at the most fundamental level. But almightiness is not the whole story. In a world reflecting a triune community, God does not monopolize the power. Were he to do so, there could be no created order, certainly not a dynamic one with free agents, and not one producing love and communion. To achieve that kind of creation, God needs to deploy his power in more subtle ways. Though no power can stand against him, God wills the existence of creatures with the power of self-determination. This means that God is a superior power who does not cling to his right to dominate and control but who voluntarily gives creatures room to flourish. By inviting them to have dominion over the world (for example), God willingly surrenders power and makes possible a partnership with the creature.[27]

Condescension is involved in God's decision to make this kind of a world. By willing the existence of significant beings with independent status alongside of himself, God accepts limitations not imposed from without. In other words, in ruling over the world God is not all-determining but may will to achieve his goals through other agents, accepting the limitations of this decision. Yet this does not make God "weak," for it requires more power to rule over an undetermined world than it would over a determined one. Creating free creatures and working with them does not contradict God's omnipotence but requires it. Only omnipotence has the requisite degree and quality of power to undertake such a project. God has the power and ability to be (in Harry Boer's words) an "ad hoc" God, one who responds and adapts to surprises and to the unexpected. God sets goals for creation and redemption and realizes them ad hoc in history. If Plan A fails, God is ready with Plan B.[28]

Divine condescension is apparent in the realm of redemption, where God manifests his power paradoxically in the cross of Christ. What an astounding way for God to deploy power, in the form of servanthood and self-sacrifice. This was the mode of power God knew in his wisdom to be appropriate for bringing about reconciliation, and it reveals that love rather than almighty power is the primary perfection of God. When love says that power will not work in a situation, power is allowed to withdraw in favor of powerlessness. God does not overcome his enemies (for example) by forcing but by loving them. God works, not in order to subject our wills but to transform our hearts. Love and not sheer power overcomes evil—God does not go in for power tactics.[29]

We could also say that love is the mode in which God's power is exercised. God neither surrenders power in order to love nor denies love in the need to rule, but combines love and power perfectly. This power creates life and then awakens and stimulates it in others. The question is not whether but in what manner God exercises power. The model cannot be domination but is one of nurturing and empowering.[30]

We must not define omnipotence as the power to determine everything but rather as the power that enables God to deal with any situation that arises. Plainly God is not at the moment all in all—this has yet to happen when the kingdom comes (1 Cor 15:28). God's power presently is more subtle, much greater in fact than the coercive power of a puppeteer. Monopoly power is easy to manage—more difficult is a power that makes free agents and governs a universe where creatures can disobey. Omnipotence does not mean that nothing can go contrary to God's will (our sins go against it) but that God is able to deal with any circumstance that may arise. The idea that it means a divine decree and total control is an alarming concept and contrary to the Scriptures. Total control is not a higher view of God's power but a diminution of it.[31] The biblical narrative plainly reveals that God has rivals and has to struggle with them.

In an attempt to preserve the notion of God's power as total control, some advocate what they call biblical compatibilism, the idea that one can uphold genuine freedom and divine determinism at the same time.[32] This is sleight of hand and does not work. Just the fact of our rebellion as sinners against God's will testifies it is not so. The fall into sin was against the will of God and proves by itself that God does not exercise total control over all events in this world. Evils happen that are not supposed to happen, that grieve and anger God. Free will theism is the best way to account for this fact. To say that God hates sin while secretly willing it, to say that God warns us not to fall away though it is impossible, to say that God loves the world while excluding most people from an opportunity of salvation, to say that God warmly invites sinners to come knowing all the while that they cannot possibly do so—such things do not deserve to be called mysteries when that is just a euphemism for nonsense.[33]

The all-powerful God delegates power to the creature, making himself vulnerable. In giving us dominion over the earth, God shares power with the creature. The fact of sin in history reveals the adverse effect that disobedience has on God's purpose. God allows the world to be affected by the power of the creature and takes risks accompanying any genuine relatedness. There is a paradox of strength and vulnerability of God according to the Scriptures. Though ontologically strong, God can be vulnerable because of the decision to make a world like this. The Lord of the universe has chosen to limit his power by delegating some to the creature. God gives room to creatures and invites them to be covenant partners, opening up the possibility of loving fellowship but also of some initiative being taken away from God and creatures coming into conflict with his plans. God gives us room to rebel against him, and when that happens patiently waits for the prodigal to return.

The theme of God's kingdom helps us to understand divine sovereignty from another angle. Jesus announces that God's rule is near but not yet in full effect. At present, God's will is resisted by powers of darkness, but the day will come when his will shall triumph. At present, evil is mounting a challenge to God's rule with considerable effect. The powers of darkness put up stiff resistance and to a degree block God's plans; that is, they can restrict God's ability to respond to a given crisis. Hence Paul says that the Spirit groans and waits with us for the final redemption (Rom 8:23). God's

ability to turn things around is circumscribed in ways we cannot understand, yet this is more than countered by the hope of the coming kingdom.
Evil may have its day, but it will not finally triumph.[34] By his decision to
create a world like ours, God showed his willingness to take risks and to
work with a history whose outcome he does not wholly decide. Theology
does not work with an abstract idea of power that confuses sovereignty with
tyranny.[35]

Divine sovereignty involves a flexible out-working of God's purposes in
history. It refers to his ability, as the only wise God, to manage things,
despite resistance to his will. Owing to the emphasis in theology on almightiness, we have tended to neglect the form of power called persuasion. It
is not the only kind of power God has at his disposal, but it is a noble form
that has been neglected in the tradition, where power tends to be associated, even equated, with coercion. The power of God's love (for example)
does not command but woos and transforms us. This power can deliver us
from evil and transform the wicked heart. Yet to reduce God's power to
persuasion would make God too passive—it would be an overreaction
against almightiness.

At the same time, however, the power of persuasion is an admirable
power. Is God's power not as wonderfully displayed in his condescension
to our weakness as in the starry heavens? It is so clear from Scripture,
illustrated in God's dealings with Moses, that God does not overpower his
servants, even though he could easily do so, but rather works with mortals
and all of their hesitations and uncertainties. God honors Moses' dignity
to the extent that when he cannot persuade him to accept the call, he
resorts to an alternate plan, calling Aaron into the picture. God aims for
the best in every situation and is even willing to work with options that are
less than the best. God accepts what people decide to do with the powers
they have been given. The future is determined by God not alone but in
partnership with human agents. God gives us a role in shaping what the
future will be. He is flexible and does not insist on doing things his way.
God will adjust his own plans because he is sensitive to what humans think
and do.[36]

Understanding God's power gives us some help with the vexed problem of evil. If this is a world in which evil is possible but not inevitable, then it can be seen as stemming primarily from the misuse of freedom. The full display of God's sovereignty would not be a present reality but something to come at the end of history, when his glory is revealed, rather than at the present time, when the Spirit suffers with us and the universe groans.[37]

We can call this model of divine openness free will theism. Upholding God's power, it understands God to be voluntarily self-limited, making room for creaturely freedom. Without making God finite, this definition appreciates God's delighting in a universe which he does not totally control.

The Immutablity of God

The Trinity is unchangeably what it is from everlasting to everlasting—and nothing can change that. Furthermore, we can always rely on God to be faithful to his promises; he is not in any way fickle or capricious. Immutability ought to focus on the faithfulness of God as a relational, personal being.

But the tradition has taken immutability far in the direction of immobility and inertness. Some have claimed that God is wholly actual and not at all potential and thus cannot change in any way. They have equated the biblical idea of faithfulness with the Greek idea that requires any changes related to God to occur only on the human side. This is the error that tempted some of the early theologians to explain the incarnation without admitting that God changed, and to explain away dozens of biblical references to God's repenting and changing.

This is a mistake from a biblical standpoint. The God of the Bible is a God of action, not inaction. God is immutable in essence and in his trustworthiness over time, but in other respects God changes. For example, God changes in his response to events in history. The Bible states that when God saw the extent of human wickedness on the earth, he was sorry that he had made humankind (Gen 6:5). The book of Jonah says that when God saw the conversion of Nineveh, he repented of the evil he said he would do to it (Jon 3:10). This latter passage is very revealing because it tells us that

God experiences temporal passage, learns new facts when they occur and changes plans in response to what humans do.

God is unchanging in nature and essence but not in experience, knowledge and action. In nature, God is consistently reliable and loving and can be depended on completely. God's character is faithful and reliable—he is a steadfast friend who binds himself to us and does not forsake us. His concern for the creature is constant and unaffected by anything. From the point of view of experience, however, God responds to the changing needs of his children and changes direction when necessary. God is changeless in nature, but his nature is that of a creative person who interacts. God's immutability does not rule out God's responsiveness, the quality that enables God to deal with every new happening and to bend it toward his objectives without violating its integrity.

When I say that God is subject to change, I am referring to a uniquely divine kind of changeability. I do not mean that God is subject to change involuntarily, which would make God a contingent being, but that God allows the world to touch him, while being transcendent over it.

The Impassibility of God
Impassibility is the most dubious of the divine attributes discussed in classical theism, because it suggests that God does not experience sorrow, sadness or pain. It appears to deny that God is touched by the feelings of our infirmities, despite what the Bible eloquently says about his love and his sorrow. How can God be loving and not pained by evil? How can God be impassible when the incarnate Son experienced suffering and death?[38]

The suffering or pathos of God is a strong biblical theme—God's love, wrath, jealousy and suffering are all prominent. God suffers when there is a broken relationship between humanity and himself. In this context, God agonizes over his people and says: "My heart recoils within me, my compassion grows warm and tender" (Hosea 11:8 RSV). God is not cool and collected but is deeply involved and can be wounded. The idea of God's impassibility arises more from Plato than from the Bible.[39]

The theme of suffering strongly brings out God's openness to the world.

Not aloof and impassive, God does not just imagine what it would be like to suffer, he actually suffers because of his decision to love. God has chosen to be open to the world and to share in its suffering because of his love. God's transcendence over the world does not prevent him from interacting with the world or from being affected by the world.

What does it mean to say that God suffers? This is a mystery of God's inner life. Plato was not altogether wrong to say that God must be free of certain kinds of passion and emotion. After all, God is not a creature; therefore, he does not suffer in exactly the ways that we do. Responding to pain, for example, must in some ways be an imaginative response to the suffering of a creature. How could God experience physical pain, if he is not physical? How could he suffer the pain of loneliness, if he is triune? Or the pain of fear when he is securely God? What we should say is that God sympathizes in his relationship with us. God risked suffering when he opened himself up to the world, when he made it possible for the creature to have an impact on him. God risked suffering when he decided to love and be loved by the creature. A lover's existence is inescapably affected by the other, especially when the loved one acts in ways that grieve and disappoint. Listen to the suffering in God's yearning for his wayward son: "Is Ephraim my dear son? Is he my darling child? For as often as I speak against him, I do remember him still. Therefore my heart yearns for him; I will surely have mercy on him" (Jer 31:20 RSV). Obviously God feels the pain of broken relationships.

At the same time, impassibility is a subtle idea with a grain of truth. We have to distinguish ways in which God can suffer from ways in which God cannot suffer. God is beyond certain modes of suffering, just as he is beyond certain modes of change. We could say that God is impassible in nature but passible in his experience of the world. Change occurs in the world and affects God when he becomes aware of it. When that change involves innocent suffering (for example), God responds tenderly to it.[40]

God's Eternity
Should we say that God is temporally everlasting or timelessly eternal?

Classical theism has made the strong claim that God is timeless, in the sense of existing outside of time and sequence. This view strongly emphasizes God's transcendence over the world. And since a timeless being would be totally actualized, it implies strong immutability and impassibility as well.[41]

However, timelessness presents many difficulties from a theological standpoint. First, it is hard to form any idea of what timelessness might mean, since all of our thinking is temporally conditioned. A timeless being could not make plans and carry them out. Second, it creates problems for biblical history, which portrays God as One who projects plans, experiences the flow of temporal passage and faces the future as not completely settled. How can a timeless God be the Creator of a temporal world? Why is God described as being involved in temporal realities? Third, it seems to undermine our worship of God. Do we not praise God, not because he is beyond time and change but because he works redemptively in time and brings about salvation? Fourth, if God did not experience events as they transpire, he would not experience or know the world as it actually is. If God's eternity were timeless, God could not be related to our temporal world. In actual fact, though, the biblical symbols do not speak of divine timelessness but of God's faithfulness over time. Though we wither and die, God abides and is not threatened or undone by time. We need an understanding of God's eternity that does not cancel or annihilate time but stands in a positive relation to it, which is for us not against us.

Experiencing temporal passage, God confronts a future that is open. The distinction between what is possible and what is actual is valid for God as well as for us. The past is actual, the present is becoming, and the future is possible. The everlasting One is active and dynamic through all of this flow, envisaging future possibilities and working to realize them. Transcendent to temporal passage, God is in the process without being involuntarily subject to it.[42]

When I say that God is eternal, I mean that God transcends our experience of time, is immune from the ravages of time, is free from our inability to remember, and so forth. I affirm that God is with us in time, experiencing the succession of events with us. Past, present and future are real to God.

This underlies the biblical claim that God is an agent who works in history, who makes plans and carries them out, who remembers the past and gives promises about the future. God's eternity embraces time and takes temporal events into the divine life.

The God of the Bible is not timeless. His eternity means that there has never been and never will be a time when God does not exist. Timelessness limits God. If he were timeless, God would be unable to work salvation in history, would be cut off from the world, have no real relationship with people and would be completely static. God is not temporal as creatures are, however, but can enter into time and relate to sequence and history. When I say that God is in time, I do not mean that God is exhaustively in time. Even in human experience, we partially transcend time through memory, imagination and reason. God's transcendence over time is vastly more perfect than is ours. Putting it positively, the Creator of time and space is at the same time the One who most perfectly experiences time. God loves time and enters into the experience of time, not only in the incarnation but always. The Bible sees God as present to the flow of history, facing the future as partly an unsettled matter. I say partly because much of the future is settled by what has already happened and by what God plans to do.[43]

Divine Knowledge

Obviously God must know all things that can be known and know them truly. To be able to know all that can be known is a dimension of God's power. Ignorance, or not to know something God needs to know in order to govern the universe and pursue his will, would be a serious limitation. However, omniscience need not mean exhaustive foreknowledge of all future events. If that were its meaning, the future would be fixed and determined, much as is the past. Total knowledge of the future would imply a fixity of events. Nothing in the future would need to be decided. It also would imply that human freedom is an illusion, that we make no difference and are not responsible.

What does the Bible say about God's knowledge? Many believe that the Bible says that God has exhaustive foreknowledge, but it does not.[44] It says, for example, that God tested Abraham to see what he would do and after the test says through the angel: "Now I know that you fear God" (Gen 22:12). This was a piece of information that God was eager to secure. In another place Moses said that God was testing the people to order to know whether they actually love him or not (Deut 13:3). Total foreknowledge would jeopardize the genuineness of the divine-human relationship. What kind of dialogue is it where one party already knows what the other will say and do? I would not call this a personal relationship. Commenting on Israel's wickedness, God expresses frustration: "nor did it enter my mind that they should do this abomination" (Jer 32:35 NRSV). God had not anticipated it. In the book of Jonah, God threatens Nineveh with destruction and then calls it off (much to Jonah's chagrin) when the people repent (Jon 3:10). Their repenting was not something God knew in advance would happen. He was planning to destroy them but changed his mind when they converted.

Often God says things like this in the Bible: "Perhaps they will understand" or "It may be that they will listen." From such phrases we must deduce that God has different options depending on people's responses that are still outstanding (see Jer 26:3; Ezek 12:3; etc.). In saying "perhaps," God also indicates that he does not possess complete knowledge of the future. The dozens of examples like this throughout Scripture establish that the Bible thinks of an open future that is not completely certain. The popular belief in God's total omniscience is not so much a biblical idea as an old tradition.[45]

The few verses that seem to go further do not require exhaustive foreknowledge. God's knowledge is wonderful and far-reaching (Ps 139:1-6) but need not be limitless with respect to the future. Isaiah records prophecies about things to come (Is 44:23-28), but these chiefly establish what God promises to do and do not prove limitless foreknowledge. Prophecies are generally open-ended and dependent in some way on the human response to them.[46]

We should not think of God's omniscience as a vast encyclopedia of past, present and future facts. The Bible does not see it this way, nor is it a helpful way to think of it. When God gave creatures freedom, he gave them an open future, a future in a degree to be shaped by their decisions, not a future already determined in its every detail. We do not limit God by saying that he can be surprised by what his creatures do. It would be a serious limitation if God could not experience surprise and delight. The world would be a boring place without anything unexpected ever happening.

Those who are unsure of this should ask themselves if they think God *could* create a world where he would not be in total control of everything, where he would experience risk and where he would not foreknow all decisions of his creatures in advance. Surely this must be possible if God is all-powerful. Then is this world not just like that? Has God not already made just such a world? Does the Bible not assume it—do we not experience it as such?

Philosophically speaking, if choices are real and freedom significant, future decisons cannot be exhaustively foreknown. This is because the future is not determinate but shaped in part by human choices. The future is not fixed like the past, which can be known completely. The future does not yet exist and therefore cannot be infallibly anticipated, even by God. Future decisions cannot in every way be foreknown, because they have not yet been made. God knows everything that can be known—but God's foreknowledge does not include the undecided.

It would seriously undermine the reality of our decisions if they were known in advance, spelled out in a heavenly register and absolutely certain to happen. It would make the future fixed and certain and render illusory the sense of our making choices between real options. We might think of this with the analogy of parents and children. As a parent, God knows what he needs to know to deal with any contingency that might arise but does not know or need to know every detail of the future. God is a person and deals with us as persons. This means that God understands us, has intuition into every situation we face and is able to deal appropriately with every situation.

This implies that God learns things and (I would add) enjoys learning them. It does not mean that God is anybody's pupil or that he has to overcome ignorance and learn things of which he should have been aware. It means that God created a dynamic and changing world and enjoys getting to know it. It is a world of freedom, capable of genuine novelty, inexhaustible creativity and real surprises. I believe that God takes delight in the spontaneity of the universe and enjoys continuing to get to know it in a love that never changes, just as we love to get to know our children as they grow up. God is the best learner of all because he is completely open to all the input of an unfolding world, whereas we are finite and slow to react, reluctant to learn and inclined to distort reality in our own interest. Rather than supposing God cannot learn, we should try to learn as God learns.[47] If this matter of God's learning surprises anyone, be reminded that simple foreknowlege also implies that God learns from what creatures do. I am not speaking in a temporal sense now but in the sense that part of what God knows depends on what creatures do.

Thus, God does not foreknow every future choice or the outcome of every human decision. God is all-knowing in the sense that he knows all that it is possible to know and powerful enough to do whatever is needed. Under these circumstances, more power and wisdom are required for God to bring his will to pass in a world that he does not control than in one that he did control. As Gregory Boyd remarks, "It takes far more self-confidence, far more wisdom, far more love and sensitivity to govern that which is personal and free than it does to govern that over which one has absolute control."[48] As a political aside, what would we think of those who contend that total control is praiseworthy as a mode of governance?

Conclusion

The God whom we love and worship is the living God who is metaphysically social and desires relationship with us. God is One whose ways are marked by flexibility and dynamism, who acts and reacts on behalf of his people, who does not exist in splendid isolation from a world of change, but relates to his creatures and shares life with them. God not only directs but interacts. No unmoved mover, God responds sensitively to what happens on earth and relates to us. God is the omnipotent Creator but exercises his power subtly and carefully in the world. By bringing other free agents into being and entering into their lives in love, God is open.

We are seeking to correct the tradition without overcorrecting the error. God is high above all yet fills all things. God is unchanging yet relates to us in a changing world. God cannot be perplexed but suffers with his people. God's power is limitless but is deployed in ways that may appear weak. God is not subject to change or decay but can relate to temporal passage. God knows everything but is still learning what the world is becoming.

The open view of God stresses qualities of generosity, sensitivity and vulnerability more than power and control. It allows us to think of God as taking risks. Instead of locating God above and beyond history, it stresses God's activity in history, responding to events as they happen, in order to accomplish his purposes. Rather than deciding the future all by himself, God made creatures with the capacity to surprise and delight him. Like a loving parent, he rejoices with them when they are happy and suffers with them when they are in pain. In and through everything, God is committed to their welfare and continually works to achieve what is best for them.

The picture of God that I receive from the Bible is of One who takes risks and jeopardizes his own sovereignty in order to engage in historical interactions with created reality. The triune God pursues this path out of the love that is fundamental to his very being. This does not make history the author of God. It portrays God as the author of history who delights in meaningful interaction with creatures as his purposes for the world are realized.[49]

4 A Philosophical Perspective

William Hasker

I n the first chapter we looked at the biblical evidence for a God who is open to us and open to the future—evidence that has often been dismissed by an a priori exegesis that knows in advance exactly what can and cannot be truly said of God. In the chapter on historical theology we saw how the tradition has handled these biblical insights, at times affirming them but at other times obscuring or even rejecting them. In the last chapter we painted a vivid and compelling portrait of a living and dynamically interacting God. The purpose of the present chapter is to provide a philosophical explication of the issues in this discussion—to exhibit the rational coherence of the theology of divine openness and to show where it is superior to competing ways of understanding God and his works. It is apparent from the historical survey that philosophy bears part of the blame for obscuring the biblical conception of God,[1] so it is fitting that philosophy should also have a part in the work of restoration.

As a matter of fact, Christian philosophers over the past several decades have been much occupied with these topics, and the results on the whole have been favorable to the theology of divine openness. I do not mean to say that a universal consensus has emerged; that rarely if ever happens in philosophy. But on many of the points that divide our view from the classical theism of Augustine and Aquinas, there is at least a strong majority of Christian philosophers who opt for the open view of God over the self-contained God of the classical tradition. And even on those points where opinion remains more evenly divided, the open conception of God has been defended with strong arguments by outstanding Christian philosophers—philosophers, moreover, who are clearly orthodox in their general theological and faith commitments.[2]

This chapter has two main sections. The first deals with the openness and responsiveness of God, while the second, longer section deals with the power and knowledge of God, and with the control that God exercises over his creation—in a word, with divine providence.

God as Open and Responsive

Without doubt a very large number of philosophical issues are involved in the difference between the divine openness view and the classical conception of God—far too many to discuss in a single chapter. My task is made somewhat easier, however, by the fact that many of the inclinations and preconceptions with which we today approach these issues are decidedly different from those which prevailed when the theological tradition was being formed. To be sure, the fact that a view was once widely held and has now been generally abandoned is not a decisive reason to reject it; truths can be forgotten and then rediscovered. But when we are assessing the merits of views supported by a long tradition, it is surely appropriate to consider the ways in which the assumptions that influenced the shaping of the tradition differ from our own.

And things have indeed changed. The philosophy of neo-Platonism, as seen in Plotinus and later on in Pseudo-Dionysius, was a powerful molding force in ancient and medieval theology. Today, however, neo-Platonism really does not exist as a living philosophy, though it continues to have considerable indirect influence through the theological tradition. The doctrine of divine simplicity, so crucial to the classical understanding of God, has been abandoned by a strong majority of Christian philosophers, though it still has a small band of defenders.[3] And the claim that God is timelessly eternal, until recently a majority view among orthodox Christian theists, has suffered massive defections in recent years.

Still, the doctrine of divine timelessness continues to enjoy greater acceptance among philosophers than does divine simplicity,[4] and it may retain
even more of its popularity among theologians. So it may be worthwhile to
state briefly the reasons for preferring the view that God is temporal—that
he lives and interacts with us through the changes of time.[5] First of all, it
is clear that the doctrine of divine timelessness is not taught in the Bible
and does not reflect the way the biblical writers understood God. In spite
of appeals by defenders of the doctrine to texts such as Exodus 3:14, John
8:58 and 2 Peter 3:8, there simply is no trace in the Scripture of the elaborate metaphysical and conceptual apparatus that is required to make sense
of divine timelessness.[6] On the positive side, the biblical writers undeniably
do present God as living, acting and reacting in time, as Nicholas Wolterstorff has powerfully argued.[7]

In the face of this, the defender of timelessness has to say either that the
scriptural texts do not mean what they seem plainly to say or that what they
say (and mean) is, strictly speaking, false: what they say may be adequate
for the religious needs of simple people, but the truly enlightened must
think of God rather in the categories of timeless eternity while still (no
doubt) "speaking with the masses" in ordinary religious contexts so as not
to give offense to those who are not up to the rigors of proper theology.
Now it might possibly be acceptable to say this sort of thing if there were
clear and compelling reasons for preferring divine timelessness to taking
the Scriptures at face value. But if such reasons are lacking, it seems much
better to take the Bible at its word and to understand God as a temporal
being.

The other main difficulty about divine timelessness is that it is very hard
to make clear logical sense of the doctrine. If God is truly timeless, so that
temporal determinations of "before" and "after" do not apply to him, then
how can God *act* in time, as the Scriptures say that he does?[8] How can he
know what is occurring on the changing earthly scene? How can he *respond*
when his children turn to him in prayer and obedience? And above all, if
God is timeless and incapable of change, how can God be born, grow up,
live with and among people, suffer and die, as we believe he did as incar-

nated in Jesus? Whether there are good answers to these questions, whether the doctrine of divine timelessness is intelligible and logically coherent, and whether it can be reconciled with central Christian beliefs such as the incarnation remain matters of intense controversy.[9]

But even if divine timelessness is not incoherent and not in conflict with other key beliefs, it seems that we have at best only a tenuous grasp on the conception of God as a timeless being.[10] Once again, this might be something we would have to accept, *if* there were compelling reasons forcing us to affirm divine timelessness. But do such reasons exist? I think not; my own conclusion on the matter is that divine timelessness is strongly dependent for its justification on neo-Platonic metaphysics, and in particular on the doctrine of divine simplicity (whose intelligibility has also been strongly challenged). Once this metaphysical taproot has been severed, the prospects for divine timelessness are not bright—nor, I think, should they be.

But our catalog of differences between ancient and modern preconceptions is not yet finished. In the philosophical lineage stretching from Parmenides to Plato to Plotinus, there is a strong metaphysical and valuational preference for permanence over change. True Being, in this tradition, must of necessity be changeless; whatever changes, on the other hand, enjoys a substandard sort of being if any at all—at best it may be, in Plato's lovely phrase, a "moving image of eternity." And this bias against change has been powerfully influential in classical theology, leading to the insistence on an excessively strong doctrine of divine immutability—which, in turn, provides key support for divine timelessness, since timelessness is the most effective way (and perhaps the only way) to rule out, once and for all, the possibility of any change in God.

For us moderns, this preference for permanence over change is scarcely compelling. Indeed, it is arguable that in our intellectual life as well as in our general culture the pendulum has swung too far in the other direction, so that if anything at all remains constant for a while our response is one of boredom and impatience. Be that as it may, the extreme valuational preference for immutability has little hold on our thinking, and the appeal of theological doctrines based on this valuation is weakened accordingly.

Finally, let us consider the doctrine of divine impassibility—the claim that God's perfection requires that God be completely self-contained, not influenced or conditioned in any way by creatures, and in particular incapable of any suffering, distress or negative emotions of any kind.[11] One of the more extreme versions of impassibility appears in Aristotle's claim that God, being perfect, cannot take any notice of lesser beings such as humans; a perfect Thinker must be one that thinks only perfect thoughts, which means that God is eternally engaged in reflecting on his own thoughts: "His thinking is a thinking of thinking." This view is so clearly in conflict with a Christian understanding of God that it has never, to my knowledge, been adopted by Christian thinkers. But in slightly less extreme forms, divine impassibility has left a lasting imprint on Christian theology. Thus, Anselm addresses God as follows: "Thou art both compassionate, because thou dost save the wretched, and spare those who sin against thee; and not compassionate, because thou art affected by no sympathy for wretchedness" (*Proslogium* 7). Plainly stated, this says that God *acts* as we would expect a compassionate person to act—but the *feeling* of compassion forms no part of the divine life and experience.

On this point, also, Nicholas Wolterstorff makes an important contribution when he connects Augustine's doctrine of divine impassibility with Augustine's own reaction at the death of a friend.[12] Augustine was endowed with a nature that was richly emotional as well as intellectually powerful, and he speaks in moving terms of the void left in his life by the departure of his friend. Yet he also severely criticizes this love of his, "a love so intense for a being so fragile that its destruction could cause such grief."[13] Such an excess of "worldly affection," he thought, should have no part in the life of the Christian—and later on, at the death of his mother, Augustine attempted (though without complete success) to restrain himself from any overt expression of grief.

Few of us today share Augustine's view of these matters. Common experience shows us (and is reinforced by psychology) that the suppression of grief is a poor strategy—that the "work of grieving" needs to be done lest one carry the grief unresolved for years to come. And the suggestion that we should not care deeply for our fellow human beings because if we care too much we expose ourselves to suffering causes us to shake our heads sadly and turn away.

But it is hard to avoid the logic of the connection Augustine makes between the ideal of human life and the perfection of God's life. If the majestic and supremely admirable Lord of all is "without passion"—if he views the world and all its sorrows and sufferings with serene, imperturbable bliss--then should not this be our aim as well?[14] Conversely, if it is fitting and good that we humans should care deeply for one another, should love one another in a way that makes us vulnerable to suffering and loss, then should not a love like this be attributed to God also? Perhaps the two ideals, of human and divine love, could be pried apart—but only at the cost of voiding the scriptural injunction to be "imitators of God" (Eph 5:1).

In order to give greater focus to the considerations of this section, it may be helpful to examine in some detail an argument for divine immutability that has been prevalent since the time of Plato. If God were to change, so the argument goes, then he would change either for the better or for the worse. But God cannot change for the better, since he is already perfect. And he cannot change for the worse, for this would mean that he would no longer be perfect. So God cannot change.

A first point to notice is that this argument is an instance of "perfect being" theology. That is, the assumption is made that God is an absolutely perfect being—in Anselm's phrase, "the being than which nothing greater can be conceived"—and then conclusions concerning God's attributes are drawn from this assumption. Clearly, perfect being theology is operative, both explicitly and implicitly, at many, many points in the theological tradition.[15]

I believe the assumption that God is an absolutely perfect being is proper and correct. It does seem to be part of our conception of God that God is deserving of absolute, unreserved and unconditional worship and devotion. But suppose that we were to discover that God was in some significant way deficient and imperfect—suppose, for example, that God's attitude toward humans was a harshly demanding one that took little or no account of our needs and frailties. We might still worship God in spite of this "fault" on God's part—but would our worship not be tinged with disappointment, with regret for what "might have been" had God not suffered from this particular imperfection? But a worship tinged with such regret is not an expression of "absolute, unreserved and unconditional devotion." I think we do well to reject such possibilities and to see in God the sum of all perfections.

The difficulties with perfect being theology do not, in my view, stem from the assumption that God is an absolutely perfect being—that he is "whatever it is better to be than not to be." Rather, difficulties have arisen because people have been too ready to assume that they can determine, easily and with little effort, what perfection *is* in the case of God—that is, what attributes a perfect being must possess. Yet it clearly is no simple matter to say what is the best kind of life for a human being or what are the ideal attributes (or virtues) for a human being to possess. So why should we assume that this is simple in the case of God? I do not think it should be taken as obvious, without long and thoughtful consideration, that it is "better" for God to be temporal *or* timeless, mutable *or* immutable, passible *or* impassible. So if we are going to object to Plato's argument, we need not reject perfect being theology as such; rather, it is the application the argument makes of divine perfection that we must question.

And we can indeed question the application in this case. In fact, Plato's argument is straightforwardly fallacious, because it rests on a false dichotomy. It rests on the assumption that all change is either for the better or for the worse, an assumption that is simply false. Consider the operation of an extremely accurate watch. A short while ago, it registered the time as five minutes after six o'clock, but now it registers twelve minutes after six. Clearly, this is a change in the watch. (Compare this watch with an "immutable" watch that always registers 10:37, day in and day out.) Is this a change for the better, suggesting a previous state of imperfection? Not at all; the watch when it registered 6:05 was perfectly accurate. Is it then a change for the worse, a decline from perfection? Again, this is clearly not the case: the time now *is* 6:12, and the watch would be inaccurate, run down or broken if it failed to register that time. So there are changes that are neither for the better nor for the worse, and the change in the watch is such a change. It is, in fact, an example of *a change that is consistent with and/or required by a constant state of excellence.*

This is not to say that the changes that occur in God are all like the changes in the watch. There are such changes in God, to be sure: God always knows what time it is. But there are other, more significant changes in God that go far beyond simply "tracking" a changing situation. When I do something wrong, God comes to be in a state of knowing that I am doing something wrong, and this is a change in God. (He could not have known ten minutes ago that I was doing something wrong, because I was not doing wrong ten minutes ago.) God also becomes displeased with me, in a way he was not before, and he may initiate actions toward me designed to remedy the situation. (For instance, the Holy Spirit may begin working in my life in such a way as to bring me to repentance for the wrong I have done.) Turning to a broader context, when God began to create the universe he changed, beginning to do something that previously he had not done. This act of creation, our faith tells us, is not something that was required in order for God to be perfect in every respect; it was sheerly a matter of free choice for God whether to create at all. Such a change, then, is consistent with, though not required by, God's maintaining a constant state of perfection.

But it is time to bring this section to a close. We have reviewed a series of divine attributes with regard to which the theology of divine openness reaches different conclusions from the classical theory of a God who is totally self-contained and unconditioned by his creation. God, we want to say, exists and carries on his life in time; he undergoes changing states. And this means that God changes—not indeed in his essential nature, his love and wisdom and power and faithfulness, but in his thoughts and deeds toward us and the rest of his creation, matching his thoughts toward the creature with the creature's actual state at the time God thinks of it. And finally, God is not impassive and unmoved by his creation; rather, in deciding to create us and love us God has opened himself to the possibility of joy and sorrow, depending on what happens to us and especially on how we respond to his love and grace.

God as Providential

With respect to all of the divine attributes considered so far, I think it is safe to say that a clear majority of Christian philosophers (and probably theologians as well) who have considered them have opted for the openness of God view in preference to the classical view. With regard to the issues now to be considered, on the other hand—issues concerning divine power, knowledge and providential governance—I cannot make such a claim. That is not to say that the classical view (or rather, views) on these topics continue to command widespread and secure acceptance. Rather, on the topics I am now going to consider there *is no* consensus, or even majority, view; instead, there are a number of competing views, each claiming impassioned supporters, but none able to boast of general acceptance.

Because of the contentious nature of these topics, I will need to proceed in a more detailed, analytical fashion. I shall begin by laying down several key definitions, which will be important for our understanding and evaluation of various theories of providence. Then I shall set out the theories in question and evaluate them, considering in each case both the logical coherence of the theory and its religious and theological usefulness, asking, To what extent does this theory give us what we need from an account of God's knowledge of, and action in, the world? I shall consider five theories:

□ theological determinism, or "Calvinism," which holds that God, by his sovereign decree, efficaciously determines everything that happens

□ middle knowledge, or "Molinism," which by ascribing a special kind of knowledge to God attributes libertarian (indeterministic) freedom to human beings and yet retains a strong doctrine of divine providential control

□ simple foreknowledge, which attributes to God complete knowledge of the actual future but not the special kind of knowledge featured in Molinism

□ the openness of God theory, or "free will theism," as developed in this book, which accepts that there are some logical limitations on God's knowledge of the future

☐ process theology, which not only holds that many aspects of the future are inherently unknowable but also imposes some very stringent inherent limitations on the way in which God is able to act in the world

As will be evident, the views are arranged here in an order beginning with the highest degree of divine control over worldly affairs (Calvinism) and ending with the lowest (process theology).

Some Definitions

If we are to understand the varying conceptions of divine providence, the ideas that most need to be clarified are the power of God, the knowledge of God and the free will of human beings. So I will set out definitions for each of these in turn. The definitions at this point are not intended to decide the issue in favor of one conception of providence or another; rather, they are general enough to be useful in our explanations of all of the different theories.[16]

Divine omnipotence. Traditionally, God is said to be "all-powerful," or omnipotent. But what exactly does this mean? I propose the following definition: To say that God is omnipotent means that *God can perform any action the performance of which is logically possible and consistent with God's perfect nature.* We should notice several things about this definition. First, the scope of God's possible actions is limited to what is logically possible, or noncontradictory. To say that God cannot create a square circle is not to say that God is less than maximally powerful; rather, the idea of a square circle is inherently self-contradictory, and the task of creating one is logically incoherent; we simply have no idea what it would mean to create such an object.[17]

Second, God's possible actions are limited by God's own perfect nature. God, for instance, cannot perform the task of climbing Mount Everest; only a limited, embodied being can perform that task—pure spirits need not apply! And if, as I believe, God's moral perfection is an essential part of his nature, then such an action as being unfaithful to his promises is absolutely impossible for God; it is not one of the things he could possibly do. Yet this certainly does not involve any weakness on God's part, any more than it implies weakness on the part of a human father if he is unable to harm his own child deliberately and maliciously. In each case, the power available is more than sufficient for the task in question, but there is also a certain *strength of character* that prevents the power from being used in the way described.

Divine omniscience. Just as God is said to be all-powerful, he is also said to be all-knowing, or omniscient. Here also we need to go beyond the mere word to a careful definition. My proposal is: To say that God is omniscient means that *at any time God knows all propositions such that God's knowing them at that time is logically possible.* One point of interest here is the suggestion that there may be propositions that God knows at one time but not at another. Consider, for example, the following proposition: "Susan was married last Sunday." Assuming that Susan does indeed marry on a Sunday, this proposition is true for exactly one week, from midnight of her wedding day to Sunday midnight a week later. And God knows the proposition for exactly one week as well: before that, he does not know it because it is not yet true, and afterward he does not know it because it is no longer true. But could there be propositions that are true at a given time, and yet it is impossible for God to know at that time that they are true? This point is deeply controversial, as we shall see. For the present, it is important to see that the definition of omniscience does not decide this question one way or the other. So far as the definition is concerned, there may be true propositions such that it is logically impossible for God to know them, or there may be no such propositions—and because of this, the definition should be equally acceptable to persons on both sides of that controversy.

The nature of free will. One of the most important questions with regard to divine providence is the nature of the free will that is attributed to human beings. Christian thinkers have almost without exception wanted to say that human beings are free in some sense. But they are deeply divided concerning the relevant sense of "free will." On the libertarian (or "incompatibilist"[18]) understanding of free will, *an agent is free with respect to a given action at a given time if at that time it is within the agent's power to perform the action and also in the agent's power to refrain from the action.* To say that the action is "within one's power" means that nothing whatever exists that would make it impossible for the power in question to be exercised. If I am free in this sense, then whether or not the action is performed depends on me; by deciding to perform the action I bring it about that things happen in a certain way, quite different from some other, equally possible, way things might have happened had I refrained from the action.

The other main understanding of free will is the compatibilist conception, which may be explained as follows: *an agent is free with respect to a given action at a given time if at that time it is true that the agent can perform the action if she decides to perform it and she can refrain from the action if she decides not to perform it.* The difference between the two definitions may not be immediately apparent, but it is of fundamental importance. On the libertarian definition, in order to be free the agent must have it in her power without qualification to perform the action and also have the power to refrain from performing it. On the compatibilist definition, on the other hand, she need only have the power to perform it *if she chooses* to do so, and likewise the power to refrain.

Now, consider a situation in which she has an overwhelmingly strong desire to perform the action, and no desire whatever to refrain. (Perhaps she has just been invited by a good friend to go to a show she has been wanting to see for weeks.) She is, no doubt, free in the compatibilist sense, since if she were to decide to refrain from the action in question, she could certainly do so. (Nothing would force her to go to the show, if she decided not to.) But she is probably not free in the libertarian sense, since it is impossible for her to *desire* to refrain from the action, and thus also impossible for her to *decide* to refrain from it. On the libertarian view, in order to be truly free she must have the "inner freedom" either to act or to refrain, but on the compatibilist view she needs only the "outer freedom" to carry out the decision either way she makes it—but the decision itself may be completely determined by the psychological forces at work in her personality. As we shall see, a lot hangs on this distinction.

Now that I have set out the definitions, I am ready to use them to explain and evaluate the different conceptions of divine providence. I begin with the one that is farthest from the "classical theism" of Augustine and Aquinas, and offers the least amount of direct divine control over the world.

Process Theology

Process theology[19] differs from the other views to be explored in that it depends heavily on a particular contemporary philosophy, the "process philosophy" created by A. N. Whitehead[20] and further developed by Charles Hartshorne, among others. Space does not permit me to explore the details of this philosophy here, but I will point out a few of the theological conclusions that are drawn from it.

One important conclusion concerning God in process theology is that God and the world are *interdependent*. This differs sharply from the one-sided dependence of the world on God, the belief on which other versions of Christian theism insist. Whitehead put it like this: "It is as true to say that God transcends the World, as that the World transcends God. It is as true to say that God creates the World, as that the World creates God."[21] God, according to process theology, is not the Creator in the absolute sense that he calls the universe into being out of nothing, but he "creates" in the sense that he *guides the development* of the cosmos in a direction that permits the achievement of rich and complex values.

Process theology ascribes to human beings freedom in the libertarian sense—indeed, freedom in something like this sense applies also to many nonhuman aspects of the world. (The way in which this works depends on technical details of the philosophy that we cannot go into here.) God is omniscient in that he knows everything that is intrinsically knowable. But process thinkers hold that many aspects of the future are inherently unknowable; many, in fact, would say that at present there is no truth to be known about (for example) how future free choices are going to turn out.

The most striking difference between process and classical theism, however, concerns the power of God and God's way of acting in the world. The process view, briefly summarized, is that God's power is always persuasive and never coercive. That is, at all times God is attempting to persuade humans, and other creatures, to follow his way; he does this by presenting to them his "initial aim" for them, the "direction" in which he wants them to go, so as to realize rich and intense values in a harmonious fashion. But this is as far as God's power goes; he does not, and indeed cannot, compel any created reality to do his will, and so the actual course of things always depends very heavily on how finite beings respond to God's persuasion. Process thinkers are quite aware that this deviates sharply from the traditional belief in divine omnipotence; their response is put rather provocatively in the title of a book by Charles Hartshorne, *Omnipotence and Other Theological Mistakes*.[22] They believe that by deviating from the tradition on this point they achieve a more adequate and satisfying account of God's nature and God's actions in the world.

Process theology undoubtedly has some impressive strengths. One such strength is found in its critique of classical theism, a critique that has been influential far beyond the bounds of process theology itself. Furthermore, process theology presents a coherent, well-developed alternative that many have found highly attractive. A strong point of this alternative is its emphasis on the persuasive activity of God—an emphasis that seems in some ways more congruent with God's actual ways of dealing with us than is the emphasis on sheer power in much traditional theism. (See the remarks on this in the previous chapter.) And finally, process theology finds itself in a rather strong position in dealing with the problem of evil—the problem, that is, of how a good and loving God could permit the vast amounts of evil that exist in the world. The process answer, simply put, is that God does not *permit* the evil, because God could not *prevent* the evils from occurring. All God can do, and what he does do, is attempt to persuade worldly beings to act in accordance with his plan; if they act differently, and evil and suffering are the result, then God suffers along with us. So the problem of evil, as an objection to belief in the existence of God, virtually disappears.[23]

However, the strengths of process theology are matched by some even more impressive weaknesses.[24] We have noted the strength of the process critique of classical theism. But having given that critique, process thinkers often proceed by what is in effect a false dichotomy—they assume, that is, that once the extreme positions of classical theism have been rejected, process theism ("neoclassical theism," as Hartshorne calls it) is the only coherent and viable alternative. But this simply is not so. A major goal of the present book, in fact, is to demonstrate that there is a third alternative, a way of understanding God and his relations to the world that embodies many of the strengths of both classical and process theism while avoiding their weaknesses.

As we have seen, the emphasis on God's persuasive power is a definite "plus" for process theism. But *limiting* God's actions in the world to persuasion is another matter entirely.[25] To say, as process theism does, that God has no direct control over anything that happens in the world, is to leave oneself with a picture of God's power and God's activity that is severely truncated, as compared to the way God is viewed in traditional theology and indeed in the Bible itself.[26] God so conceived cannot create the heavens and the earth out of nothing, nor can he part the Red Sea for the people of Israel, nor can he raise Jesus from the dead as a pledge of victory over sin and eternal life. Nor, it seems, is God in a position to guarantee the eventual triumph of righteousness and the coming of his kingdom. God no doubt *hopes* for these things and *works* for them to the best of his ability. But as we have see, all that God can actually *do* to achieve his purposes is to make creatures aware of the "aim" toward the goal—and this he has already been doing to the limit of his ability. But the outcome depends entirely on the obedient, cooperative response of the creatures—and judging from the results so far, it is difficult to be extremely optimistic. True, the prevalence of evil is less serious as an objection against the existence of the process God—but that is because this God is very, very limited in his ability to *do* anything about evil.

There is a certain irony that we should note before we leave this topic. As we have seen, classical theism has been subjected to severe, and no doubt largely warranted, criticism because it has so heavily "bought into" Greek philosophical assumptions about the nature of a "perfect being." And much of this criticism is due to process theologians. Yet it would seem that process theology itself is also vulnerable to criticism for excessive deference to philosophy—in this case, to the process philosophy of Whitehead. And it seems to many of us that the results of this "synthesis" are even more damaging to the biblical conception of God than was the neo-Platonism of the early church fathers.[27]

Calvinism

The theory of theological determinism to be discussed here is called Calvinism because of its association with Calvin, but it by no means originated with him.[28] The first real "Calvinist" was Augustine, and some prominent medieval theologians, notably Thomas Aquinas,[29] held essentially deterministic views of the God-human relationship. And Luther and Zwingli were just as deterministic as was Calvin.

The central idea of Calvinism is quite simple: everything that happens, with no exceptions, is efficaciously determined by God in accordance with his eternal decrees. As Augustine said, "The will of God is the necessity of things." God's power to achieve whatever he desires is limited only by logical possibility—and that is no real limitation, for it is inconceivable that God would have an incoherent desire for a self-contradictory state of affairs. The conception of free will affirmed by a Calvinist must, of course, be a compatibilist conception: people are, in many circumstances, free to do what they choose to do, but this "freedom" has to be consistent with the fact that God has infallibly predetermined what they will choose, and there is no real possibility of their choosing otherwise.[30]

Calvinism gives us as strong a conception of God's providential control as anyone could desire—and it might seem that this speaks decisively in its favor. It has been said that "nothing is more depressing than the thought that God is not in control"—but this, clearly, is a thought the Calvinist need never entertain. Do not Christians pray, along with their Lord, that "your will be done"? And Calvinism guarantees, in the strongest possible way, the fulfillment of this prayer.

On further reflection, however, these advantages are not compelling. The point of the prayer that God's will be done is that we, like Jesus, willingly submit to the will of God for our lives; but human submission, willing or otherwise, is irrelevant to the efficacious divine decrees postulated by Calvinism. Indeed, when a person "hardens his heart" and rejects God, this also is the fulfillment of "God's will" in the sense of God's efficacious decree! Calvinists respond to this paradox by postulating different senses of "God's will"—for instance, between God's "secret will" and his "revealed will."[31] Such distinctions are not necessarily illegitimate, but the fact that they are needed underscores the point that the sense in which, according to Calvinism, God's will is always done is quite different from the sense in which we pray for God's will in our lives.

The notion of God's being "in control" is similarly ambiguous. The parents of small children certainly desire to be "in control" of what happens in their children's lives, and often manage this to a considerable degree. But they do not, if they are wise, attempt to exercise this control by determining every detail of what their children do and experience. On the contrary: in large measure, they seek to create suitable conditions for the child to explore for itself the possibilities for its life, and to encourage it to take advantage of those opportunities. Their policy could well be described as the deliberate and intensive application of "persuasive power"—though to be sure, coercive power is there in reserve, should the child start to run out into a busy roadway. Should not a similar account be given of God's control over us?

A major objection to Calvinism is found in its effect on our understanding of the personal relationship that we have with God. That believers enjoy such a relationship is a fundamental part of Christian faith—but does not Calvinism undermine this notion? (Please note that I am not denying that many Calvinists do in fact enjoy a rich and intimate relationship with their Lord. What I am suggesting is that their theory, if taken seriously at this point, undercuts the reality of the relationship that they experience.) The Calvinist understanding of the God-human relationship has been compared to a puppet-master controlling the movements of a puppet, or of a ventriloquist having a "conversation" with his dummy. Calvinists, to be sure, reject these analogies as inappropriate. Perhaps a closer comparison would be with a computer wizard who has assembled a lifelike robot and, through a thorough knowledge of the robot's programming, is able to anticipate and manipulate the robot's responses to an indefinitely large variety of situations.[32] I think that reflecting on these and similar examples will convince most people that Calvinism is distinctly unappealing as an account of our personal relationship with God.

But by far the strongest objections to Calvinism are found in the phenomena of sin and moral evil. How can we say that God desires for all to be saved, when he has eternally decreed that some will be lost?[33] It is not that God "reluctantly permits" those who reject him to go their own way; rather, that is the way God wanted it all along. And in general, all the evil that is done in the world—from the murder of Abel to "ethnic cleansing" in Bosnia—is precisely what God wanted to happen. At this point Calvinists usually take refuge in the inscrutable wisdom of God[34]—often, at the same time, lashing out indignantly at those who have the temerity to raise such questions. But all else aside, does not Calvinism attribute to God an attitude toward evil that is logically incoherent? God, the Calvinists say, is wholly good; everything that occurs God has willed to occur in preference to any other logically possible state of affairs God might have chosen. And then a just and loving God assumes toward part of what he himself has chosen to create and bring about—namely, sin and moral evil—an attitude of utter, implacable hostility. So the Calvinist must believe—but is this even coherent, let alone plausible?

Molinism

The theory of "middle knowledge" was devised by the sixteenth-century Jesuit theologian Luis de Molina as a way of avoiding these difficulties.[35] Molina was convinced of the necessity of attributing to human beings free will in the libertarian sense, rather than the compatibilist free will that is consistent with theological determinism. But he also desired to maintain a strong doctrine of divine providential control, which he accomplished by attributing to God the knowledge of certain propositions that have recently come to be called "counterfactuals of freedom." These propositions specify, concerning every possible free agent that God might create, exactly what that agent would freely choose to do in every possible situation of (libertarian) free choice in which the agent might find itself.

This theory supplies us with an answer to the question of how God can know with certainty the future free actions of his creatures. God knows which creatures he will create and which situations those creatures will find themselves in. And in virtue of his knowledge of the counterfactuals of freedom, God knows exactly which choices will be made in each such situation, thus enabling him to know the future in its entirety.

Beyond this, however, Molinism lends itself to an extremely strong view of divine providence, probably the strongest view possible if we reject Calvinism. If human beings possess libertarian free will, then God cannot simply determine by decree what their choices shall be, as he does according to Calvinism. It seems plausible that this would introduce a kind of uncertainty and riskiness into God's plan for the world: how things ultimately turn out will depend on how free agents, such as human beings, respond to the choices that they are offered. But Molinism shows how God can entirely avoid taking any risks. Prior to his decision to create anything or to place any free agent in a situation where she would make a choice, God knows exactly what choice would be made in any possible situation. This means that God can survey all the possible ways in which things might turn out—all the "feasible worlds," as they have come to be called—and select the very one that most closely fits his desire and purpose for his creation.

God's choice is not as unconstrained as it is for Calvinism, because God is limited by the counterfactuals of freedom: if the relevant counterfactual says that, in the given situation, Adam would choose to eat the apple, then God cannot bring it about that *in that very situation* Adam freely chooses to refrain from eating it. But this is the *only* limitation on God's ability to get what he wants; in particular, there is no risk or uncertainty whatever about God's plan being executed exactly as he has conceived it. Alfred J. Freddoso, a leading contemporary Molinist, puts the point succinctly:

God, the divine artisan, freely and knowingly plans, orders, and provides for all the effects that constitute His artifact, the created universe with its entire history, and executes His chosen plan by playing an active causal role sufficient to ensure its exact realization. Since God is the perfect artisan, not even the most trivial details escape His providential decrees.[36]

Serious questions have been raised concerning the coherence and logical possibility of Molinism, the most important of which concern the very existence of true counterfactuals of freedom.[37] These questions become very involved logically, and we cannot go into them in detail here. One way to look at the matter is this: If Adam is free with respect to eating the apple, then it seems reasonable to say that he *might* eat the apple, and also that he *might not* eat it. But if it is true that he might eat it, then (according to the principles of counterfactual logic) it is false that he *would not* eat it—and conversely, if it is true that he might not eat the apple, then it is false that he *would* eat it. So if he is free with respect to eating the apple, then it is true that he might eat it and also true that he might not eat it, but it is not true *either* that he (definitely) *would* eat it *or* that he (definitely) *would not* eat it. Thus, if he is free in his decision to eat or not, then there *is no* true counterfactual of freedom describing what he would do in the situation. And if there are no true counterfactuals of freedom in situations like this, the theory of middle knowledge collapses.

As I have said, these arguments become extremely complex, and if at this point the reader is bewildered rather than enlightened, he has plenty of company. But I think it is fair to say that the majority of philosophers who have considered these and similar arguments have concluded that there are serious questions about the coherence and logical possibility of middle knowledge, though this conclusion is certainly not unanimous.

As has been noted, middle knowledge can afford God a very high degree of providential control over the world. But a price must be paid for this. The effect on our understanding of a personal relationship with God is similar to what we saw for Calvinism: God becomes the archmanipulator, knowing in every case exactly "which button to push" in order to elicit precisely the desired result from his creatures. The analogy of the cyberneticist and the robot applies here also, with one change:[38] we must suppose that part of the programming of the robot was done by a third party. (This, of course, represents the counterfactuals of freedom.[39]) But the robot-master still knows all about that part of the program and is able just as before to fine-tune the situations that the robot encounters so as to achieve just the desired result. Whether the change from Calvinism to Molinism makes the situation appreciably better in this regard is left for the reader to decide.

Molinism is undeniably better off than Calvinism with respect to the problem of evil. The reason is precisely that in Molinism God has somewhat less control than he does according to Calvinism: specifically, God has no control over the counterfactuals of freedom. And this means that there may be certain logically possible states of affairs that God cannot cause to be actual—for instance, God may be unable to bring about a state of affairs in which Adam freely resists the temptation to sin. Alvin Plantinga has made use of this in order to argue that it may be impossible for God to bring about the existence of a world in which creatures have libertarian freedom to choose between good and evil, but in fact always choose good.[40] And if God could not have created such a world, then it is not a moral fault on God's part that he did not do so.

But Molinism still has plenty of trouble over the problem of evil. As Freddoso pointed out, according to Molinism God specifically "plans, orders, and provides for" each of the events that actually happen—the evil along with the good. So God specifically planned the Holocaust, Saddam Hussein's invasion of Kuwait, the ethnic cleansing in Bosnia—and on and on. But how, we may ask, could God intentionally bring about such horrible evils? So far as I can see, only one answer to this even begins to make sense. I believe that the Molinist is virtually compelled to affirm what Michael Peterson has termed "meticulous providence," which holds that every single instance of evil that occurs is such that God's permitting either that specific evil or some other equal or greater evil is necessary for some greater good that is better than anything God could have brought about without permitting the evil in question.[41] Peterson argues forcefully that Christians should not affirm meticulous providence, and I believe he is right. Without going into the matter at length, doesn't it strain one's credulity almost beyond limits to believe that none of the evils mentioned—or a thousand more that could have been added—could have been prevented without creating an even greater evil, or without losing some good that is great enough to outweigh those truly horrendous evils? Yet this is what the Molinist must affirm, unless he is content to say that God has deliberately arranged for these horrible evils to occur *without* there being any outweighing good that compensates for them.[42]

Simple Foreknowledge

The theory of simple foreknowledge agrees with Molinism that human beings possess libertarian free will and that God has comprehensive knowledge of the future. But it does not accept that God possesses "middle knowledge," knowledge of the counterfactuals of freedom. (This is what makes simple foreknowledge simple!) Since they do not affirm middle knowledge, proponents of simple foreknowledge cannot avail themselves of the explanation it offers of *how* God knows the future, so they need an alternative account of this. The only plausible answer seems to be that God somehow has "direct vision" of the future—that he "sees" it as if in a telescope, or perhaps a crystal ball.

By this time it should come as no surprise that there are serious questions concerning the logical compatibility of comprehensive divine foreknowledge and libertarian free will. The idea, roughly, is this: If God knows already what will happen in the future, then God's knowing this is part of the past and is now fixed, impossible to change. And since God is infallible, it is completely impossible that things will turn out differently than God expects them to. But this means that the future event God knows is also fixed and unalterable, and it cannot be true of any human beings that they are both able to perform a certain action and able not to perform that action. If God knows that a person is going to perform it, then it is impossible that the person fail to perform it—so one does not have a free choice whether or not to perform it. There are dozens of different versions of this argument; one of my favorites concerns a certain Clarence, known to be addicted to cheese omelets. Will Clarence have a cheese omelet for breakfast tomorrow morning, or won't he? The argument proceeds as follows:

1. It is now true that Clarence will have a cheese omelet for breakfast tomorrow. (Premise)

2. It is impossible that God should at any time believe[43] what is false, or fail to believe anything that is true. (Premise: divine omniscience)

3. God has always believed that Clarence will have a cheese omelet tomorrow. (From 1,2)

4. If God has always believed a certain thing, it is not in anyone's power to bring it about that God has not always believed that thing. (Premise: the unalterability of the past)

5. Therefore, it is not in Clarence's power to bring it about that God has not always believed that he would have a cheese omelet for breakfast. (From 3,4)

6. It is not possible for it to be true both that God has always believed that Clarence would have a cheese omelet for breakfast, and that he does not in fact have one. (From 2)

7. Therefore, it is not in Clarence's power to refrain from having a cheese omelet for breakfast tomorrow. (From 5,6) So Clarence's eating the omelet tomorrow is not an act of free choice. (From the definition of free will)[44]

What this argument shows is that it is logically impossible that God should have foreknowledge of a genuinely free action. It follows from this that if there *are* actions that are free in the libertarian sense, it is logically impossible for God to know in advance how such actions will turn out. And in the light of our definition of omniscience, God's failure to know what logically cannot be known in no way detracts from God's omniscience. As soon as these truths become available, God will be the first to know them! (On the other hand, the definition of omniscience given in step 2 of the argument above is faulty, because it fails to allow for the possibility of truths that are intrinsically unknowable.)

There is a minor cottage industry among philosophers of religion seeking to devise an escape from this argument. I cannot go into all of this here;

I will simply record my conviction (shared by the other authors of this book) that none of the evasions are successful. Probably the most common answer makes a point of the claim that God's knowledge of what Clarence will do does not *cause* Clarence to eat the omelet. This may be true, but it is irrelevant to the argument as presented, which does not make any claim to the effect that God's beliefs are the cause of human actions. But the reader who wishes to pursue this matter further must consult the relevant literature.[45]

Leaving this aside for the moment, if God *did* possess simple foreknowledge, how would this affect our understanding of divine providence? The answer, rather surprisingly, is not at all! That is to say: If we assume that God has comprehensive knowledge of the past and present, including the causal powers, dispositions, tendencies and so forth of every creature, then it adds nothing at all to God's providential control over the world if we add the assumption that God possesses "simple foreknowledge" as described in this section.

To see why this is so,[46] let us begin with the example (borrowed from David Basinger) of a young woman, Susan, who is seeking God's guidance concerning which of two men she should marry. What sort of guidance might God choose to give her? God knows, of course, everything there is to know concerning the personality, temperament, physical condition and so on of each of the three persons involved, as well as their potential for future happiness under various conditions. He knows far more, then, than even the wisest and most skillful human marriage counselor. But what more would be added if we assume that God somehow "sees" the actual future? Suppose he looks into the future and sees Susan unhappily married to Tom. Could not God, on the basis of this, warn Susan that she had better accept Kenneth's offer instead? A moment's reflection will show this to be incoherent. What God knows is the *actual* future, the situation in which she actually is married to Tom. So it is nonsensical to suggest that God, knowing the actual future, could on the basis of this knowledge influence things so that this would *not* be the actual future, which would mean that God would not know Susan as being married to Tom . . . I trust the point is clear.[47]

In general, to assume that God does anything in the present *on the basis of* his knowledge of the actual future *which could have an effect on that future* immediately leads us into the philosophical morass of circular explanation and circular causation. So if God did possess simple foreknowledge, it would be impossible that he should act on it, and the foreknowledge would do him (and us) no good. Simple foreknowledge, unlike middle knowledge, simply does not "help" God in providentially governing the world.

The recognition of this point introduces a certain irony into the situation. The theory of simple foreknowledge is fairly widely held among Christian philosophers; it may represent a plurality, if not a majority, view among those who take a position on the question. Most of these philosophers, however, have not taken account of the "religious uselessness" of simple foreknowledge, as argued in the preceding paragraph. It is reasonable to suppose that when they do become cognizant of this, many of them will be inclined to abandon simple foreknowledge in favor of one of the alternatives. Some may accept views such as Calvinism or Molinism, which (for all their problems) do provide a basis for a stronger view of divine providential control. Others will move in the direction of a more consistent acceptance of the openness of God.[48] But even without that, many of those who affirm simple foreknowledge are in agreement with the open view of God regarding most of the other topics discussed in this book, and we are more than happy to consider them our allies.[49]

The Openness of God

The portrait of a God who is open to us and to the future was presented vividly and, I think, very appealingly in the previous chapter. Any reader who does not find that picture of God attractive is unlikely to be convinced by any of the arguments offered in this book. At this point I will not try to repeat what Clark Pinnock has already done so well, but instead will limit myself to commenting on some of the implications of divine openness in relation to the topics developed in this chapter.

According to the open view of God, or "free will theism," God is strictly omnipotent as defined earlier in this chapter—he is able to do anything that is logically possible and consistent with God's perfect nature. It is worth stressing the point that God as so conceived is in no way deficient in power as compared with God as viewed by Calvinism. We believe that God is completely capable of creating a universe every detail of whose history is solely determined by his sovereign decree. But it seems to us that a wise and good God would not want—and, in fact, has not chosen—to create such a universe. We in turn would ask the Calvinist, Is God as you conceive him unable to create a world in which there are free creatures who voluntarily enter into a relationship of love and friendship with him? Or does he prefer a world in which he alone monopolizes control, leaving nothing to be decided by his creatures? And why should we think that he would prefer a world like that?

God is also omniscient, in that he knows everything that logically can be known. The argument that free actions logically cannot be known with certainty in advance has already been given, and I will not repeat it here. (Note, however, that God has a vast amount of knowledge about the *probabilities* that free choices will be made in one way rather than another.) To be sure, God could have created a world in which he would have full foreknowledge of every detail, simply by creating a world in which everything that happens is fully controlled by his sovereign decrees. But it seems to us that God found such a world less desirable—less appealing to his creative goodness—than a world that contains genuinely free creatures.

It is evident that free will theism does not have the problems encountered by Calvinism and Molinism in conceiving our personal relationship with God. God knows an immense amount about each one of us—far more, in fact, than we know about ourselves—but he does not, because he cannot, plan his actions toward us on the basis of a prior knowledge of how we will respond. And this means that God is a risk-taker; in expressing his love toward us, he opens himself up to the real possibility of failure and disappointment. God does not, of course, "need" us in all of the ways that we need one another (Clark Pinnock has explained this very well in the previous chapter), but he does genuinely and deeply care about us; he is saddened when we reject his love, and rejoices when one of us turns to him in repentance and faith.

Free will theism is also in a better position than Calvinism or Molinism to deal with the problem of evil. Regarding Calvinism, this should be obvious: Calvinism asserts that, unconstrained by any requirement other than his own will, God has deliberately chosen to cause all of the horrible evils that afflict our world. Our theory says nothing of the sort, attributing much evil instead to the rebellious wills of creatures. Molinism, of course, also affirms libertarian free will and in that respect is better off than Calvinism. But Molinism still leaves us with an uncomfortably close connection between the will of God and specific instances of evil. As we have seen, according to Molinism God specifically "plans, orders, and provides for" each of the events that actually happen in the world. This means, for example, that God, fully knowing Hitler's counterfactuals and the use he would make of his free will, specifically chose a world in which Hitler would come into existence and be confronted with precisely those situations that led to the incalculable evil of the Holocaust. And we are then left to wonder (but without much hope of an answer) what "greater good" was achieved as a result of these horrible events.

According to free will theism, on the other hand, God knows that evils will occur, but he has not for the most part specifically decreed or incorporated into his plan the individual instances of evil. Rather, God governs the world according to *general strategies* which are, as a whole, ordered for the good of the creation but whose detailed consequences are not foreseen or intended by God prior to the decision to adopt them. As a result, we are able to abandon the difficult doctrine of "meticulous providence" and to admit the presence in the world of particular evils God's permission of which is not the means of bringing about any greater good or preventing any equal or greater evil. Much more needs to be said, of course, and this is hardly the place to take up the task of constructing a theodicy.[50] I believe, however, that these differences between free will theism and Molinism are extremely helpful as we attempt to compose a strong and plausible reply to the problem of evil.[51]

Critics of the openness of God theory typically claim that God as we conceive him would be unable to do the kinds of things that Scripture represents God as doing.[52] One such complaint deals with the subject of prophecy—if God does not know everything about the future, how can he tell us about it? Fortunately, Richard Rice has dealt capably with this issue in the first chapter of this book, so I can limit myself here to a brief summary. We have available to us three different ways of understanding biblical prophecies, consistent with God's openness to the future. Some prophecies are conditional on the actions of human beings, others are predictions based on existing trends and tendencies, while still others are announcements of what God himself intends to bring about.[53] We believe (though I cannot argue here in detail) that these approaches can lead one to a satisfying understanding of the phenomena of biblical prophecy.

I will take time here to consider just one more objection to the open view of God. It is sometimes asserted that God as we conceive him would not be able to ensure the fulfillment of his plan *even in the most general respects.* If every single human being has it in his or her power to accept or reject God's offer of salvation, and if God has no advance knowledge of how a person will respond, then it would be possible for every person without exception to reject salvation—and if this were to occur, there would be no "people of God," no church, and a key element in God's plan would be frustrated. As things actually stand, to be sure, this has not happened, but it could have happened; that it has not is attributable to nothing but "God's luck."

To answer this fully, we should have to know exactly what methods and resources are available to God in his providential governance of the world. But this is something we certainly do not know and cannot expect to know—and without it, any answer to the objection must be based on speculation. We certainly should not underestimate the tremendous resourcefulness of God in adapting his responses to human actions—even willful and disobedient human actions—so as to achieve his wise and loving purposes. But even if it is possible, on the open view of God, for all human beings without exception to reject salvation, still this might be overwhelmingly improbable—so improbable that the risk of such an outcome is negligible. Consider a parallel: According to modern physics, there is a finite probability that all of the oxygen in a room should concentrate itself in a small volume, leaving the rest of the room devoid of oxygen and unable to sustain life. But the probability of this happening is so minute that rational persons can and do disregard the possibility in conducting their lives; I am completely confident that not a single one of my readers goes about with bottled oxygen in order to protect himself in the event of such an occurrence! So why should our inability to show how God can logically guarantee that humans will respond to his love constitute a serious objection?

This book has put forward a picture of God as majestic yet intimate, as powerful yet gentle and responsive, as holy and loving and caring, as desiring for humans to decide freely for or against his will for them, yet endlessly resourceful in achieving his ultimate purposes. In spite of all of the arguments that have been set forth and discussed, it is in the end out of the question for anyone to "prove" that a particular conception of God is the correct one. Rather, one simply finds that a particular way of understanding the things of God makes the most sense, and provides the greatest illumination, in the overall context of one's thinking and living. And so we offer a challenge to the reader, to "try and see" whether he or she cannot find a rich and satisfying understanding of Scripture, of the Christian faith generally and of our life in Christ, seen through the lens of the openness of God.

5 Practical Implications

David Basinger

As we have seen, there are a number of distinct ways to conceive of the relationship between God and our world. Within some of these conceptual models God is viewed as totally unaffected by what occurs on earth, while within others varying degrees of affective response are allowed. Within some God is considered the all-determining ruler, while within others it is believed that control over earthly affairs is voluntarily (or involuntarily) shared with other beings. Within some God is characterized as knowing infallibly all that will occur in the future, while within others it is held that God's knowledge is limited to that which has occurred and is now occurring.

The purpose of this book has not been to discuss all of these conceptual models in detail, but rather to discuss one such model—what we have called the open view of God[1]—emphasizing how it differs from its leading competitors. The purpose of this final chapter is to consider in a comparative manner the practical implications of conceiving of God in this fashion. Specifically, I will consider the implications of affirming the open view of God for five issues of importance to Christians: the efficacy of petitionary prayer, the discernment of God's will, the appropriate Christian explanation(s) for evil, the appropriate Christian response to social problems and the Christian's evangelistic obligations.

We have noted and discussed throughout this book the basic characteristics of the God of the open model, but it is important to reemphasize the five that are most significant for our present purpose:

1. God not only created this world ex nihilo but can (and at times does) intervene unilaterally in earthly affairs.

2. God chose to create us with incompatibilistic (libertarian) freedom—freedom over which he cannot exercise total control.

3. God so values freedom—the moral integrity of free creatures and a world in which such integrity is possible—that he does not normally override such freedom, even if he sees that it is producing undesirable results.

4. God always desires our highest good, both individually and corporately, and thus is affected by what happens in our lives.

5. God does not possess exhaustive knowledge of exactly how we will utilize our freedom, although he may well at times be able to predict with great accuracy the choices we will freely make.

With these divine characteristics in mind, let us now consider what it means in practice to commit oneself to an "open" understanding of the God-world relationship.

Petitionary Prayer

All Christian traditions emphasize the importance of prayer. And for some types of prayer—prayers of worship, praise, confession and so forth—the view of God that one holds may not be very relevant. However, within most Christian traditions it is quite clearly held, to use the words of David Mason, that believers "are to ask God for things" and that God "hears, is affected by our importunities, and responds adequately to them."[2] That is, most Christians engage in petitionary prayer, prayer that they believe changes things. And the view of God one holds does significantly affect the way in which the efficacy of petitionary prayer can justifiably be understood—the way in which it can justifiably be said that petitionary prayer changes things.

Some Christians—some Calvinists and others sympathetic to the Reformed tradition[3]—affirm what I will label "specific sovereignty." God, they believe, has total control over everything in the sense that all and only that which God wants to occur will occur. He could have created any number of self-consistent systems but chose to create exactly what we now have. Thus, this world represents God's preordained, perfect plan.[4]

Many in this camp are compatibilists who claim that God retains total control over human activity by unilaterally influencing the voluntary decision-making process of all individuals in such a way that they always make the exact decisions he would have them make.[5] However, some in this camp, perhaps surprisingly, are incompatibilists. They deny that God can unilaterally control the voluntary decision-making process itself, but believe that in some paradoxical manner beyond our ability to comprehend, God is still able to ensure unilaterally that all individuals always freely make the exact decisions that he has determined should be made.[6]

However, in whatever manner the means of divine control are explicated, all proponents of specific sovereignty deny that human decision-making can in any way limit God's providential activity in our world. God may use human choice as a means to accomplish desired goals. But our choices, and thus our activities, never thwart or hinder in any way God's perfect plan.

The implications of this view of God for petitionary prayer are significant. Proponents of specific sovereignty remain free to distinguish between God's *secret* will, which "pertains to all things which He wills either to effect or permit and which are therefore absolutely final," and his *revealed* will, which "prescribes the duties of man." Thus they remain free to claim that petitionary prayer is justified because God has requested (indeed commanded) that we petition him.[7] Moreover, proponents of specific sovereignty can justifiably maintain that prayer of this type may affect petitioners themselves—for example, make them more sensitive to the role they might play in the context in question. And they can justifiably maintain that such prayer may significantly affect those people who are aware of the fact that petitions are being offered on their behalf.[8]

However, most Christians also continue to believe firmly that whether God directly intervenes in our world depends at times on whether we use the power of choice over which God has given us control to request such intervention. That is, most Christians continue to believe that God has granted us the power to decide whether to request his assistance and that at times the decision we make determines whether we receive the help desired. Or, to state this important point differently yet, most continue to believe that at times "we have not because we ask not" in the sense that certain states of affairs that God can and would like to bring about do not occur because we have chosen not to request that he intervene.

But proponents of specific sovereignty cannot maintain justifiably that petitionary prayer is efficacious in this sense. They do, of course, remain free to maintain that God has decided to bring about some states of affairs in response to requests that he do so. And thus they are free to maintain justifiably that petitionary prayer may well "change things" in the sense that God may at times intervene in our world in ways that he would not have intervened if petitions had not been offered. They remain free, for example, to maintain that God has touched a fevered body or guided the thinking of a world leader or granted peace to a troubled mind in ways he would not have if petitions had not been offered.

But proponents of specific sovereignty maintain, remember, that God not only can but does unilaterally ensure that we always freely make the exact decisions that he would have us make. Thus, for proponents of specific sovereignty, it can never be the case that God is prohibited from bringing about that which he can and would like to bring about—a healing, guidance and the like—because we have not requested that he do so. That is, it can never be the case that whether God brings about some state of affairs in our world depends on whether we utilize the power of choice over which God has given us control to petition his assistance.[9] Rather, as Thomas Aquinas, John Calvin and Martin Luther all clearly understood, if a God with specific sovereignty has decided to bring about some state of affairs in response to a prayer offered freely, he can always ensure that this prayer will be offered freely and thus that the desired state of affairs will come about. No person ever has it in his or her power to make it otherwise.[10]

Process theists, on the other hand, have a radically different understanding of the God-world relationship. They believe that all entities—human and nonhuman, animate and inanimate—always possess some power of self-determination (some freedom of choice). Thus, even though they believe that God displays his concern for our world by presenting to every entity at every moment the best option available and then attempting to persuade each entity to act in accordance with it, they deny that God can ever unilaterally intervene in any sense in earthly affairs.[11]

Hence, we should not be surprised that process theists must also deny that petitionary prayer can ever be efficacious in the sense that it initiates unilateral divine activity that would not have occurred if it had not been freely requested. Like proponents of specific sovereignty, process theists can justifiably maintain that petitionary prayer can be efficacious in the sense that it affects petitioners and those for whom petitions are offered. But since process theists believe that every entity always possesses some power of self-determination and that God is already doing all that is possible to persuade each entity to make the choices that he would have it make, they can never claim that petitionary prayer brings it about that God becomes more involved than he would otherwise have been. God is already involved in earthly affairs—for instance, in the sharing of wisdom or peace—to the extent that any petitioner could request that he be.[12]

For those of us who affirm an open view of God, however, the situation is quite different. Unlike proponents of specific sovereignty, we do not believe that God can unilaterally ensure that all and only that which he desires to come about in our world will in fact occur. We maintain, rather, that since God has chosen to create a world in which we possess significant freedom, and since we can be significantly free only if he does not unilaterally control how this freedom is utilized, God voluntarily forfeits control over earthly affairs in those cases where he allows us to exercise this freedom.

However, unlike proponents of process theism, we maintain that God does retain the right to intervene unilaterally in earthly affairs. That is, we believe that freedom of choice is a gift granted to us by God and thus that God retains the power and moral prerogative to inhibit occasionally our ability to make voluntary choices to keep things on track.[13]

Consequently, those of us who affirm an open view of God are not limited to conceiving of the efficacy of petitionary prayer in only those ways in which such efficacy can justifiably be affirmed by proponents of specific sovereignty and process theism. Like proponents of both of these perspectives, we can justifiably maintain that prayer is efficacious in the sense that it can affect petitioners and those for whom petitions are offered. And, like proponents of specific sovereignty, we believe that God can use petitionary prayer to bring about desired ends.

However, it is also possible for proponents of the open model to conceive of petitionary prayer as efficacious in the crucial sense in which it is not possible for proponents of either specific sovereignty or process theism to maintain that it is. Since proponents of specific sovereignty believe that God always ensures that we freely make the exact decisions that he would have us make, and since process theists deny that God can ever unilaterally intervene in earthly affairs, those in neither camp can justifiably maintain that petitionary prayer initiates unilateral divine activity that would not have occurred if we had not utilized our God-given power of choice to request such divine assistance. However, since we who affirm the open view deny that God can unilaterally control human decision-making that is truly voluntary but affirm that God can unilaterally intervene in earthly affairs, it does become possible for us to maintain justifiably that petitionary prayer is efficacious in this sense—that is, to maintain justifiably that divine activity is at times dependent on our freely offered petitions.[14] It becomes possible to maintain justifiably, for instance, that God does at times give guidance to a leader or soothe a troubled mind because we have utilized our God-given power of choice to request that he do so.

This does not mean, though, that all proponents of the open view are equally comfortable with all of the ways in which Christians commonly petition God. It is not unusual for Christians to ask God to involve himself in the lives of other people—to offer assistance to a friend in need, for example. But a key assumption in the open model is that God so values the inherent integrity of significant human freedom—the ability of individuals to maintain control over the significant aspects of their lives—that he will not as a general rule force his created moral agents to perform actions that they do not freely desire to perform or manipulate the natural environment in such a way that their freedom of choice is destroyed. Accordingly, most of us who affirm the open view of God doubt that he would override the freedom of one individual primarily because he was freely asked to do so by another. We doubt, for instance, that God would override the freedom of someone in a troubled marriage primarily because he was freely petitioned to do so by a friend of the couple.

What if we assume, however, that what is being asked of God is not that he override the freedom of others but rather only that he influence their lives in such a way that it will be more likely that things will work out for the best? Does this not resolve the difficulty? The answer depends on what we who affirm the open model mean when we say that God loves all individuals in the sense that he is always seeking the highest good for each. For some of us this means that God would never refrain from intervening beneficially in one person's life simply because someone else has failed to request that he do so. And, accordingly, we naturally find prayers requesting even noncoercive divine influence in the lives of others to be very problematic.[15]

Other proponents of the open model, though, see no necessary incompatibility in affirming both that God always seeks what is best for each of us and that God may at times wait to exert all the noncoercive influence that he can justifiably exert on a given person until requested to do so by another person. And thus they readily acknowledge the potential efficacy of prayers of this type.[16]

Christians, however, do not only ask God to help others; they also at times ask God to intervene beneficially on their own behalf. And with respect to petitioning of this type, there is much less debate among those who affirm the open model of God. Since we believe that God greatly respects our freedom of choice, all of us find it quite reasonable to assume that God will at times refrain from doing all that he would like to do for us until we personally request such assistance.

Some of us, it must be admitted, believe that it is important to qualify the scope of such efficacy. Since the God of the open model wishes us to become morally mature individuals, it is quite unlikely, we argue, that God would respond positively to requests that he, for example, take total control of our lives or relieve us of the responsibility of doing or discovering what we can do or discover for ourselves.[17]

But we all agree that it is, at the very least, quite reasonable to view petitionary prayer as a means whereby we grant God the permission to influence our noncognitive states of mind and/or share with us those cognitive insights concerning ourselves and others that will help us better live out our Christian commitment in this world.

Accordingly, even granting the reality of a number of "intramural debates," it should not be surprising that those who affirm the open model believe the status of petitionary prayer within this model to be one of its most attractive features. All Christian perspectives on the God-world relationship can justifiably consider petitionary prayer to be a meaningful, efficacious activity. But the open model of God is one of the few in which petitionary prayer is efficacious in the manner still presupposed by most Christians: as an activity that can initiate unilateral divine activity that would not have taken place if we had not utilized our God-given power of choice to request his assistance.

Divine Guidance

We as Christians do not only believe it is important that we share our thoughts and concerns with God. We also want God to share his thoughts and concerns with us. That is, we desire God's guidance when deciding how to think and act.

But Christians do not agree on the type of knowledge God possesses, and this has important implications for the type of guidance available. As noted in the last chapter, while some Christians believe that God knows only what *will* happen to us beforehand—that he possesses only simple foreknowledge—others believe that he also knows beforehand what *would* happen, given each of the options open to us—that he possesses middle knowledge. And, of course, if God does possess middle knowledge, then a great deal of very specific guidance is available to us.[18] If God possesses middle knowledge, for instance, then he knows much more than simply whether a couple appear at present to be well suited for each other or even whether they will in fact marry. Rather, he possesses very useful comparative information about their potential marriage: he knows exactly what will happen if they do marry and exactly what will happen if they do not marry, and can offer guidance on this basis.[19]

However, proponents of the open view do not believe that God possesses middle knowledge—that God always knows beforehand what would happen, given each option open to us.[20] In fact, we do not even believe that God always knows beforehand exactly how things *will* turn out in the future—that God possesses simple foreknowledge.

We maintain, rather, that God possesses only what has come to be called "present knowledge." God, we acknowledge, does know all that has occurred in the past and is occurring now. Moreover, God does know all that will follow deterministically from what has occurred, and can, as the ultimate psychoanalyst, predict with great accuracy what we as humans will freely choose to do in various contexts. God, for instance, might well be able to predict with great accuracy whether a couple would have a successful marriage. But since we believe that God can know only what can be known and that what humans will freely do in the future cannot be known beforehand, we believe that God can never know with certainty what will happen in any context involving freedom of choice. We believe, for example, that to the extent that freedom of choice would be involved, God would not necessarily know beforehand exactly what would happen if a couple were to marry. Accordingly, we must acknowledge that divine guidance, from our perspective, cannot be considered a means of discovering exactly what will be best in the long run—as a means of discovering the very best long-term option. Divine guidance, rather, must be viewed primarily as a means of determining what is best for us now.

Is this a negative aspect of our model? Many conservative Christians may think so. Most have been taught that God can furnish them with comparative, long-term divine guidance. Hence many may find the fact that our model does not allow for such guidance to be an unappealing feature.

However, proponents of the open model believe there to be significant theological benefits in denying that God has exhaustive knowledge of the future. For instance, many Christians who believe that God has exhaustive knowledge of the future believe as a result that he has a specific plan for their lives. That is, they believe that God has identified for them the ideal way in which their lives would run, if all went as God desired. But some in this category also believe that it is possible to stray from this plan; they therefore expend a great deal of time and energy trying to determine whether they are within God's perfect will at any given moment and, if not, what can be done to reenter it or at least what would have occurred if they had not settled for "second best."

This is obviously not an issue with which open view theists need to grapple in the same sense. The God of the open model does have a general will for each of us. He does want us to live in accordance with the principles that he has established. And he does at every moment know which available option is "best" for us and desire that we actualize this short-term ideal. Thus it is perfectly reasonable for those of us who affirm the open view to wonder whether we are in God's will in the sense of wondering whether we are now acting in accordance with what God has identified as the best present course of action. And it is perfectly reasonable for us to resolve to be more diligent in our attempts to identify and actualize this ideal in the future. In fact, it is even reasonable for us to feel that we may have failed to follow God's leading in the past and have thus missed an opportunity that might have led to a better, more satisfying life than we now lead.

However, since we do not believe that God has exhaustive knowledge of the future, it makes no sense for us to think in terms of some perfect, preordained plan for our lives and, hence, to worry about whether we are still within it. Accordingly, we need never feel—no matter what has happened in the past—that we must now settle for "second best" in this rigid sense.

Moreover, we see a second, related benefit in assuming that God does not have exhaustive knowledge of the future. Christians are often convinced at one point in time that they have correctly discerned God's will, but later come to wonder whether this was actually so. A student, for example, who was totally convinced that God was guiding her into a given field of study may come to question whether this was really God's leading when she cannot find related employment.

Of course, certain possibilities are open to all Christians in such cases. As will be discussed in some detail later, it is always possible that what a given individual thought was God's will initially really was not. It is always possible, for instance, that a person's own intense desire to enter a profession was wrongly interpreted as God's will. Moreover, it is always possible that what an individual has identified as God's specific will in a given context really is God's will and that the reason things have not worked out as expected is that God has always had something else in mind.

But for open view theists another explanation is available. We seek and trust in God's guidance. Only he is aware of all the relevant factors, and only he is in a position to determine the best course(s) of action given these factors. However, since God does not necessarily know exactly what will happen in the future, it is always possible that even that which God in his unparalleled wisdom believes to be the best course of action at any given time may not produce the anticipated results in the long run. For example, given that God may not know exactly what the state of the economy will be over the next five or ten years, it is possible that what God in his wisdom believes at present to be the best course of study for a student may not be an option that will allow her after graduation to pursue the profession for which she has prepared.

In other words, as we see it, a person who finds that her attempts to follow God's will do not produce what she perceives to be a positive state of affairs need not assume automatically either that she did not properly discern God's will in the first place or that what appears not to be a positive state of affairs in some mysterious way actually is (and thus that she ought not attempt to change anything). Since it is always possible that what will occur as the result of following God's specific will at a given time will not be exactly what even God envisioned, she can justifiably assume that this may have occurred in her case. Of course, it does not follow from the fact that this may have occurred in her case that this is what did actually occur. But if, after consideration, an individual remains convinced that she was indeed following God's will initially and can over time discern no hidden benefit in maintaining the status quo, then, given the open view, she is free to turn to God without remorse or guilt to attempt to discern his new specific will for her life.

There remains, though, one other practical issue related to God's will that we should consider: In what way(s) does God attempt to share his will—his guidance—with us? This is a question with which all Christians must grapple. However, those who affirm the open model are committed to a response that is somewhat different from that of either process theists or proponents of specific sovereignty.

Process theists clearly believe that God attempts to share his will with us. In fact, as we have seen, they believe that God is at every moment presenting to each of us the best available option and attempting to persuade us to chose it. However, process theists do not view this process—God's presentation of the best available option—as something of which individuals are normally aware at the conscious level. Rather, in the words of process theist John Cobb, the process whereby God shares his desires with us "is most of the time below the level of consciousness or at its fringes. Clear conscious decisions in relation to clear conscious knowledge of possibilities is a rare phenomenon."[21]

For those who affirm the open model of God, things are, in principle, much different. We do not necessarily deny that God is at all times trying to persuade individuals at the subconscious level to act in accordance with his general will—for instance, to treat others with respect. However, we also believe, as do proponents of specific sovereignty, that God does at times break through to give specific, conscious guidance to individuals—for instance, that God does at times furnish specific, conscious guidance with respect to marriage or career options.

However, the relationship between such guidance and human decision-making differs significantly within the two models in question. Those who affirm specific sovereignty deny that God is in any sense dependent on human choice and thus deny that such choice can ever thwart or hinder in any way God's perfect plan. This does not mean that proponents of specific sovereignty cannot justifiably seek God's "revealed will"—that which "God is pleased to have his creatures do."[22] But it can never be the case within this model that someone fails to become aware of guidance that God desires to make available because this person has decided not to seek God's will. If God desires a given individual to receive certain guidance— if this is part of God's perfect plan—then that person will receive the guidance in question.[23]

However, this is not the case for proponents of the open model. Since we believe that God does not as a general rule override human freedom and/or the natural order, we acknowledge that numerous reasons exist why individuals might fail to receive that which God desires to share with them. Some might, for instance, fail to ask for such guidance. Or there may exist psychological or physiological conditions that prohibit some from clearly receiving or understanding God's guidance, even when it is sought with sincerity. For instance, some individuals may find it difficult to discern God's specific will for a possible marriage because of the very strong hormonal or psychosocial impulses involved. Or the influence of friends or respected spiritual leaders might so overwhelm some individuals that they simply cannot discern clearly what God would have them do.

Accordingly, open view theists have good reason to take very seriously a series of well-known, practical checks and balances when attempting to discern God's specific will. We have good reason, for instance, to test seemingly direct divine guidance against general scriptural principles or to wait to see whether this "guidance" stays consistent over time.

There is, however, one very popular method for discerning God's guidance on which we who affirm the open model cannot rely heavily: the "opening and closing of doors" by God. It is not uncommon for Christians to maintain that if they cannot discern in some clear, direct way God's leading in a given context, they should proceed in a given direction and wait for God to respond. If God does not approve of the direction in which they are moving, he will close the door—for instance, he will bring it about that the schools to which they apply will not accept them or that the individuals they desire to marry will refuse their proposals—while if God approves, the door will remain open.[24]

To affirm the open view of God does not categorically rule out guidance of this fashion. After all, we who affirm the open view do not deny that God can, and even does, occasionally intervene in earthly affairs by overriding human freedom and/or the natural order. However, since we believe that God unilaterally intervenes quite infrequently, there can be no assurance, from our perspective, that what happens—including what happens as the result of a person's decision to proceed in a certain direction—is God's will. There can be no assurance, or even strong probability, for instance, that a school's decision to accept or reject an application or a person's decision to accept or reject a marriage proposal is a "closed door." Given the open view, such occurrences are more likely to be the result of human decision-making over which God has not exercised control.

We must acknowledge that some (or even many) Christians may consider this a negative aspect of the open model. However, we believe just the opposite to be true. While those who rely on the "closed door" technique must guard against becoming quite passive—against simply sitting back and assuming that they are on the "right track" unless God puts some barrier in their way—proponents of the open model do not face this danger. Since we can never be certain that what occurs naturally is a "sign" from God, we must be quite proactive in our attempts to discern God's will. And, as we see it, this is a very positive consequence of commitment to our model.[25]

Human Suffering

Here is a common situation: a house catches fire and a six-month old baby is painfully burned to death. Could we possibly describe as "good" any person who had the power to save this child and yet refused to do so? God undoubtedly has this power yet in many cases of this sort he has refused to help. Can we call God "good"?[26]

Sometimes philosophers and theologians are said to be out of touch with the thoughts and feelings of nonacademics. But this is certainly not the case with respect to what is called the problem of evil. For centuries "professionals" and laypersons alike have struggled with the question posed above: If God exists, why is there so much evil?

In response, few Christian deny that there is a great deal of pain and suffering in this world. Moreover, no Christian believes that God finds human pain and suffering intrinsically valuable in the sense that God delights in its occurrence. No Christian, for example, believes that God derived pleasure from the fact that so many died horrible deaths during the Holocaust. But Christians do differ significantly on the question of the types of evil our world contains and on the question of how "responsible" God is for its occurrence. And these differences have important implications for how we explain and react to the evil we experience.

For those who believe in specific sovereignty—who deny that human decision-making can ever thwart or hinder in any way God's perfect plan— all evil must be considered nongratuitous. That is, all evil must be viewed as a necessary means to a greater good in the sense that it is something that God causes or allows because it is a necessary component in his preordained plan.[27]

On the other end of the spectrum is process theism. Proponents of this model, as we have seen, do not deny that some of the evil we experience may happen to be nongratuitous—that it may lead to a greater good of some kind. But since they believe that all entities possess some power of self-determination, they maintain that God can never unilaterally bring about or prohibit any state of affairs. What occurs always depends in part on the "decisions" made by such entities. Accordingly, since they also believe that self-determining beings not only can, but often do, choose less than the best option available, process theists quite naturally assume that much of the evil we as humans experience may well be gratuitous—may well not lead to any greater good.[28]

Those of us who affirm an open view of God are much closer to process theists at this point. Unlike process theists, we believe that God *could* have ensured that this world contained no gratuitous evil by refraining from granting other entities significant freedom. And unlike process theists, we believe that God may at times allow the occurrence of an evil state of affairs in order to bring about some greater good. But we believe that God has chosen to create a world in which individuals possess significant freedom, and hence that God does not as a general rule unilaterally intervene in earthly affairs. And we, like process theists, maintain that humanity not only can, but often does, choose less than the best option available. Thus we, like process theists, believe that much of the pain and suffering we encounter may well be gratuitous—may well not lead to any greater good.[29]

Moreover, viewing evil in this manner has practical significance. For instance, it means that we, unlike proponents of specific sovereignty, need not assume that some divine purpose exists for each evil that we encounter. We need not, for example, assume when someone dies that God "took him home" for some reason, or that the horrors many experience in this world in some mysterious way fit into God's perfect plan. We can justifiably assume, rather, that God is often as disappointed as are we that someone's earthly existence has ended at an early age or that someone is experiencing severe depression or that someone is being tortured.

This does not mean, it must quickly be added, that those who affirm the open model cannot justifiably maintain that God is involved in our lives. As we see it, God at every moment experiences with us whatever evil is at hand and desires that we turn to him for comfort. Nor do we deny that something good can come out of even the most tragic occurrence. Even process theists can justifiably contend that something positive or redemptive can be found in every situation. But even in those cases where something of value appears, we who affirm the open model need not assume that God caused or allowed the evil in question as a means to this end. We remain free to assume that such evil was an undesired byproduct of misguided human freedom and/ or the normal outworking of the natural order.[30]

But why would any Christian want to make this assumption? Would not every Christian like to be able to assume instead that all evils are necessary components in God's overall plan for this world? In response, we must acknowledge that this may be the case for some Christians, especially in relation to individual instances of tragedy. Some Christians may prefer to assume, for instance, that the death of a child who has been hit by a drunk driver or the failure of a student to be accepted into graduate school is part of some meaningful, perfect divine plan.[31]

However, this is not the case for most of us who accept the open view. From our perspective, to view specific tragedies in this world as the result of a system over which God has chosen not to exercise complete control is more appealing than to view such events as the outworking of some specific, preordained divine plan. We find it more comforting, for example, to view the death of a child hit by a drunk driver as the result of faulty human decision-making, or the failure of an individual to be accepted into graduate school as the result of insufficient preparation or discrimination or a careless selection process.[32]

Moreover, all Christians at times wonder about the seemingly unjust distribution of evil in our world. Why are millions of individuals in the Third World starving while many of us in North America have much more to eat than we need? Why are so many innocent children sexually abused by individuals who are never made to pay for what they have done? Why do so many "good" people live in their own private mental "hell" while so many "bad" people seem to enjoy life to the fullest?

Proponents of specific sovereignty can offer a self-consistent answer: the amount and type and location of all evil are necessary components in some preordained plan, although we as humans may never understand how this could be. But we who affirm the open model need not maintain that God's creative goals require that many people in the Third World be allowed to starve or that many children be allowed to suffer abuse. We are free to maintain, rather, that these evils, and also their patterns of distribution, are byproducts of a world containing freedom—byproducts that God, as well as each of us, wishes had not occurred. And most of us find the ability to respond in this fashion to be a psychological, as well as theological, benefit.[33]

Social Responsibility
Closely related to the problem of evil is the question of social responsibility.

All Christians are rightly concerned about the devastating problems facing many in our world today: starvation, disease, racism and sexism, to name a few. But to what extent is it our responsibility as Christians to help rid the world of such evils?

For those Christians who believe in specific sovereignty, remember, human decision-making can never in any sense thwart God's will. All and only that which God has preordained to occur will occur. This does not mean, it is important to note, that proponents of this perspective must consider our actions totally irrelevant to the social ills we face. They can justifiably maintain that a direct causal relationship exists between these problems and our actual behavior. They can legitimately maintain, for example, that many individuals in Third World countries are starving in part because we in Western cultures consume too much or have not done enough to create a more equitable global economic system. Thus they can justifiably maintain that changes in our behavior might very well have a beneficial impact.

However, given specific sovereignty, it can never be maintained justifiably that the primary reason our world continues to face pervasive social problems is what we as humans have freely chosen to do or not do. For example, it cannot be said that the primary reason that so many face starvation is that we as humans have failed to choose freely to do what we can to rectify the situation. Since we can in no sense thwart God's perfect will, the primary reason we continue to face problems such as mass starvation is that God has preordained that it be so. He might, of course, decide to have us freely modify our behavior in such a way that social conditions will improve. But whether he does so or not is his decision alone.[34]

For proponents of process theism, not surprisingly, the situation is much different. Since process theists believe that every entity always possesses some power of self-determination, they maintain that there can be no guarantee that what God desires that we do will ever in fact come about. Thus within the process system, we humans bear a tremendous amount of responsibility for that which occurs in those social contexts where human decision-making is relevant. For instance, since God can unilaterally ensure nothing, it is true not only that the fate of hundreds of millions of starving people, but that the very survival of the human race itself depends primarily on whether enough of us make the right choices.

Not surprisingly, proponents of the open model believe that process theists are much closer to the truth on this issue. Since the God of the open model can unilaterally intervene on occasion, we who affirm this model do not believe that humanity bears quite as much responsibility for what occurs as process theists believe. Specifically, unlike process theists, we believe that God has a very general plan for humanity that he will not allow human decision-making to alter. For example, we believe that whether our race survives is ultimately dependent on God and not on us.

However, since we also believe that God does not as a general rule intervene in earthly affairs, we quite naturally assume, like process theists, that humanity bears primary responsibility for much of what occurs in those contexts in which human decision-making is involved. We assume, for instance, that to the extent that starvation and cancer are the result of human decision-making, humanity bears primary moral responsibility for such states of affairs. Accordingly, it becomes very important for us to attempt to discover ways in which we can remedy social problems.

Evangelistic Responsibility

Christians, though, are not only concerned about the social ills we humans confront. Almost all Christians (even process theists) believe that many people are not properly related to God personally and, accordingly, that it is also important to share with them the "good news"—the joy and excitement of being properly related to God. In short, almost all Christians also support some form of evangelistic effort.

On the basis of what has already been said, however, it should not be surprising that the primary basis for such evangelistic concern differs significantly among the models of divine-human interaction that we have been discussing.

Proponents of specific sovereignty can justifiably feel an obligation to share the good news with others. After all, they are commanded by God to do so. But given specific sovereignty, remember, human decision-making can never in any sense thwart God's will. God may use human effort as a means to accomplish his purposes, but humans are never the primary initiators of what occurs.

Thus, according to this perspective, it can never be said that we bear direct moral responsibility for the status of any other person's relationship with God. This does not mean, of course, that proponents of specific sovereignty must deny the existence of any significant causal connection between our actions and someone else's relationship with God. They can justifiably claim, for example, that parents often do in fact have a great impact on their children's spiritual well-being. However, given specific sovereignty, it can never be the case that someone either comes to be rightly related to God, or fails to do so, primarily because of decisions we as humans have made. God may well use us as "tools" by which he brings someone into a proper relationship with himself. But all and only those whom God desires to be "saved" will be saved. And thus the fear that some will fail to enter into a proper relationship with God because of some negligence on our part can never serve as a justifiable basis for evangelistic efforts.[35]

The situation is in some ways quite different for process theists. As they see it, everyone is in one sense automatically related to (connected with) God to the extent possible: God is always offering to every individual, at the subconscious level, the best options available, and every individual is always feeling, at the subconscious level, some compulsion to act in accordance with this guidance. However, process theists also maintain that we often fail to appropriate consciously the benefits of this relationship to the extent that we could. Accordingly, proponents of this perspective can justifiably maintain that we ought to encourage others to be as open as possible to what God is "saying." But it remains the case, given process thought, that we need never fear that someone else will fail to establish or maintain the *capacity* to interact fully with God because of some failure on our part.

The situation, though, is very different for those who are proponents of the open model. We agree with process theists that individuals can fail to appropriate consciously all that God has to offer and, hence, agree that we should encourage each other in this respect. But, unlike process theists, we also believe that a significant initial separation exists between God and humans—an initial inability for God and humans to interact to the extent possible—that can be bridged completely only when we choose freely to enter into a relationship with God. And thus we believe that we also have a responsibility to help others become rightly related to God in this sense.

This is not to say, it must quickly be added, that all proponents of the open model are necessarily committed to the contention that some will spend eternity separated from God because we have failed to share the "good news" with them. While proponents of the open view do believe in an afterlife, many maintain that each person's eternal destiny will ultimately be determined by God on the basis of the "light" available to him or her (or by other criteria).[36]

But those who affirm the open view are clearly committed to the contention that some may fail to relate properly to God at least in this life because of our failure to share the "good news" with them. Moreover, we are clearly committed to the contention that a personal relationship with God is what gives this life its fullest meaning. Thus, given the open view, the fear that some will fail to enter fully into a relationship with God—that some might not avail themselves of the totality of God's transforming power—because of some negligence on our part can justifiably serve as an important basis for evangelistic efforts.

Or, to state this important point in a slightly different manner, while proponents of all three models rightly feel an obligation to obey God's command to "preach the gospel," it is within the open model that our decision to obey or disobey this command has the most significant impact on whether others will develop their relationship with God in this life to the fullest extent possible. And while we who are proponents of the open view find this sobering, we also find it highly motivating.[37]

Conclusion

My primary purpose in this chapter has been to set forth what I believe to be the most significant implications of affirming an open view of God. However, it is obvious from the manner in which I have discussed these implications that I, like the other authors of this book, consider the open model not only to be significantly different from its main competitors but to be superior. Accordingly, it is important in closing that I clearly identify the exact manner in which I consider this to be so.

I do not consider our model to be logically superior to all others in the sense that I believe ours to be the only self-consistent, comprehensive model that can justifiably be claimed by its proponents to be a plausible perspective on the relationship between God and the world. Nor do I believe the open model to be experientially superior in the sense that I believe it to be the only model that any thoughtful, sincere person could reasonably find satisfying. Just as not all children will agree on the most appealing parenting style, and not all students will agree on the most appealing teaching style, not all Christians will agree on the most appealing type of divine-human interaction. And I see no objective basis for denying that proponents of other models can justifiably continue to view their perspectives on the relationship between God and our world as the most fulfilling personally.

But I do believe the open model to be superior in the sense that I personally find it to be the most plausible, appealing conceptualization of this relationship. And thus I, along with the other authors, invite those Christians who have not seriously thought about this issue or who are not totally comfortable with their present perspective to consider carefully the God-world relationship outlined in this book. There are certain risks involved. Things do not always turn out as expected or desired. But the God to whom we are committed is always walking beside us, experiencing what we are experiencing when we are experiencing it, always willing to help to the extent consistent with our status as responsible creations of his. And we find this to be both exciting and spiritually rewarding.

Notes

Chapter 1: Biblical Support for a New Perspective/Rice

[1]Millard J. Erickson, *Christian Theology*, 3 vols. (Grand Rapids, Mich.: Baker Book House, 1983), 1:351-54.

[2]Stephen Charnock, *Discourses upon the Existence and Attributes of God*, 2 vols. (Grand Rapids, Mich.: Baker Book House, 1979), 1:310-62.

[3]Ibid., 1:455.

[4]Ibid., 1:321-22.

[5]Ibid., 1:454.

[6]Ibid., 1:434.

[7]This is why biblical scholars often object to expressions like "the biblical view of" or "according to the Bible." They insist that there are biblical *views*, but no one biblical view. While it is *not* true, in spite of what some people claim, that you can make the Bible say anything you want it to say, different passages often seem to support different points of view. To cite a familiar example, many people do not see how the same God could command Israel on occasion to utterly destroy its foes (Josh 6:17; 1 Sam 15:2-3) and through Jesus instruct us to love our enemies (Mt 5:44).

[8]See, for example, Paul Tillich: "The statement that God is being-itself is a nonsymbolic statement. . . . However, after this has been said, nothing else can be said about God as God which is not symbolic" (*Systematic Theology*, 3 vols. [Chicago: University of Chicago Press, 1951-1963], 1:238-39).

[9]Proponents of the traditional view of God are often quick to discount the importance of many biblical descriptions of God on the grounds that they are nothing more than metaphors, mere figures of speech.

[10]Terence Fretheim, *The Suffering of God: An Old Testament Perspective* (Philadelphia: Fortress, 1984), p. 11.

[11]Another possible definition appears in John 4:24: "God is spirit." According to Wolfhart Pannenberg, these two statements are the Bible's only "clearcut saying[s] about God's essential nature" (*Systematic Theology*, trans. Geoffrey W. Bromiley [Grand Rapids Mich.: Eerdmans, 1991], 1:395-96).

[12]Eberhard Jüngel, *God as the Mystery of the World,* trans. Darrell L. Guder (Grand Rapids, Mich.: Eerdmans, 1983), p. 314.

[13]Jer 33:11; Ps 100:5; 106:1; 107:1; 118:1-4; 136:1-26; Ezra 3:11.

[14]Abraham Joshua Heschel, *The Prophets* (New York: Harper & Row, 1962), p. 291.

[15]Ibid., p. 297.

[16]Ibid., pp. 290, 289.

[17]Ibid., p. 291.

[18]Karl Barth, *Church Dogmatics* 2/1, ed. G. W. Bromiley and T. F. Torrance (Edinburgh: T & T Clark, 1957), pp. 272-73.

[19]Ibid., p. 275.

[20]Ibid., p. 279.

[21]Emil Brunner, *Dogmatics,* vol. 1, *The Christian Doctrine of God,* trans. Olive Wyon (Philadelphia: Westminster Press, 1949), p. 185.

[22]Walter Kasper, *The God of Jesus Christ,* trans. Matthew J. O'Connell (New York: Crossroad, 1984), p. 195. Kasper sees God's self-communicating love as the starting point for the understanding of the Trinity (ibid.).

[23]Pannenberg, *Systematic Theology,* 1:396.

[24]Barth, *Church Dogmatics* 2/2, pp. 283-84.

[25]"The LORD, the LORD, the compassionate and gracious God, slow to anger, abounding in love and faithfulness."

[26]Pannenberg, *Systematic Theology,* 1:432.

[27]It would exceed the scope of this discussion to pursue this further, but it is significant that many theologians, including those just mentioned, see the identification of God's very being with his act of love as the basis for the doctrine of the Trinity, the distinctive Christian idea of God. If love is what God *is,* then God must experience love within himself from all eternity, and the understanding of Father, Son and Spirit as relations of love within the divine reality makes this comprehensible.

[28]On the preeminence of God's love see Fritz Guy, "The Universality of God's Love," in *The Grace of God, the Will of Man: A Case for Arminianism,* ed. Clark H. Pinnock (Grand Rapids, Mich.: Zondervan, 1989), pp. 33-36. Applying this idea to the divine wrath, for example, we see God's anger not as a contradiction of his love but as an expression of it. To quote Heschel again, "God's concern is the prerequisite and source of His anger. It is because He cares for man that His anger may be kindled against man. Anger and mercy are not opposites but correlatives" *(Prophets,* p. 283). If we apply the same principle to divine power, we must not say merely that God is both powerful and loving, nor that God's love is more important than his power, nor even that God's power and love are intimately connected. Instead, we must say that God's love is the source of his power. God is supremely powerful precisely because of the intensity and immensity of his love. In the final analysis, divine power is nothing other than the power of love.

[29]The work of Terence E. Fretheim includes the following: *The Suffering of God: An Old Testament Perspective* (Philadelphia: Fortress, 1986); "Prayer in the Old Testament: Creating Space in the World for God," in *A Primer on Prayer,* ed. Paul Sponheim (Philadelphia: Fortress, 1988), pp. 51-62; "Suffering God and Sovereign God in Exodus: A Collision of Images," *Horizons in Biblical Theology* 11 (1989): 31-56; "The Repentance of God: A Key to

Evaluating Old Testament God-Talk," *Horizons in Biblical Theology* 10 (1988): 47-70; "The Repentance of God: A Study of Jeremiah 18:7-10," *Hebrew Annual Review* 11 (1987): 81-92; "The Color of God: Israel's God-Talk and Life Experience," *Word & World* 6 (1986): 256-65; "Divine Foreknowledge, Divine Constancy and the Rejection of Saul's Kingship," *The Catholic Biblical Quarterly* 47 (1985): 595-602.

[30]Still other references are: "But Samuel replied: 'Does the LORD delight in burnt offerings and sacrifices as much as in obeying the voice of the LORD? To obey is better than sacrifice, and to heed is better than the fat of rams' " (1 Sam 15:22). "May those who delight in my vindication shout for joy and gladness; may they always say, 'The LORD be exalted, who delights in the well-being of his servant' " (Ps 35:27). "The LORD abhors dishonest scales, but accurate weights are his delight" (Prov 11:1). "The vineyard of the LORD Almighty is the house of Israel, and the men of Judah are the garden of his delight. And he looked for justice, but saw bloodshed; for righteousness, but heard cries of distress" (Is 5:7). "No longer will they call you Deserted, or name your land Desolate. But you will be called Hephzibah, and your land Beulah; for the LORD will take delight in you, and your land will be married" (Is 62:4).

[31]The expression is that of Tikva Frymer-Kensky in *In the Wake of the Goddesses: Women, Culture and the Biblical Transformation of Pagan Myth* (New York: Fawcett Columbine, 1992), p. 144. Her illuminating study identifies the dialogue between humankind and God as "the essential insight of monotheism" (p. 117).

[32]Ibid, pp. 148-49.

[33]Ibid., p. 147 (emphasis hers).

[34]Ibid., p. 149.

[35]"Hear, O Israel: The LORD our God, the LORD is one" (Deut 6:4) has been the prayer of devout Jews for centuries. "You shall have no other gods before me," reads the first of the Ten Commandments (Ex 20:3).

[36]Heschel, *Prophets,* p. 223.

[37]Ibid., p. 56.

[38]Ibid., pp. 224-25, 231.

[39]Ibid., p. 226.

[40]The NRSV translates this verse "The LORD changed his mind about the disaster that he planned to bring on his people."

[41]R. Alan Cole, *Exodus: An Introduction and Commentary* (Downers Grove, Ill.: InterVarsity Press, 1973), p. 217.

[42]Charnock, *Existence and Attributes of God,* 1:345.

[43]George A. F. Knight, *Theology as Narration: A Commentary on the Book of Exodus* (Grand Rapids, Mich.: Eerdmans, 1976), p. 187.

[44]Terence E. Fretheim, *Exodus* (Louisville, Ky.: John Knox Press, 1991), p. 283.

[45]Ibid., p. 285.

[46]RSV reading. Fretheim points out that evil refers to "anything in life that makes for less than total well-being, including divine judgment and its effects" (ibid., p. 286). God never repents of sin, of course.

[47]Ibid., p. 287.

[48]Unlike so-called self-fulfilling prophecies, God evidently hopes that his forecasts of judgment

will be "self-refuting prophecies"!

[49]Fretheim, "Repentance of God: Jeremiah," pp. 88-89.

[50]Adrio König, *Here Am I! A Believer's Reflection on God* (Grand Rapids, Mich.: Eerdmans, 1982), p. 66.

[51]According to König, "The other texts which are used to deny that God repents (i.e. Ps. 110:4; Jer. 4:28; Ezek. 24:14; Zech. 8:14), actually presuppose that the Lord can repent, and therefore emphasize that under certain circumstances he will not repent" (ibid.).

[52]Fretheim, "Repentance of God: Old Testament God-Talk," p. 56.

[53]The conversation mentioned earlier between God and Abraham is a well-known example (Gen 18).

[54]G. Ernest Wright and Reginald H. Fuller, *The Book of the Acts of God: Contemporary Scholarship Interprets the Bible* (Garden City, N.Y.: Doubleday/Anchor Books, 1960).

[55]Fretheim, "Repentance of God: Jeremiah," p. 87.

[56]Cf. "God was in Christ," as many versions translate 2 Corinthians 5:19.

[57]I am indebted to John Sanders for this emphasis on the father's humiliation.

[58]Once again, however, we see the father's surprising love for his children. Instead of shrugging off the killjoy's rudeness, he comes out to plead for a change of heart.

[59]König, *Here Am I*, p. 43.

[60]Millard J. Erickson, for example, cites vv. 8 and 9 without mentioning v. 7 as support for the attribute of divine transcendence, the idea that "God is separate from and independent of nature and humanity" (*Christian Theology*, 1:312).

[61]König, *Here Am I*, p. 79.

[62]Kenneth Leech, *Experiencing God: Theology as Spirituality* (San Francisco: Harper & Row, 1985), p. 300.

[63]Ibid., p. 316.

[64]For a fuller discussion of these issues, see my book *God's Foreknowledge and Man's Free Will* (Minneapolis: Bethany House, 1985).

[65]König, *Here Am I*, p. 89.

[66]E. M. Good, "Love in the OT," in *The Interpreter's Dictionary of the Bible*, ed. George Arthur Buttrick (New York: Abingdon, 1962), 3:165; Ethelbert Stauffer, *agapao, Theological Dictionary of the New Testament*, ed. Gerhard Kittel, trans. Geoffrey W. Bromiley (Grand Rapids, Mich.: Eerdmans, 1964-1976), 1:41.

[67]"God is not a man, that he should lie, nor a son of man, that he should change his mind. Does he speak and then not act? Does he promise and not fulfill?" (Num 23:19). "He who is the Glory of Israel does not lie or change his mind; for he is not a man, that he should change his mind" (1 Sam 15:29).

[68]This is where proponents of the open view of God differ from process philosophers and theologians. For process philosophy, God needs the world as much as the world needs God. The ultimate reality, therefore, is not God, period, it is God-and-world. True, God would be God no matter what actual world existed, but there must be some actual world or other. In harmony with the classical theistic tradition, supporters of the open view of God accept the asymmetry of God's relation to the world as far as the divine existence is concerned. This means that God could exist without a creaturely world. But if there is such a world, then the actual content of his experience depends in part on the specific content of that world.

[69]Terence Fretheim puts the point this way: it is God's openness to change "that reveals what it is about God that is unchangeable: God's steadfastness has to do with God's love; God's faithfulness has to do with God's promises; God's will is for the salvation of all. God will always act, even make changes, in order to be true to these unchangeable ways and to accomplish these unchangeable goals" (*Exodus*, p. 287).

[70]Lester J. Kuyper on the exegetical efforts of Charles Hodge, William G. T. Shedd, A. H. Strong and L. Berkhof. He also describes Stephen Charnock's exposition as moving "from proper exegesis of Scripture to interpretations controlled by presuppositions" ("The Suffering and the Repentance of God," *Scottish Journal of Theology* 22 [1969]: 266-67).

[71]According to Emil Brunner, it is a "disastrous misunderstanding" to treat this expression as an ontological definition of God (*Christian Doctrine of God*, pp. 120, 128-29).

[72]Pannenberg, *Systematic Theology*, 1:205.

[73]For a helpful discussion of this approach to the passage, see John Courtney Murray, *The Problem of God Yesterday and Today* (New Haven, Conn.: Yale University Press, 1964), pp. 8-15.

[74]König, *Here Am I*, p. 43.

[75]For many conservative Christians, fulfilled prophecy is one of the strongest indications of the Bible's divine inspiration.

[76]Francis J. Beckwith critiques the open view of God in light of a single "Biblical test of a prophet," namely, the ability to predict the future accurately ("Limited Omniscience and the Test for a Prophet: A Brief Philosophical Analysis," *Journal of the Evangelical Theological Society* 36 [1993]: 357-62). Equating an "unfulfilled prophecy" with a "false prediction" (p. 362), Beckwith argues that unless a prophet is "correct about the future in every possible world," "the alleged spokesperson does not speak for God" (p. 358). Beckwith ignores the texture and complexity of biblical prophecy. He says nothing about conditional prophecy. And his rigid standard of prophetic authenticity would clearly require us to discredit Jonah, in view of the unfulfilled predictions he made.

[77]Jonathan Edwards, *Freedom of the Will*, ed. Paul Ramsey (New Haven, Conn.: Yale University Press, 1957).

[78]See William L. Craig, *The Only Wise God: The Compatibility of Divine Foreknowledge and Human Freedom* (Grand Rapids, Mich.: Baker Book House, 1987).

[79]Fretheim argues that Pharaoh only gradually reached the point where his refusal was final (*Exodus*, pp. 96-103).

[80]At the same time, from the fact that God's creatures have significant freedom it does not follow that God cannot, if he chooses, ever act on his own. We must avoid both over- and underestimating the amount of freedom that God's creatures enjoy. The fact that God sometimes requires creaturely cooperation does not mean that he always does so.

[81]William G. MacDonald makes a strong case for the corporate nature of election, and for Christ as the One in whom all are chosen for salvation, in his article "The Biblical Doctrine of Election," in *Grace of God*, ed. Pinnock, pp. 219, 222-23.

[82]William Klein, *The New Chosen People: A Corporate View of Election* (Grand Rapids, Mich.: Zondervan, 1990). Unfortunately, Klein's traditional view of divine foreknowledge detracts from his impressive study. Says Klein, "God's omniscience includes knowledge of the future—all its contingencies and eventualities" (p. 278).

[83]Ibid., pp. 258-59; "Election is not God's choice of a restricted number of individuals whom he wills to save, but the description of that corporate body which, in Christ, he is saving" (p. 266).

[84]Ibid., p. 279.

[85]Ibid., p. 272.

Chapter 2: Historical Considerations/Sanders

[1]Étienne Gilson, *God and Philosophy* (New Haven, Conn.: Yale University Press, 1959), p. 19.

[2]This anticipates the criticism of Feuerbach that what has no predicates lacks existence.

[3]G. S. Kirk and J. E. Raven, *The Presocratic Philosophers* (New York: Cambridge University Press, 1962), p. 273.

[4]For a survey of the various positions see John P. Rowan, "Platonic and Christian Theism," in *God in Contemporary Thought: A Philosophical Perspective*, ed. Sebastian A. Matczak (New York: Learned Publications, 1977), pp. 385-413.

[5]Plato *Republic* 381. References are to *Dialogues of Plato*, trans. B. Jowett, 2 vols. (New York: Random House, 1937).

[6]*Philebus* 33.

[7]*Symposium* 200-203.

[8]*Parmenides* 134.

[9]*Symposium* 203.

[10]*Laws* 900-907.

[11]Plato does say that God established a "general plan" by which evil will be overcome, but it does not seem that God gets very involved in accomplishing this plan (*Laws* 903-5). He claims that the wicked may be prospering now, but one must remember that God makes "all things work together and contribute to the great whole" and "you are created for the sake of the whole, and not the whole for the sake of you." This idea would later be emphasized by the Stoics.

[12]*Republic* 379-85; *Laws* 900-902; and *Phaedo* 63c.

[13]*Laws* 901.

[14]*Timaeus* 37-38.

[15]*Sophist* 265c; *Laws* 886e, 889b-e; *Philebus* 26e; *Timaeus* 28-30.

[16]*Laws* 818, 741; *Timaeus* 48, 30.

[17]For an overview and a bibliography see Joseph Owens, "Aristotle on God," in *God in Contemporary Thought*, ed. Matczak, pp. 415-42.

[18]Aristotle *On the Heavens* 270; *Metaphysics* 1071-75. References are to *The Basic Works of Aristotle*, ed. Richard McKeon (New York: Random House, 1941).

[19]*Physics* 256-58; *Metaphysics* 994.

[20]*Metaphysics* 1071-75.

[21]To know anything external entails a need for the object, which means that the knower is less than perfectly self-sufficient. See his *Eudemian Ethics* 7. Yet in criticizing Empedocles he implies that divine perfection includes knowledge of all that exists (*Metaphysics* 1000b)!

[22]*Eudemian Ethics* 1244b; *Nicomachean Ethics* 1159a. Aristotle does say that the gods are our friends (*Nicomachean Ethics* 1179a), but this most likely refers to the Olympian gods, and it is a fair question whether this remark is a concession to popular opinion. For a discussion

of this issue in Aristotle see Owens, "Aristotle on God."

[23]*Nicomachean Ethics* 1178b.

[24]*Eudemian Ethics* 1249b.

[25]*Metaphysics* 1073a; *Physics* 267b.

[26]*Metaphysics* 1072b.

[27]See Benjamin Wirt Farley, *The Providence of God* (Grand Rapids, Mich.: Baker Book House, 1988), pp. 61-70.

[28]Augustine made use of this idea, as do many modern Christians who respond to some tragic event by saying, "God must have had a specific purpose for this to have happened. It is all part of God's plan for your life." However, contemporary Christians generally interpret such events individualistically rather than corporately, as did the Stoics. This involves a strong understanding of the principle of sufficient reason.

[29]See Farley, *Providence of God,* pp. 67-70.

[30]Cicero *De Divinatione* 2.5-8. Alexander of Aprodisias (second century A.D.) developed these same arguments. See R. T. Wallis, "Divine Omniscience in Plotinus, Proclus and Aquinas," in *Neoplatonism and Early Christian Thought,* ed. H. J. Blumenthal and R. A. Markus (London: Variorum, 1981), pp. 224-25.

[31]He got this from Exodus 3:14. The Hebrew text reads, "I am who I am" or "I will be who I will be," which, in context, is saying either that God will be faithful to Moses or that Moses has no control over God (Moses had asked God for his name, which in Semitic thinking gave the one knowing the name power over the one named). The Septuagint translation of Exodus 3:14 shows Hellenistic influence, as it reads "He who is" *(ho ôn).* But Philo renders this in the neuter *(to on),* thus further undermining the personal God of the Bible. The Semitic meaning of the text is far removed from the Hellenistic necessarily existent one. On the history of this text as a metaphysical definition see Walter Kasper, *The God of Jesus Christ,* trans. Matthew O'Connell (New York: Crossroad, 1984), pp. 147-52.

[32]Philo *On the Change of Names* 11.

[33]In ascribing anonymity to God, Philo was following the LXX, which never uses a name for God: *Yahweh* is always translated *kyrios.* See T. E. Pollard, "The Impassibility of God," *Scottish Journal of Theology* 8 (1955): 355-56, and Adrio König, *Here Am I! A Believer's Reflection on God* (Grand Rapids, Mich.: Eerdmans, 1982), p. 67.

[34]See Samuel Sandmel, *Philo of Alexandria* (New York: Oxford University Press, 1979), pp. 91-93.

[35]Farley, *Providence of God,* p. 73, believes that Philo is being innovative here since Greek philosophy had considered reason and being *(nous* and *ontos)* as identical—there being no higher reality than reason. Philo's God, however, is a step beyond reason. In my opinion this idea was latent in Plato and is seen in texts where he suggests that reason cannot attain to the highest reality—only a mystical experience will suffice. Philo and the neo-Platonic tradition would develop this sentiment more fully.

[36]This is the "God beyond God" so popular in writers from Plotinus to Tillich. N. T. Wright, *The New Testament and the People of God* (Minneapolis: Fortress, 1992), p. 248 n. 15, claims that Philo "dehistoricized and hence deeschatologized the whole Jewish world view."

[37]Philo *On the Unchangeableness of God* 32.

[38]For discussion see Harry Wolfson, *Philo: Foundations of Religious Philosophy in Judaism, Chris-*

tianity and Islam, 2 vols. (Cambridge, Mass.: Harvard University Press, 1947), 2:137-38.

[39]He knows that Deuteronomy 8:5 says that God trains us as a son but he says that this verse is for the instruction of the common person and is not, in fact, true. This is *theoprepēs* in action.

[40]For elaboration see Wolfson, *Philo,* 2:446-56, and Joseph C. McLelland, *God the Anonymous: A Study in Alexandrian Philosophical Theology,* Patristic Monographs 4 (Cambridge, Mass.: Philadelphia Patristic Foundation, 1976), p. 44.

[41]H. P. Owen, *Concepts of Deity* (New York: Herder and Herder, 1971), p. 1. Owen and G. L. Prestige, *God in Patristic Thought* (London: SPCK, 1975) both defend this synthesis.

[42]See Henry Chadwick, *Early Christian Thought and the Classical Tradition: Studies in Justin, Clement and Origen* (New York: Oxford University Press, 1966); Richard A. Norris, *God and the World in Early Christian Thought: A Study in Justin Martyr, Irenaeus, Tertullian and Origen* (New York: Seabury, 1965); and Frederick Copleston, *A History of Philosophy,* 7 vols. (Garden City, N.Y.: Image, 1961), 2:1.27-54.

[43]Ignatius *Epistle to Polycarp* 3.2 and *Epistle to Ephesians* 7.2.

[44]For helpful historical studies and bibliographies on impassibility and immutability see J. K. Mozley, *The Impassibility of God* (New York: Cambridge University Press, 1926); Joseph Hallman, *The Descent of God* (Minneapolis: Fortress, 1991); Richard Bauckham, "Only the Suffering God Can Help: Divine Passibility in Modern Theology," *Themelios* 9 (April 1984): 6-12; Lester Kuyper, "The Suffering and Repentance of God," *Scottish Journal of Theology* 22 (1969): 257-77; and Rem. Edwards, "The Pagan Dogma of the Absolute Unchangeableness of God," *Religious Studies* 14 (1978): 305-13.

[45]Justin *First Apology* 20 and *Second Apology* 13.

[46]*First Apology* 13, 61 and *Second Apology* 6.

[47]*First Apology* 28.

[48]Ibid. 28, 43.

[49]Ibid. 43-45. On the history of providence, foreknowledge and free will, see Farley, *Providence of God,* and Roger Forster and V. Paul Marston, *God's Strategy in Human History* (Minneapolis: Bethany House, 1973), pp. 243-95.

[50]Anthenagoras *Plea* 10. See also *Plea* 8.

[51]*Plea* 8.

[52]Irenaeus *Against Heresies* 1.12.2; 2.12.1; 2.13.3-4; 2.28.4; 3.8.3; 3.16.6; 4.11.2; 4.21.2. It is interesting that for the most part the Gnostics and fathers agreed on these points. The Gnostics failed, however, to connect God with creation.

[53]*Against Heresies* 5.27.2. Contrary to Irenaeus's intentions, the doctrines of immutability and impassibility are pressuring God out of direct relationship with history and humanity.

[54]*Against Heresies* 2.1-2; 2.6, as opposed to Eusebius, who said that God cannot be involved in time, hence the need for a middle being. See Jensen, *Triune Identity,* pp. 78-79.

[55]*Against Heresies* 4.37.1-2.

[56]Tertullian *Against Marcion* 2.24.

[57]See Hallman, *Descent of God,* pp. 51-66, and Jensen, *Triune Identity,* pp. 70-74.

[58]*Against Marcion* 2.16.

[59]*On the Flesh of Christ* 5.

[60]*Against Marcion* 2.5-6, 23-24. See Farley, *Providence of God,* pp. 95-97.

[61]*Against Praxeas* 29.

[62]*Against Hermogenes* 12.

[63]*Against Marcion* 1.8.

[64]See R. A. Norris, *God and the World in Early Christian Theology* (New York: Seabury, 1965), p. 112.

[65]For references and discussion see McLelland, *God the Anonymous*, pp. 50-125; Farley, *Providence of God*, pp. 87-90; Hallman, *Descent of God*, pp. 36-46; and Mozley, *Impassibility of God*, pp. 59-63.

[66]See Origen, *On Prayer*, in *Classics of Western Spirituality*, trans. Rowan Greer (New York: Paulist, 1979), pp. 90-97.

[67]See *De Principles* 2.4.4; *Contra Celsus* 4.37, 72; 6.53.

[68]See *Contra Celsus* 4.14-15, and McLelland, *God the Anonymous*, pp. 108-22. McLelland points out that history is not significant for Origen since history and incarnation are but temporary accommodations until the final cure of humanity is complete and Christians ascend to full participation in divine being.

[69]The text is known as *Ad Theopompum*. See Mozley, *Impassibility of God*, pp. 63-72, and Hallman, *Descent of God*, pp. 46-49.

[70]See Mozley, *Impassibility of God*, pp. 48-52, and Hallman, *Descent of God*, pp. 66-70.

[71]See Arnobius *Against the Heathen* 1.27.

[72]See Hallman, *Descent of God*, p. 79 nn. 5-6, for bibliography on the Arians. The Arians had other reasons as well for going the direction they did. See Catherine LaCugna, *God for Us: The Trinity and Christian Life* (New York: HarperCollins, 1991), pp. 30-37.

[73]See LaCugna, *God for Us*, pp. 37-39, and Hallman, *Descent of God*, pp. 78, 83-85.

[74]Robert W. Jenson, *The Triune Identity* (Philadelphia: Fortress, 1982), p. 85.

[75]LaCugna, *God for Us*, pp. 14, 63-66.

[76]See Jenson, *Triune Identity*, pp. 106-7, 111-14.

[77]Gregory of Nyssa *Against Eunomius* 1.42.

[78]Nevertheless, the Cappadocians exhibit a tension between this idea and their insistence that we cannot know the essence *(ousia)* of God. Does this mean that God's relationality is not actually part of his essence? If so, then is God actually supremely relational or is there a static conception behind the relations? See Jenson, *Triune Identity*, p. 108.

[79]Yet even here there was not consensus. See Chadwick, *Early Christian Thought*, pp. 46-47, 85. Moreover, some fathers speculated that God created out of his goodness (nature), which by definition must diffuse itself. See Wolfhart Pannenberg, *Basic Questions in Theology* (Philadelphia: Fortress, 1971), 2:175. On the history of the idea that God necessarily creates see Arthur Lovejoy, *The Great Chain of Being* (Cambridge, Mass.: Harvard University Press, 1964).

[80]See Pannenberg, *Basic Questions*, 2:162-65.

[81]See LaCugna, *God for Us*, chap. 4. Eventually this led to changes in the perception of Jesus as remote and a stern judge, which in turn led to the rising importance of Mary as mediator.

[82]Augustine is no emanationist, but he does say that Plotinus's *Enneads* teach the same thing as John 1:1 *(Confessions* 7.9).

[83]Augustine *Confessions* 7.11; 11.18; 12.15; 13.16; *The Trinity* 1.1.3; 5.2.3; 4.5-6; 7.5.10; and *City of God* 8.6; 11.10; 22.2. See also Mozley, *Impassibility of God*, pp. 104-9, Hallman, *Descent of God*, pp. 105-23, Farley, *Providence of God*, pp. 101-6, and Christopher Kaiser, *The Doctrine of God*

(Westchester, Ill.: Crossway, 1982), pp. 75-81.

[84]Augustine *City of God* 8.6; *Confessions* 7.11; and *Studies in John* 1.8.

[85]*Confessions* 11.12.

[86]Ibid. 11.12-13. See also *City of God* 11.14, 21 (here he explicitly refers to Plato's *Timaeus);* 12.15, 17; and *Trinity* 1.1.3. It is interesting to compare this answer with that of Irenaeus, who said that we do not know what God was doing before the creation since Scripture is silent on the subject *(Against Heresies* 2.28.3).

[87]*Confessions* 12.15; 13.16.

[88]*City of God* 11.21.

[89]See *City of God* 5.9-10.

[90]See *Confessions* 11.18; *City of God* 11.21; 5.10; *Psalms* 106.31; and *Gift of Perseverance* 15.

[91]See his *Predestination of the Saints; Gift of Perseverance;* and *Enchiridion* 24-28.

[92]Augustine acknowledged that God works through secondary causes, but he failed to see that this did not settle the problem of determinism. What he did was to argue that fate and human responsibility were incompatible and that fate and divine causality are different. Thus, he thought, divine causality and human responsibility are compatible. But this is no solution, since arguing that A is incompatible with B and A is different from C does not yield the conclusion that B is compatible with C. See W. T. Jones, *History of Western Philosophy* (New York: Harcourt, Brace & World, 1969), 2:99-100.

[93]*Enchiridion* 26. See also 24.

[94]Ibid. 27.

[95]See his *Perseverance* and *Rebuke and Grace* 10-21.

[96]*On Free Will* 3.68. See also *Enchiridion* 24.

[97]*City of God* 14.9.

[98]Ibid.

[99]*Trinity* 1.1.2.

[100]*Psalms* 106.31; *City of God* 11.18, 21; 14.9, 11.

[101]*Psalms* 132.11.

[102]*City of God* 9.5.

[103]See Hallman, *Descent of God,* p. 112.

[104]*City of God* 22.2.

[105]See Hallman, *Descent of God,* pp. 120-21.

[106]*Trinity* 5.16.17. See also Kaiser, *Doctrine of God,* p. 80.

[107]See LaCugna, *God for Us,* pp. 86-87.

[108]Augustine rejected the Cappadocian doctrine of relations as absurd in favor of his simplicity axiom. See Jenson, *Triune Identity,* p. 119. Augustine has here lost sight of the historical Jesus and what he reveals about the being of God. Instead he is using the neo-Platonic distinction between relations and substance. See Kaiser, *Doctrine of God,* pp. 77-78.

[109]See LaCugna, *God for Us,* pp. 93-103, and Kaiser, *Doctrine of God,* pp. 75-77.

[110]*Trinity* 12.5-7.

[111]Jaroslav Pelikan, *The Christian Tradition: A History of the Development of Doctrine,* 5 vols. (Chicago: University of Chicago Press, 1971), 2:296.

[112]See LaCugna, *God for Us,* p. 101; Kaiser, *Doctrine of God,* p. 81; and Emil Brunner, *The Christian Doctrine of God,* vol. 1 of *Dogmatics,* trans. Olive Wyon (Philadelphia: Westminster

Press, 1949), p. 239.

[113]See Joseph O'Leary, *Questioning Back: The Overcoming of Metaphysics in Christian Tradition* (New York: Winston, 1985), chap. 4.

[114]LaCugna, *God for Us,* p. 87.

[115]See *Pseudo-Dionysius: The Complete Works,* trans. Colm Luibheid, Classics of Western Spirituality (New York: Paulist, 1987); Kaiser, *Doctrine of God,* pp. 81-84; and Justo González, *A History of Christian Thought,* 3 vols. (Nashville: Abingdon, 1971), 2:81-84.

[116]See González, *History,* 2:128-35; Jones, *History of Philosophy,* 2:172-84; Hallman, *Descent of God,* pp. 125-26; and Mozley, *Impassibility of God,* pp. 109-11.

[117]John Scotus Erigena, *The Division of Nature,* quoted in Mozley, *Impassibility of God,* p. 110.

[118]Anselm *Proslogium* 8.

[119]The following discussion is based on his *Summa Theologica,* part 1, questions 1-26.

[120]See Farley, *Providence of God,* pp. 127-30.

[121]See Norman Kretzmann, "Goodness, Knowledge and Indeterminacy in the Philosophy of Thomas Aquinas," *Journal of Philosophy* 80, no. 10 suppl. (October 1983): 631-49. The problem here is how a non-Calvinist can explain divine knowledge of *evil* free actions if God is the cause of his own knowledge. This consideration may have led Aquinas to back away from the notion of causal knowledge in his later work. See R. T. Wallis, "Divine Omniscience in Plotinus, Proclus and Aquinas," in *Neoplatonism and Early Christian Thought,* ed. H. J. Blumenthal and R. A. Markus (London: Variorum, 1981), p. 231.

[122]See Paul Althaus, *The Theology of Martin Luther,* trans. Robert Schultz (Philadelphia: Fortress, 1963), p. 31.

[123]Martin Luther, *The Bondage of the Will,* trans. J. I. Packer and O. R. Johnston (Old Tappan, N.J.: Revell, 1957), p. 80.

[124]See Farley, *Providence of God,* pp. 139-41.

[125]Brunner, *Christian Doctrine of God,* p. 173.

[126]John Calvin, *Institutes of the Christian Religion,* ed. John McNeill, 2 vols. (Philadelphia: Westminster Press, 1960), 1.10.2.

[127]Ibid. 1.2.2; 1.13.2; 1.17.13; 1.18.3; 3.2.6; and *Treatise on the Eternal Predestination of God,* in *Calvin's Calvinism,* trans. Henry Cole (Grand Rapids, Mich.: Eerdmans, 1950), pp. 182-85.

[128]*Institutes* 3.23.2. Yet Calvin does say that God must do good (*Institutes* 2.3.5). This understanding of the divine will had tremendously negative consequences on the doctrines of creation, redemption and the divine relationality to the creation. See Colin Gunton, *The One, the Three and the Many: God, Creation and the Culture of Modernity* (New York: Cambridge University Press, 1993), pp. 57-58.

[129]*Institutes* 1.16.3. See also 1.17.1; 1.18.3. On Calvin's definition of power see Anna Case-Winters, *God's Power: Traditional Understandings and Contemporary Challenges* (Louisville, Ky.: Westminster/Knox, 1990), pp. 44, 50, 89.

[130]*Institutes* 3.23.6. See also 3.23.7; 3.21.5. Calvin's teaching on predestination is quite similar to that of Aquinas. His views became so familiar, however, because he placed the subject within the doctrine of salvation and made it a matter of preaching.

[131]In his theodicy Calvin uses circular reasoning and equivocation, resorts to name-calling and, when he gives up on rational argument, appeals to mystery. See Case-Winters, *God's Power,* pp. 73-80.

¹³²*Institutes* 1.16.3; 1.17.1.

¹³³Brunner, *Christian Doctrine of God,* p. 315.

¹³⁴See Case-Winters, *God's Power,* pp. 45, 84-85.

¹³⁵*Institutes* 1.17.12-14.

¹³⁶Ibid. 3.20.11-16. Furthermore, in his commentary on Jeremiah (18:7-10) he vacillates back and forth between the "theologically correct" speech of absolute omnipotence that does not respond to anything and the "preaching voice" of divine responsiveness that does not control everything. He even says that the Israelites' sin was the *cause* of the divine judgment.

¹³⁷See McLelland, *God the Anonymous,* p. 169. According to Farley, Protestant Scholasticism and Reformed theology in particular have tended to define God along lines derived from Greek influence (*Providence,* p. 226).

¹³⁸*The Writings of James Arminius,* trans. James Nichols, 3 vols. (Grand Rapids, Mich.: Baker Book House, 1956), 1:440; 2:34, 45-49. Also see Richard Muller, *God, Creation and Providence in the Thought of Jacob Arminius* (Grand Rapids, Mich.: Baker Book House, 1991), chap. 8.

¹³⁹Arminius also made use of the doctrine of "middle knowledge" (God knows how we would respond differently if circumstances were different), which makes God's knowledge, in part, conditioned by the creature. See Muller, *God, Creation and Providence,* pp. 156-66.

¹⁴⁰Paul Tillich, *Systematic Theology,* 3 vols. (Chicago: University of Chicago Press, 1951-1963). John Hick holds to divine anonymity, calling God "the Real." See his *An Interpretation of Religion: Human Responses to the Transcendent* (New Haven, Conn.: Yale University Press, 1989).

¹⁴¹Tillich, *Systematic Theology,* 1:271-72.

¹⁴²Ibid., 1:223.

¹⁴³Ibid., 3:120. See also 3:192. In this way Tillich attempts to overcome the "subject-object" schema.

¹⁴⁴See David Basinger, *Divine Power in Process Theism* (Albany: State University of New York Press, 1988).

¹⁴⁵See, for example, Herman Bavinck, *The Doctrine of God,* trans. William Hendriksen (Grand Rapids, Mich.: Baker Book House, 1951), pp. 145-52; A. W. Tozer, *Knowledge of the Holy* (New York: Harper, 1978), p. 45; Charles Ryrie, *Basic Theology* (Wheaton, Ill.: Victor Books, 1986), pp. 37-38; and J. I. Packer, *Knowing God* (Downers Grove, Ill.: InterVarsity Press, 1973), pp. 67-72. Virtually all these writers cite Plato's dictum: If God can change in any way, it can only be change for the worse.

¹⁴⁶Tozer, *Knowledge,* p. 60.

¹⁴⁷W. Bingham Hunter, *The God Who Hears* (Downers Grove, Ill.: InterVarsity Press, 1986), pp. 52-53.

¹⁴⁸Carl F. H. Henry, *God, Revelation and Authority,* 6 vols. (Waco, Tex.: Word, 1982), 5:304. The relevant sections are vol. 5, chaps. 6, 12, 14-16, and 6:84-85. At one point Henry says that at every moment in history God has alternatives open (5:304). This must be seen as rhetoric, however, given what he says immediately following.

¹⁴⁹J. Rodman Williams, *Renewal Theology,* 3 vols. (Grand Rapids, Mich.: Zondervan, 1988), 1:47-81.

¹⁵⁰Louis Berkhof, *Systematic Theology* (Grand Rapids, Mich.: Eerdmans, 1978), p. 71. Charles Ryrie says, "Love in God is seeking the highest good and glory of *His* perfections" (*Basu*

Theology, p. 39; emphasis mine).

[151]Charles Hodge, *Systematic Theology*, 3 vols. (Grand Rapids, Mich.: Eerdmans, 1949), 1:428.

[152]Millard Erickson, *Christian Theology* (Grand Rapids, Mich.: Baker Book House, 1986), pp. 263-300, 405-6. Yet he also holds that God is timeless, which, he says, means that there can be no change in God's interests, knowledge or will. For him, prayer should not be understood as an attempt to change God's mind. Rather, God wills our prayers as the means by which he accomplishes his plans.

[153]James Oliver Buswell Jr., *A Systematic Theology of the Christian Religion*, 2 vols. (Grand Rapids, Mich.: Zondervan, 1962), 1:56.

[154]Nicholas Wolterstorff, "God Everlasting," in *God and the Good*, ed. Clifton Orlebeke and Lewis Smedes (Grand Rapids, Mich.: Eerdmans, 1975), pp. 181-203; Stephen Davis, *Logic and the Nature of God* (Grand Rapids, Mich.: Eerdmans, 1983). The open view of God enjoys widespread discussion in the journals *Faith and Philosophy* and *Religious Studies*.

[155]Jack Cottrell, *What the Bible Says About God the Ruler* (Joplin, Mo.: College Press, 1984), p. 217. For Cottrell, God's foreknowledge is conditioned by what his creatures decide.

[156]Richard Foster, *Prayer: Finding the Heart's True Home* (New York: HarperCollins, 1992), pp. 181, 225, 247, 249, and *Celebration of Discipline: The Path to Spiritual Growth*, rev. ed. (New York: HarperCollins, 1988), pp. 35, 40.

[157]Foster, *Celebration of Discipline*, p. 35.

[158]Donald Bloesch, *Essentials of Evangelical Theology*, 2 vols. (New York: Harper & Row, 1982), 1:31. See also 1:27-31; 2:57-58.

[159]Gabriel Fackre, *The Christian Story*, rev. ed. (Grand Rapids, Mich.: Eerdmans, 1984), 1:250-65.

[160]Among those who affirm the full openness of God are Richard Rice, *God's Foreknowledge and Man's Free Will* (Minneapolis: Bethany House, 1985); William Hasker, *God, Time and Knowledge* (Ithaca, N.Y.: Cornell University Press, 1989); Clark Pinnock, "Between Classical and Process Theism," in *Process Theology*, ed. Ronald Nash (Grand Rapids, Mich.: Baker Book House, 1987), and "God Limits His Knowledge," in *Predestination and Free Will*, ed. David Basinger and Randall Basinger (Downers Grove, Ill.: InterVarsity Press, 1986); John Sanders, "God as Personal," in *The Grace of God, the Will of Man*, ed. Clark Pinnock (Grand Rapids, Mich.: Zondervan, 1989); Greg Boyd, *Trinity and Process: A Critical Evaluation and Reconstruction of Hartshorne's Di-polar Theism Towards a Trinitarian Metaphysics* (New York: Peter Lang, 1992), and *Letters from a Skeptic* (Wheaton, Ill.: Victor Books, 1994). From the Reformed side see Harry Boer, *An Ember Still Glowing* (Grand Rapids, Mich.: Eerdmans, 1990). It has also been held by numerous Arminian theologians, among whom the work of L. D. McCabe stands out as he discusses virtually every biblical text relating to foreknowledge. See his *Divine Nescience of Future Contingencies a Necessity* (New York: Phillips and Hunt, 1882), and *The Foreknowledge of God* (Cincinnati: Cranston and Stowe, 1887). Gordon Olson, *The Foreknowledge of God* and *The Omniscience of the Godhead* (Arlington Heights, Ill.: Bible Research Corporation, 1941, 1972), closely follows McCabe.

Other theologians do not always affirm the full openness of God, but do speak of divine responsiveness and temporality. See William Pratney, *The Nature and Character of God* (Minneapolis: Bethany House, 1988); James Daane, "Can a Man Bless God?" in *God and the Good*, ed. Orlebeke and Smedes, pp. 165-73. Philip Yancey, *Disappointment with God: Three Questions*

No One Asks Aloud (Grand Rapids, Mich.: Zondervan, 1988), speaks of God taking risks and limiting himself (pp. 59-61, 140), of a give-and-take relationship with us (p. 149) and of suffering with us (p. 91), and says that even though God has foreknowledge and is timeless he "learns" in the sense of taking on new experiences (pp. 63, 197-99). Gilbert Bilezikian, *Christianity 101* (Grand Rapids, Mich.: Zondervan, 1993), says that God freely chooses not to know the future. John Boykin, *The Gospel of Coincidence: Is God in Control?* (Grand Rapids, Mich.: Zondervan, 1990), argues for a nondetermining God and seems to suggest (p. 80, n. 2) that even though God has foreknowledge, we can prevent what God knows will happen.

[161]See Terence Fretheim, *The Suffering of God* (Philadelphia: Fortress, 1984), and *Exodus*, Interpretation (Louisville, Ky.: John Knox, 1991).

[162]Thomas Torrance, *Space, Time and Incarnation* (New York: Oxford University Press, 1969), pp. 74-75.

[163]Thomas Oden, *The Living God* (San Francisco: Harper & Row, 1987), pp. 53-130. Oden, however, always puts the best "spin" on the fathers and generally fails to criticize the biblical-classical synthesis. Also, he affirms divine simplicity, timelessness and exhaustive foreknowledge without explaining how these cohere with his understanding of God's responsiveness.

[164]Jürgen Moltmann, *Theology of Hope* (London: SCM, 1967), *The Crucified God* (New York: Harper & Row, 1974); Wolfhart Pannenberg, *Systematic Theology*, 2 vols. (Grand Rapids, Mich.: Eerdmans, 1991, 1994). A caution must be given, however, since these two theologians are heavily influenced by Hegel and utilize the dialectic method. Hence certain passages suggest the open God while others seem to take it back, intimating that God is not genuinely involved in the temporal process, only in the dialectical (logical) process.

[165]See Jenson, *Triune Identity*.

[166]Brunner, *Christian Doctrine of God;* Hendrikus Berkhof, *Christian Faith*, trans. Sierd Woudstra (Grand Rapids, Mich.: Eerdmans, 1979); Eberhard Jüngel, *God as the Mystery of the World* (Grand Rapids, Mich.: Eerdmans, 1983); König, *Here Am I;* Colin Gunton, *The Promise of Trinitarian Theology* (Edinburgh: T & T Clark, 1991); Thomas Finger, *Christian Theology: An Eschatological Approach*, 2 vols. (Scottdale, Penn.: Herald, 1989), 2:481-508. C. S. Lewis says that God grants significant freedom to his creatures and allows a certain amount of free play to his own plans, which can be modified in response to our prayers *(God in the Dock: Essays on Theology and Ethics,* ed. Walter Hooper [Grand Rapids, Mich.: Eerdmans, 1970], p. 106).

[167]LaCugna, *God for Us*, and Elizabeth A. Johnson, *She Who Is: The Mystery of God in Feminist Theological Discourse* (New York: Crossroad, 1992).

[168]See Keith Ward, *Holding Fast to God: A Reply to Don Cupitt* (London: SPCK, 1982), and *Divine Action* (San Francisco: Torch, 1991). For the others see chapter four, notes 48 and 49.

[169]See Jenson, *Triune Identity*, pp. 4, 58-60.

[170]The notion that God's foreknowledge is indeed dependent on what humans decide to do is a significant attempt to soften this. In a sense it could be said that God "learned," since he would not have had the foreknowledge he possesses had it not been for the decisions the creatures made. There are still problems, however, explaining how a timeless God with total foreknowledge could repent, plan, deliberate or respond, since such actions involve sequence, duration and a degree of uncertainty. See W. Kneale, "Time and Eternity in Theology," *Proceedings of the Aristotelian Society* 61 (1960): 87-108; Wolterstorff, "God Everlasting," pp. 197-200; and Eleanore Stump and Norman Kretzmann, "Eternity," *Journal of Phi-*

losophy 78 (August 1981): 446.

Chapter 3: Systematic Theology/Pinnock

[1]The vision has been described by the present authors elsewhere: see Richard Rice, *God's Foreknowledge and Man's Free Will* (Minneapolis: Bethany House, 1985); David Basinger and Randall Basinger, eds., *Predestination and Free Will* (Downers Grove, Ill.: InterVarsity Press, 1986), pp. 143-62; Clark H. Pinnock, ed., *The Grace of God, the Will of Man: A Case for Arminianism* (Grand Rapids, Mich.: Zondervan, 1989); William Hasker, *God, Time and Knowledge* (Ithaca, N.Y.: Cornell University Press, 1989); and David Basinger, *Divine Power in Process Theism: A Philosophical Critique* (Albany, N.Y.: State University of New York Press, 1988).

[2]Dealing with the concept of God, see Thomas V. Morris, *Our Idea of God: An Introduction to Philosophical Theology* (Downers Grove, Ill.: InterVarsity Press, 1991), and Keith Ward, *The Concept of God* (London: Collins, 1977). On the larger search to understand God's identity, see Karen Armstrong, *A History of God: The 4000 Year Old Quest of Judaism, Christianity and Islam* (New York: Knopf, 1993).

[3]On the importance of doctrine, see Alister McGrath, *Understanding Doctrine: Its Relevance and Purpose for Today* (Grand Rapids, Mich.: Zondervan, 1990).

[4]As Schubert M. Ogden notes in *The Reality of God* (New York: Harper & Row, 1966), chap. 1. Gordon D. Kaufman makes the concept of God central to his work *In Face of Mystery: A Constructive Theology* (Cambridge, Mass.: Harvard University Press, 1993).

[5]On theology as an unfinished task see Michael Bauman, *Pilgrim Theology: Taking the Path of Theological Discovery* (Grand Rapids, Mich.: Zondervan, 1992).

[6]On the use of models in theology see Richard Rice and John Sanders in *Grace of God*, ed. Pinnock, pp. 130-37, 167-78.

[7]The open view of God is also sketched out in Keith Ward, *Holding Fast to God: A Reply to Don Cupitt* (London: SPCK, 1982), chap. 3.

[8]See Robert A. Morey, *Battle of the Gods: The Gathering Storm in Modern Evangelicalism* (Southbridge, Mass.: Crown, 1989). Morey equates the open view of God with what he calls finite godism. What troubles me about his view is not the charge of heresy so much as the distance I feel between his vision of God and the loving heart of the Father.

[9]Emil Brunner discusses this problem in *The Christian Doctrine of God* (Philadelphia: Westminster Press, 1950), pp. 151-56. John Macquarrie speaks of the dialectical in *In Search of Deity: An Essay on Dialectical Theism* (London: SCM, 1984), chap. 13.

[10]See the discussion of this in Adrio König, *Here Am I! A Believer's Reflection on God* (Grand Rapids, Mich.: Eerdmans, 1982), pp. 67-68, and Walter Kasper, *The God of Jesus Christ* (New York: Crossroad, 1986), p. 148.

[11]Wolfhart Pannenberg reviews the attempt at integration in a classic essay, "The Appropriation of the Philosophical Concept of God as a Dogmatic Problem of Early Christian Theology," in *Basic Questions in Theology*, vol. 2 (Philadelphia: Fortress, 1971).

[12]Joseph M. Hallman discusses this in *The Descent of God: Divine Suffering in History and Theology* (Minneapolis: Fortress, 1991).

[13]Hendrikus Berkhof speaks of the distortion in *Christian Faith: An Introduction to the Study of the Faith* (Grand Rapids, Mich.: Eerdmans, 1979), pp. 106-11.

[14]Thomas Oden has a point in his *Systematic Theology* when he calls us back to ancient tra-

ditions, but surely not all traditions deserve our commitment. On the necessity of rethinking things, see Stanley J. Grenz, *Revisioning Evangelical Theology: A Fresh Agenda for the 21st Century* (Downers Grove, Ill.: InterVarsity Press, 1993).

[15]Walter Kasper points this out in *The God of Jesus Christ* (New York: Crossroad, 1986), pp. 152-57.

[16]The attempt to achieve balance between transcendence and immanence is the motif around which Stanley J. Grenz and Roger E. Olson analyze modern theology in *20th-Century Theology: God and the World in a Transitional Age* (Downers Grove, Ill.: InterVarsity Press, 1992). I have tried to find the middle way in "Between Classical and Process Theism," in *Process Theology*, ed. Ronald Nash (Grand Rapids, Mich.: Baker Book House, 1987), pp. 309-27.

[17]The social analogy of the Trinity is gaining ground; see Ted Peters, *God as Trinity: Relationality and Temporality in Divine Life* (Louisville, Ky.: Westminster/Knox, 1993); Colin E. Gunton, *The Promise of Trinitarian Theology* (Edinburgh: T & T Clark, 1991), chap. 5; Wolfhart Pannenberg, *Systematic Theology*, vol. 1 (Grand Rapids, Mich.: Eerdmans, 1991), chap. 5; and Jürgen Moltmann, *The Trinity and the Kingdom: The Doctrine of God* (San Francisco: Harper & Row, 1981).

[18]On God as three persons in communion, see Catherine M. LaCugna, *God for Us: The Trinity and the Christian Life* (San Francisco: HarperSanFrancisco, 1991), especially chap. 8, and Cornelius Plantinga Jr., "The Hodgson-Welch Debate on the Social Analogy of the Trinity," Ph.D. diss., Princeton University, 1982.

[19]Moltmann accents this in *Trinity and the Kingdom,* chap. 6. Like LaCugna, he is sensitive to a relational ontology.

[20]This is the basic point of Gregory A. Boyd's entire thesis; see *Trinity and Process: A Critical Evaluation and Reconstruction of Hartshorne's Di-polar Theism Towards a Trinitarian Metaphysics* (New York: Peter Lang, 1992), pp. 332-33.

[21]H. P. Owen, *Concepts of Deity* (New York: Herder and Herder, 1971), p. 9.

[22]John Piper's book has a noble title: *The Pleasures of God* (Portland, Ore.: Multnomah Press, 1991).

[23]Karl Barth, *Church Dogmatics* 2/1 (Edinburgh: T & T Clark, 1957), pp. 272-321.

[24]Otto Weber, *Foundations of Dogmatics* (Grand Rapids, Mich.: Eerdmans, 1981), 1:440-47.

[25]Boyd discusses God's benevolence in creation in *Trinity and Process*, pp. 374-93.

[26]Hugh Montefiore, *The Probability of God* (London: SCM, 1985), shows us how to craft a new teleological argument out of the evidences of modern science in relation to the immanence of God the Spirit.

[27]Feminists understandably handle this issue with finesse, having experienced the dominating male power. See Sheila G. Davaney, *Divine Power: A Study of Karl Barth and Charles Hartshorne* (Philadelphia: Fortress, 1986), and Anna Case-Winters, *God's Power: Traditional Understandings and Contemporary Challenges* (Louisville, Ky.: Westminster/Knox, 1990).

[28]Harry R. Boer, *An Ember Still Glowing: Humankind in the Image of God* (Grand Rapids, Mich.: Eerdmans, 1990), chap. 8. As an Arminian I can only wish for more Calvinists like this. For a rendition of divine providence after this fashion by an Arminian, see Jack Cottrell, *God the Ruler* (Joplin, Mo.: College Press, 1984).

[29]Douglas J. Hall, *God and Human Suffering* (Minneapolis: Augsburg, 1986), chap. 4.

[30]Elizabeth A. Johnson, *She Who Is: The Mystery of God in Feminist Theological Discourse* (New

York: Crossroad, 1992), pp. 369-70. This book parallels my thesis about the openness of God despite the fact that Johnson identifies her position with panentheism (pp. 230-31). In reality she denies that the world exists necessarily and that God needs the world ontologically. She uses the word *asymmetrical* to describe the relation between God and the world and therefore should not be using the term *panentheism.* Not to be overbold, I would say that Johson needs a term like *the openness of God* to describe her view.

[31]In opposition to Carl F. H. Henry (for example), "The Sovereignty of the Omnipotent God," chap. 16 in *God, Revelation and Authority,* vol. 5 (Waco, Tex.: Word Books, 1982).

[32]For example, J. I. Packer, *Evangelism and the Sovereignty of God* (Downers Grove, Ill.: Inter-Varsity Press, 1961), pp. 18-24.

[33]See D. A. Carson, *Divine Sovereignty and Human Responsibility* (London: Marshall, Morgan & Scott, 1981). Carson needs to distinguish *contradiction* from *mystery.* A circle is not and cannot ever be at the same time a square. An action is not and cannot be at the same time determined by God and freely chosen in a significant sense. To say it can be is not mysterious but self-contradictory. Trusting the Bible is not the issue—the issue is whether we wish to attribute nonsense to Scripture in our interpretation of it. See David Basinger, "Biblical Paradox: Does Revelation Challenge Logic?" *Journal of the Evangelical Theological Society* 30 (1987): 205-13, and Bauman, *Pilgrim Theology,* pp. 29-30.

[34]Walter Wink, "Prayer and the Powers," chap. 16 in *Engaging the Powers* (Minneapolis: Fortress, 1992).

[35]Pannenberg, *Systematic Theology,* 1:416.

[36]This insight is well brought out by Terence E. Fretheim, *Exodus* (Louisville, Ky.: John Knox, 1991), throughout the book.

[37]On evil and the openness of God, see Rice, *Openness of God,* chap. 4.

[38]Terence E. Fretheim, *The Suffering of God: An Old Testament Perspective* (Philadelphia: Fortress, 1984), and Paul S. Fiddes, *The Creative Suffering of God* (Oxford: Clarendon, 1988).

[39]In his book *The Pleasures of God,* John Piper is right to say that God takes pleasure in being God, but he omits saying that God's heart can be wrenched. Piper also attributes pleasures to God that God does not own—like the pleasure of deliberately not electing some sinners to be saved—and denies God the pleasure that comes from genuine interaction with creaturely persons, because he supposes that God wants total control.

[40]On the subtleties of impassibility, see Richard E. Creel, *Divine Impassibility: An Essay in Philosophical Theology* (Cambridge: Cambridge University Press, 1986).

[41]See Stephen T. Davis, *Logic and the Nature of God* (Grand Rapids, Mich.: Eerdmans, 1983), and Ronald H. Nash, *The Concept of God* (Grand Rapids, Mich.: Zondervan, 1983).

[42]Let the reader who still worries about this sounding too much like process theism consult the last note of the chapter.

[43]Nelson Pike, *God and Timelessness* (New York: Schocken Books, 1970), and Hasker, *God, Time and Knowledge.*

[44]It is generally assumed that the Bible teaches that God has total foreknowledge; from Stephen Charnock (d. 1680), *The Existence and Attributes of God* (Ann Arbor, Mich.: Sovereign Grace, 1967), pp. 181-260, to John Piper, *Pleasures of God,* chap. 2.

[45]Fretheim is helpful in *Suffering of God,* chap. 4, though William L. Craig does not agree; see his *The Only Wise God: The Compatibility of Divine Foreknowledge and Human Freedom* (Grand

Rapids, Mich.: Baker Book House, 1987).

[46]On prophecy and foreknowledge, see Rice, *God's Foreknowledge,* chap. 7.

[47]See John M. Hull, *What Prevents Christian Adults from Learning?* (Philadelphia: Trinity Press International, 1991), pp. 219-38.

[48]Boyd, *Time and Process,* p. 336.

[49]Anticipating the criticism that the open view of God is a form of process theology, let me reiterate two chief ways in which it differs. First, God is ontologically other than the world, which is not necessary to God—the world exists only because God wills it. Therefore, God is not dependent on the world out of necessity but willingly, because he chose to create a world in which there would be mutuality and relational interdependence. Second, God not only sustains the world as the ground of its being but also acts in history to bring about salvation. God was particularly active in that stream of human history which culminated in the life, death and resurrection of Jesus, and involved himself in marvelous actions that go beyond his undergirding of the world process. God is also active in the entire history of the world by the Spirit, which sustains and directs all things.

Chapter 4: A Philosophical Perspective/Hasker

[1]I don't wish to create the impression that I think it was simply a mistake for the early fathers to utilize the resources of Greek philosophy in formulating the Christian conception of God. On the contrary, I regard the availability of philosophy for this purpose as a manifestation of divine providence, allowing the church to make progress in clear and rigorous thinking about God that might otherwise have been impossible to achieve. But it is clear that great discernment was required in applying philosophical conceptions to the biblical God, and we need not assume that the church fathers made the correct decisions in every case.

[2]Here and throughout this chapter, *orthodoxy* is to be understood in terms of the Nicene Creed, the one confession that is almost universally accepted as a touchstone of Christian faith.

[3]Two recent defenses are Eleonore Stump and Norman Kretzmann, "Absolute Simplicity," *Faith and Philosophy* 2 (October 1985): 353-82, and William E. Mann, "Divine Simplicity," *Religious Studies* 18 (1982): 451-71 Critiques may be found in Thomas Morris, "On God and Mann: A View of Divine Simplicity," in *Anselmian Explorations* (Notre Dame, Ind.: University of Notre Dame Press, 1987), and in Christopher M. Hughes, *On a Complex Theory of a Simple God: An Investigation in Aquinas' Philosophical Theology* (Ithaca, N.Y.: Cornell University Press, 1989).

[4]Two important recent defenses are found in Eleonore Stump and Norman Kretzmann, "Eternity," *Journal of Philosophy* (1977): 429-58, and Brian Leftow, *Time and Eternity* (Ithaca N.Y.: Cornell University Press, 1991).

[5]The core of what I mean by saying that God is "in time" is that God experiences changing mental states. Physical time—time as measured by physical changes, such as the rotation of planets or the vibrations of quartz crystals—did not exist prior to or apart from the creation of those physical realities by which it is measured. And conventional time—calendar time and clock time—depends for its existence on the human beings who adopted the conventions. But apart from all of this we can maintain that a change of state, and therefore of time, does exist in God, who is thus present in every "now" of time rather than in the "eternal

Now."

[6] The case that the scriptural conception is not of a timeless God is made forcefully by Alan G. Padgett in *God, Eternity and the Nature of Time* (New York: St. Martin's Press, 1992), chap. 2.

[7] See Nicholas Wolterstorff, "God Everlasting," in *God and the Good*, ed. Clifton J. Orlebeke and Lewis B. Smedes (Grand Rapids, Mich.: Eerdmans, 1975).

[8] See the excellent presentations of scriptural evidence of divine action in the chapters by Rice and Pinnock.

[9] In chap. 8 of *God, Time and Knowledge* (Ithaca, N.Y.: Cornell University Press, 1989; referred to hereafter as *GTK*), I argue that the doctrine of divine timelessness has not been shown to be logically incoherent; in chap. 9 I give my own reasons for rejecting the doctrine. Alan Padgett gives a strong critique of divine timelessness in *God, Eternity and the Nature of Time*.

[10] My own observation is that many who affirm divine timelessness have hardly begun to think through such questions, and in fact what they say on the topic often leaves one more or less in the dark concerning what they understand the doctrine of divine timelesness to mean. As an example, consider the *Systematic Theology*, 3rd ed., by the well-respected Reformed theologian Louis Berkhof (Grand Rapids, Mich.: Eerdmans, 1946). Berkhof defines eternity as *"that perfection of God whereby He is elevated above all temporal limits and all succession of moments, and possesses the whole of His existence in one indivisible present"* (p. 60, emphasis his). But throughout the volume Berkhof consistently speaks about God and his actions in temporal language; concerning such questions as those raised in the text, he says only that "the relation of eternity to time constitutes one of the most difficult problems in philosophy and theology, perhaps incapable of solution in our present condition" (ibid.). It seems to me that the doctrine of timelessness is not a living part of Berkhof's theology but rather a mere remnant of tradition—a tradition that he might better have reexamined critically.

[11] The best recent book on this topic is Richard Creel, *Divine Impassibility* (Cambridge: Cambridge University Press, 1986). Creel defends a modified version of impassibility, but in other respects his conclusions about God are very much in harmony with those presented in these pages.

[12] Nicholas Wolterstorff, "Suffering Love," in *Philosophy and the Christian Faith*, ed. Thomas V. Morris (Notre Dame, Ind.: University of Notre Dame Press, 1988), pp. 196-237.

[13] Ibid., p. 196 (the words quoted are Wolterstorff's).

[14] To be sure, Augustine holds that true *apatheia* is not something we can attain, or even properly aim at, in the present life. Rather, we should indeed experience the "passions" of fear and grief because of our sins—and because of the sins of our fellow humans, with whom we have some kind of solidarity. It remains true, however, that we should *not* experience fear, or grief, over the *temporal condition* of ourselves or others—nor is it appropriate to have some special attachment to those close to us by blood or friendship, which we do not have to men and women in general (see the quotation from *Of True Religion*, which Wolterstorff discusses in ibid., pp. 232-34).

[15] A good recent discussion of perfect being theology may be found in Morris, *Anselmian Explorations*.

[16] I believe that the definitions used here are defensible, but the reader should be aware that

questions concerning the correct definitions of the divine attributes are extremely complex, going well beyond what can be discussed in the next few pages. For a discussion of some of these complexities, see Edward Wierenga, *The Nature of God: An Inquiry into Divine Attributes* (Ithaca, N.Y.: Cornell University Press, 1989).

[17]This point is sometimes made by saying that expressions like "square circle" are "meaningless." But this is a mistake. "Square circle" is a *contradictory* expression—and in order for us to know that it is contradictory, we must know its meaning. (In contrast, I have no idea whether Lewis Carroll's expression "slithy toves" [from "Jabberwocky"] is contradictory; in fact, I suspect there is no answer to that question, since so far as I know no meaning has been assigned to those words.)

[18]So called, because this kind of free will is incompatible with determinism.

[19]An excellent introduction to process theology is John B. Cobb Jr. and David Ray Griffin, *Process Theology: An Introductory Exposition* (Philadelphia: Westminster Press, 1976).

[20]The classic source is A. N. Whitehead, *Process and Reality,* ed. David Ray Griffin and Donald W. Sherburne, corrected ed. (New York: Free Press, 1978).

[21]Ibid., p. 348.

[22]Charles Hartshorne, *Omnipotence and Other Theological Mistakes* (Albany: State University of New York Press, 1984).

[23]There remains the point that God could have prevented a great deal of evil if he had guided the world's development differently—for instance, by not encouraging the development of sentient or rational beings. But this course of action would also have eliminated many of the possibilities for good that exist in the world as we know it.

[24]For a collection of essays critical of process theology, see Ronald Nash, ed., *Process Theology* (Grand Rapids, Mich.: Baker Book House, 1987). Insightful criticism of process theism from a Roman Catholic standpoint may be found in W. Norris Clarke, *The Philosophical Approach to God* (Winston-Salem, N.C.: Wake Forest University Press, 1980).

[25]An excellent, and extremely readable, critical discussion is David Basinger, *Divine Power in Process Theism: A Philosophical Critique* (Albany: State University of New York Press, 1988).

[26]David and Randall Basinger nicely illustrate this point by the following comparison: "The relationship between the God of process theism and the world can be compared to the relationship between a conductor and her orchestra. Without the orchestra, the conductor could not express herself (after all, she plays no instrument). . . . Moreover, the conductor—no matter how competent—cannot unilaterally guarantee that the piece will be played exactly as she has decided it should be played. . . . The extent to which what she envisions is actualized is finally up to the ability and responsiveness of those playing the instruments" (unpublished manuscript, used by permission). In applying this to the actual world, of course, we must keep in mind that many of the players refuse even to acknowledge the conductor's existence, and a great many more pay only the most cursory attention to her direction.

[27]We could also plausibly describe the process theory as a "classical-biblical synthesis." Whitehead's thought was deeply influenced by Plato, and the process conception of God is similar in many respects (though not in all) to Plato's Demiurge.

[28]Many of the themes discussed in the remainder of this chapter are developed further in my "Providence and Evil: Three Theories," *Religious Studies* 28 (1992): 91-105, as well as in *GTK.*

[29]There is some debate as to whether Aquinas was a theological determinist, but I believe the

preponderance of evidence favors the view that he was.

[30]This leaves open, however, the question whether and to what extent deterministic causal connections hold within the created world. A Calvinist may, for example, affirm physical causation according to deterministic natural law, or she may reject it. But whether or not there are *creaturely* sufficient causes for all or most things that happen, there is always the *divine* cause as reflected in the eternal decrees.

[31]See L. Berkhof, *Systematic Theology*, pp. 77-78.

[32]The robot's behavior, even if completely deterministic, would eventually escape the human roboticist's ability to anticipate it—but of course, this can never happen to God.

[33]Some Calvinists, to be sure, wish to say that God predestined the elect for salvation but did not specifically predestine others for damnation; rather, he simply "passed over" them and they are damned as a result of their own sins. This way of putting it has a softer sound, but it really does not make the situation any better. The sins they commit are the sins that God decreed they should commit, and he failed to choose them for salvation knowing that, in the absence of his choice, they will inevitably be damned. Whether or not this is described as a "decree of reprobation" is merely a verbal matter.

[34]Here Berkhof is perhaps typical: "The problem of the relation of God to sin has proved to be insoluble" (*Systematic Theology*, p. 123).

[35]Molina's theory can be found in Luis de Molina, *On Divine Foreknowledge (Part IV of the Concordia)*, trans. and introduction by Alfred J. Freddoso (Ithaca, N.Y.: Cornell University Press, 1988). Freddoso's introduction is the best overall exposition and defense of the doctrine in the recent literature. The modern philosophical revival of middle knowledge was initiated by Alvin Plantinga; see his *The Nature of Necessity* (New York: Oxford University Press, 1973) and, on a more popular level, his *God, Freedom and Evil* (Grand Rapids, Mich.: Eerdmans, 1977).

[36]Alfred J. Freddoso, introduction to *On Divine Foreknowledge*, p. 3.

[37]Robert M. Adams initiated this aspect of the discussion of Molinism with his article "Middle Knowledge and the Problem of Evil," *American Philosophical Quarterly* 14 (1977): 109-17; see also his recent "An Anti-Molinist Argument," *Philosophical Perspectives* 5 (1991): 343-53. My own work on the topic is found in *GTK* chap. 2; for further discussion see Thomas P. Flint, "Hasker's *God, Time and Knowledge*," *Philosophical Studies* 60 (1990): 103-15, and William Hasker, "Response to Thomas Flint," *Philosophical Studies* 60 (1990): 117-26.

[38]To be sure, the human being is assumed to have libertarian free will, whereas the robot is deterministic. But given middle knowledge, this difference between the robot and the human being makes no difference with respect to the way in which they can be controlled. In either case, God knows exactly "which buttons to push" so as to obtain, within the inherent limitations of the robot or of the human being, the exact response he desires.

[39]It does make a difference how the programming was done—that is, what sorts of counterfactuals of freedom God was confronted with in the "creation situation." The counterfactuals (over which God has no control) might have been very favorable for God's purposes, so that he could create a large number of free creatures that would always, or almost always, do exactly what he wished for them to do; in that case, we might have expected him to create a world that was virtually or entirely free from sin. On the other hand, the counterfactuals might have been very unfavorable—so bad, perhaps, that God would not have chosen to

create any world containing free creatures. Presumably the Molinist will not suppose that either of these extreme possibilities was realized. It seems to me that many Molinists in effect assume that while God cannot obtain just any result he desires, the creative options open to him include a feasible world that he takes as his end in the sense that he fully endorses its actualization, so that he is able to say of his creation that it is "very good."

[40]See Plantinga, *Nature of Necessity* and *God, Freedom and Evil.*

[41]See Michael Peterson, *Evil and the Christian God* (Grand Rapids, Mich.: Baker Book House, 1982), pp. 79-99. (The definition given here is my own.)

[42]It is fair to state here that David Basinger thinks that I (and several other philosophers) tend to overstate the importance of middle knowledge for providence and the problem of evil. See his "Middle Knowledge and Divine Control: Some Clarifications," *International Journal for Philosophy of Religion* 30 (1991): 407-22; and William Hasker, "How Good/Bad Is Middle Knowledge? A Reply to Basinger," *International Journal for Philosophy of Religion* 33 (1993): 111-18.

[43]The term *believe* is used here instead of *know* for technical philosophical reasons; it does not imply that God's "beliefs" are tentative or uncertain.

[44]*GTK*, p. 69.

[45]A number of important articles on this topic are collected in John Martin Fischer, ed., *God, Foreknowledge and Freedom* (Stanford, Calif.: Stanford University Press, 1989). And see *GTK*, chaps. 4-7.

[46]For a more detailed development of the argument presented here, see *GTK*, chap. 3; also important is David Basinger, "Middle Knowledge and Classical Christian Thought," *Religious Studies* 22 (1986): 407-22.

[47]Note that things would be quite different if we were to assume that God has middle knowledge. In that case, God would be able to know what Sue's future *would* be like if she were to marry Tom, and what it *would* be like if she married Kenneth, and what it *would* be like if she were to remain unmarried—all this before Susan has made any decision concerning what she will actually do.

[48]Among the philosophers who affirm the open view are A. N. Prior, "The Formalities of Omniscience," *Philosophy* 32 (1962): 119-29; J. R. Lucas, *The Freedom of the Will* (Oxford: Oxford University Press, 1970), and *The Future: An Essay on God, Temporality and Truth* (London: Basil Blackwell, 1989); Peter Geach, *Providence and Evil* (Cambridge: Cambridge University Press, 1977); Richard Swinburne, *The Coherence of Theism* (Oxford: Oxford University Press, 1977); and Richard Purtill, "Fatalism and the Omnitemporality of Truth," *Faith and Philosophy* 5 (1988): 185-92. Thomas V. Morris (*Our Idea of God: An Introduction to Philosophical Theology* [Downers Grove, Ill.: InterVarsity Press, 1991]) is very close to the open view but does not in the end commit himself concerning the nature of God's knowledge.

[49]I would place in this category Stephen T. Davis, *Logic and the Nature of God* (Grand Rapids, Mich.: Eerdmans, 1983), Linda Zagzebski, *The Dilemma of Freedom and Foreknowledge* (New York: Oxford University Press, 1991), and Nicholas Wolterstorff.

[50]Admittedly, some difficulty still remains so long as we hold that God had the power to intervene to prevent these evils but did not do so. The process theologian does have an easier time of it on this point, but this is outweighed (we believe) by the deficiencies of process theology in other respects, especially its severe limitations on the power of God.

[51]Michael Peterson's *Evil and the Christian God* is, I believe, the best presentation now available of a theodicy that is consistent with the open view of God. John Hick's *Evil and the God of Love,* rev. ed. (San Francisco: Harper & Row, 1978), while written from a less orthodox perspective, contains much valuable material. And see William Hasker, "Suffering, Soul-Making and Salvation," *International Philosophical Quarterly* 28 (March 1988): 3-19, and "The Necessity of Gratuitous Evil," *Faith and Philosophy* 9 (January 1992): 23-44.

[52]For the claim that this view of providence is inadequate, see the review of *God, Time and Knowledge* by Alfred J. Freddoso in *Faith and Philosophy* 10 (January 1993): 99-107.

[53]And this points us to an important difference between free will theism and process theism with regard to the extent of God's knowledge. Formally the two theories are in agreement here: God knows what it is logically possible for him to know, and this does not include what depends on the future free actions of his creatures. But according to free will theism, God is able to know quite a lot more than according to process theism, because he is able to do more to ensure the completion of his plans.

Chapter 5: Practical Implications/Basinger

[1]This model is also called "free will theism" by Clark Pinnock and William Hasker, chapters three and four herein.

[2]David Mason, "Reflections on 'Prayer' from a Process Perspective," *Encounter* 45 (Autumn 1984): 347-48.

[3]I am not claiming that all who consider themselves Calvinists can justifiably be placed in this category. John Feinberg, for example, considers himself a Calvinist but does not affirm specific sovereignty. See Feinberg, "God Ordains All Things," in *Predestination and Free Will,* ed. David Basinger and Randall Basinger (Downers Grove, Ill.: InterVarsity Press, 1986). However, some self-proclaimed Calvinists such as Gordon H. Clark and G. C. Berkouwer clearly do affirm specific sovereignty. See, for example, Clark, *Religion, Reason and Revelation* (Philadelphia: Presbyterian & Reformed, 1961), and Berkouwer, *The Providence of God* (Grand Rapids, Mich.: Eerdmans, 1972).

Nor am I claiming that all who affirm specific sovereignty necessarily consider themselves Calvinists. I am not certain exactly what theological label J. I. Packer or Vernon Grounds prefers, but both clearly affirm specific sovereignty. See, for example, Packer, *Evangelism and the Sovereignty of God* (Downers Grove, Ill.: InterVarsity Press, 1961), and Grounds, "The Postulate of Paradox," paper presented at the Evangelical Theological Society annual meeting, March 1978.

[4]See, for example, Clark, *Religion, Reason and Revelation,* pp. 221-41, and Berkouwer, *Providence of God,* chaps. 4 and 6.

[5]See, for example, Berkouwer, *Providence of God,* chap. 5. John Feinberg, as I have already noted, does not affirm specific sovereignty, but he does believe that it is possible for God to unilaterally control our voluntary decision-making process itself and that at times God does so. See Feinberg, "God Ordains All Things."

[6]See, for example, Packer, *Evangelism and the Sovereignty of God,* pp. 19-35; R. B. Kuiper in *The Authority of God,* ed. G. W. Marston (Philadelphia: Presbyterian & Reformed, 1960), p. 16. Don Carson and John Piper may also fit into this category, but their exact positions on some of these points are not totally clear. See, for example, Carson, *Divine Sovereignty and Human*

Responsibility (Atlanta: John Knox Press, 1981), and Piper, *The Pleasures of God* (Portland, Ore.: Multnomah Press, 1991).

[7]Louis Berkhof, *Systematic Theology* (Grand Rapids, Mich.: Eerdmans, 1978), pp. 77-78.

[8]Some also believe that our prayers can, apart from God, directly affect even those who are not consciously aware of the fact that petitions are being offered on their behalf. See, for example, Frank Laubach, *Prayer: The Mightiest Force in the World* (Old Tappan, N.J.: Revell, 1959); Marjorie Suchocki, "A Process Theology of Prayer," *American Journal of Theology and Philosophy* 2 (May 1981).

[9]Again, I am not claiming that this holds for all those who consider themselves Calvinists or proponents of some other branch of the Reformed tradition, since not everyone in these categories affirms specific sovereignty.

[10]Aquinas states this most clearly: "we pray not in order to change the divine disposition, but for the sake of acquiring through petitionary prayer what God has been disposed to achieve by prayer" (*Summa Theologiae* 1A, q. 19, a. 8, r. 2). See also John Calvin, *Institutes of the Christian Religion*, trans. Henry Beveridge (Grand Rapids, Mich.: Eerdmans, 1979), 2:147, and Martin Luther, *Martin Luther: Selections from His Writings*, ed. John Dillenberger (Garden City, N.Y.: Anchor Books, 1961), p. 217.

[11]The most accessible introduction to basic process thought remains John B. Cobb Jr. and David Griffin, *Process Theology: An Introductory Exposition* (Philadelphia: Westminster Press, 1976).

[12]See again Suchocki, "Process Theology of Prayer."

[13]I discuss below the question why God does not utilize this power to prevent more evil.

[14]This is true for any theological model in which it is believed that God cannot unilaterally control voluntary human choice.

[15]For example, this is the position I support in "Why Petition an Omnipotent, Omniscient, Wholly Good God?" *Religious Studies* 19 (1983): 24-41.

[16]This is, for instance, the position of William Hasker and John Sanders.

[17]Basinger, "Why Petition?"

[18]Proponents of middle knowledge readily acknowledge, though, that we may not always do what is necessary on our part to receive the guidance that is available to us—for instance, we may not seek or be open to God's leading.

[19]The most accessible discussions of middle knowledge are found in William Hasker, *God, Time and Knowledge* (Ithaca, N.Y.: Cornell University Press, 1989), and William Craig, *The Only Wise God* (Grand Rapids, Mich.: Baker Book House, 1987). For a more detailed discussion of the type of comparative guidance middle knowledge makes possible, see David Basinger, "Middle Knowledge and Classical Christian Thought," *Religious Studies* 22 (1986): 407-22.

[20]Some, such as William Hasker, argue that middle knowledge is not possible. Others (myself included) maintain only that theists should not assume that God possesses knowledge of this type.

[21]John B. Cobb Jr., "Spiritual Discernment in a Whiteheadian Perspective," in *Religious Experience and Process Theology*, ed. Harry Cargas and Bernard Lee (New York: Paulist, 1976), pp. 360-61.

[22]Berkhof, *Systematic Theology*, p. 77.

[23]Once again, I must emphasize that only those Christians—for example, only those Calvin-

ists—who affirm specific sovereignty are committed to this understanding of the nature of divine guidance.

[24]It is not clear, though, that those who rely heavily on the "open door" technique are always consistent. Some are quite willing to maintain that God often leads us by opening and closing doors but then want to distance themselves from the tremendous amount of direct manipulation of human freedom and/or the natural environment that the frequent use of this method of divine guidance presupposes. See John Boykin, *The Gospel of Coincidence* (Grand Rapids, Mich.: Zondervan, 1990), for a good discussion of this point.

[25]The general assumption in this section has been not only that God has a specific will for our lives in most cases of significance—for example, with respect to whom we marry—but that his primary concern is that we discern his will and act in accordance with it. However, not all proponents of the open model believe this to be the case. Some (such as John Sanders) believe that while God may well have an opinion in many cases—may well believe that one decision would be better than another—his primary concern is not that we make a specific decision but rather that the decision we do make be made in a godly manner. See also Gary Friesen, *Decision Making and the Will of God* (Portland, Ore.: Multnomah Press, 1980).

[26]B. C. Johnson, "God and the Problem of Evil," in *Philosophy and Contemporary Issues*, ed. J. Burr and M. Goldinger, 6th ed. (New York: Macmillan, 1992), p. 159.

[27]Technically, "gratuitous evil" is best defined as that evil which is a necessary means to a greater good *or the avoidance of some greater evil*. The best-known version of this argument is set forth by Leibniz in his *Theodicy*. But a more contemporary version appears in Gordon H. Clark, *Religion, Reason and Revelation* (Philadelphia: Presbyterian & Reformed, 1961), chap. 5.

[28]The most thorough discussion of process theodicy is found in David Griffin, *Evil Revisited* (Albany: State University of New York Press, 1991).

[29]The most accessible discussion of this perspective is found in Hasker, *God, Time and Knowledge*, chap. 10.

[30]This assumption can be made by any Christian—for instance, any Calvinist—who denies specific sovereignty. See Feinberg, "God Ordains All Things."

[31]Some of these same Christians, though, want to distance God from pervasive, horrific evils such as the Holocaust or mass starvation. See Basinger and Basinger, introduction to *Predestination and Free Will*, for a more detailed discussion of this sort of theological vacillation.

[32]Some Christians not only find it more comforting to assume that some instances of evil are not a preordained part of God's plan but go so far as to say that they can affirm the existence of God only if they assume that God is at times not directly involved. See, for instance, *Evil* in the videotape series Questions of Faith (United Methodist Communcations, 1991).

[33]See, for example, David P. Hunt, "Middle Knowledge and the Soteriological Problem of Evil," *Religious Studies* 27 (March 1991): 3-26.

[34]Some proponents of specific sovereignty believe, though, that God can hold us morally responsible for what he unilaterally determines that we do or do not do. See, for example, Clark, *Religion, Reason and Revelation*, pp. 221-41.

[35]Once again, this holds only for those who affirm specific sovereignty.

[36]See my "Divine Omniscience and the Soteriological Problem of Evil: Is the Type of Knowl-

edge God Possesses Relevant?" *Religious Studies* 28 (1991): 1-18, for a discussion of the various theological perspectives on how one comes to be rightly related to God. Also see Clark Pinnock, *A Wideness in God's Mercy: The Finality of Jesus Christ in a World of Religions* (Grand Rapids, Mich.: Zondervan, 1992), and John Sanders, *No Other Name: An Investigation into the Destiny of the Unevangelized* (Grand Rapids, Mich.: Eerdmans, 1992).

[37]This is not to say that those who affirm specific sovereignty are not in practice highly motivated to share the gospel. The argument here is only that those in this camp cannot justifiably be motivated by the fear that some lack of effort on their part will negatively affect some other person's eternal destiny.